Beginning Excel 2013

1st Edition

Contents

Introduction

Welcome! Congratulations to taking the first step to learning Excel 2013!

Beginning Excel 2013 covers all the foundations you need to create your own excel spreadsheets. We also cover the basics of charting and data analysis. We can't cover everything, but we zoom in on what most regular people create with Excel.

Who this book is written for

Whether you are using Excel 2013 for your work, studies, and you just want to figure out how to best get your stuff done, or you are a newcomer who wants to become a spreadsheet expert, this is definitely the book for you.

How this book is structured

This book is best read as a reference to Excel as each chapter is independent of the rest. Lookup the table of contents and the topic of interest. You can of course still read it cover to cover.

In each chapter, we cover the most efficient ways to do a particular tasks. Once you have mastered that, you can experiment with other methods on your own.

What tools do I need?

You should already have Excel 2013 installed on your computer.

Do you have a cheatsheet?

Just drop us an email at support@i-ducate.com and we will send a Excel 2013 cheatsheet containing instructions and shortcuts to you!

Contact

We look forward to hearing from you at support@i-ducate.com. Now wait no further and get started on your Excel 2013 learning journey!

1. The Excel 2013 User Experience

Introduction

In this chapter, we will

- ➤ Get familiar with Excel 2013 program.
- ➤ Learn how to use the Excel program button.
- ➤ Get familiar with Backstage view.
- ➤ Customize the Quick Access Toolbar.
- ➤ Learn to use the Excel Ribbon effectively.
- ➤ Have fun with Formula Bar.
- ➤ Deal with the Worksheet area.
- ➤ Show off the Status bar.
- ➤ Learn how to use online help.

Let's Get Started

To open an Excel 2013 document, you need to have Microsoft Office 2013 installed on your machine. Once it is installed, you can go to Start → All Programs → Microsoft Office 2013 → Excel 2013 which will open a screen similar to the one shown in Figure 1-1.

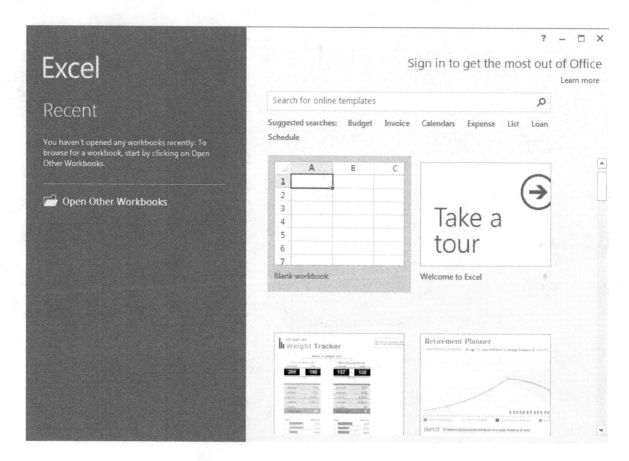

Figure 1-1 Excel 2013 Start Screen

You can select a template from the available list. You could find a number of templates for daily work schedule, event budget, retirement financial planner, vacation planner and so on. If you could not find the one that suits your needs from the available list, you can look for online templates from the search box given (circled in red in Figure 1-2).

If you do not want any specific template or if you could not find a template that matches your needs even from the online collection, then you can open a blank workbook (the first option). If you have already worked with some Excel files, then the recently opened files will also be displayed in the Start screen so that you can quickly reopen it for further editing.

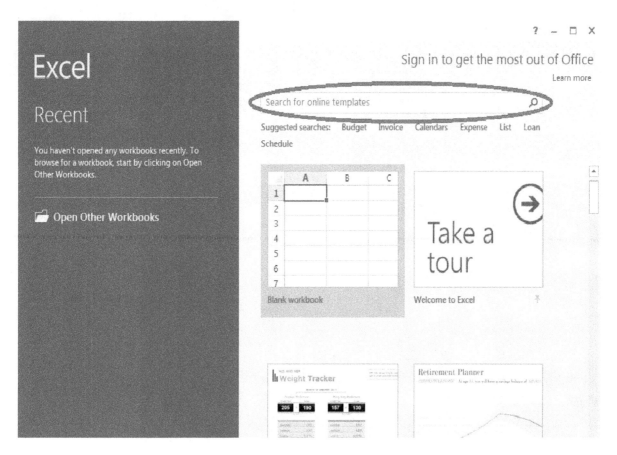

Figure 1-2: Textbox to search for online templates

Once you select the Blank workbook from the Start screen (Figure 1-1), the Excel opens a new workbook, named Book1, with an initial worksheet, named Sheet1. There will be changes in the name of the workbook and worksheet if you are opening an existing template. The screen you get in case of opening a blank workbook will be similar to the one shown in Figure 1-3.

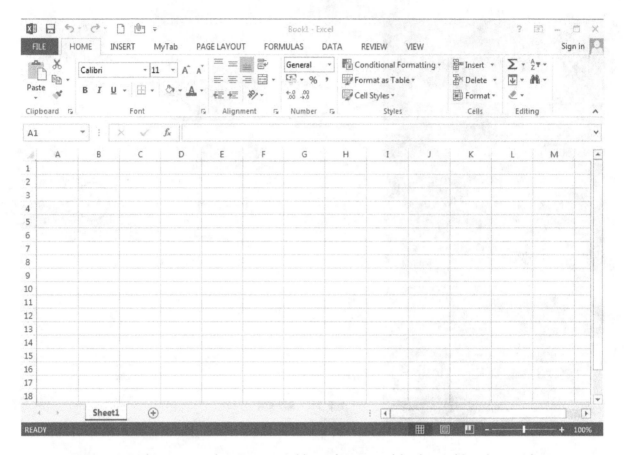

Figure 1-3 The screen that is opened by selecting a blank workbook template

You could find the following components in this screen:

1. **Excel Program button**: The Excel Program button is at the top left corner of the screen.

Figure 1-4 The Excel Program button

Once clicked, it displays a drop-down menu with options to change the size (minimize, maximize, size) and position (restore) of the window as well as to exit (close) the application.

2. **The File button**: The File button is situated at the top left of the screen (just below the Excel Program button).

Figure 1-5 The File button

12

Once clicked, it opens the backstage view. The left side menu contains all the document related commands such as Info, New, Open, Save, Save As, Print, Share, Export and Close. It also provides an Account option that displays the User and Product information as well as an Options item that allows user to change many of the default settings of Excel. Once you click the back arrow at the top left of the screen, you can exit the backstage view.

3. **Quick Access Toolbar**: Quick Access Toolbar is situated at the top left of the screen just to the right of the Excel Program button.

Figure 1-6 Quick Access Toolbar

It is a customizable toolbar where you can include buttons for the most common commands, so that you do not have to go the corresponding menu in the ribbon or outside the ribbon each time to do the task. For example, you can add the Save option in the Quick Access Toolbar so that you do not have to click the File button and click Save every time you want to save a file. You just need to click the Save button in the Quick Access Toolbar which will save your time of course.

4. **Ribbon**: Ribbon is positioned just to the right of the File button.

Figure 1-7: Excel Ribbon

It contains almost all Excel commands grouped into a number of tabs ranging from Home through View. In other words, all the most commonly used Excel commands are available at our fingertips because of this single strip called Ribbon.

5. **Formula Bar**: Formula bar is positioned just below the Ribbon.

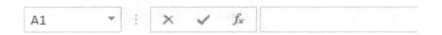

Figure 1-8 Formula bar

It displays the address of the current cell along with the data inside that cell.

6. **Worksheet Area**: Worksheet area is the section below the formula bar.

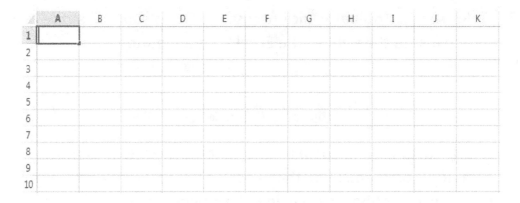

Figure 1-9 Worksheet area

The Worksheet area is the actual working area that consists of cells of the worksheet. Each cell is identified by a combination of letters and numbers. Each column is identified using letters and each row is identified using numbers. The first cell in the first column will be identified as A1.

7. **Status bar**: Status bar is positioned at the bottom of the screen.

Figure 1-10 Status bar

It displays the current mode in which the workbook appears. You can also select a different worksheet view and even zoom in and zoom out the view by dragging the slider.

Using the Excel Program Button

The Excel Program button positioned at the top left corner allows you to change the size and position of the window as well as to exit the application. When you select the button, a dropdown similar to the one shown in Figure 1-11 appears.

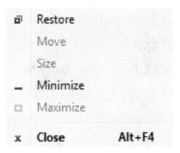

Figure 1-11 Dropdown menu with Move, Size and Maximize options disabled

The Move, Size or Maximize options will not be enabled if the current window fits to the full screen. If the window is not in its full size, the dropdown menu will look like similar to Figure 1-12.

Figure 1-11 Dropdown menu with Move, Size and Maximize options enabled

If you click the Minimize option, the window will be minimized. If you click the Size option, you will see a message "Use arrow keys to size" in the status bar. You can increase or decrease the size of the window by using the arrow keys. If you click the Maximize option, the window will be maximized. If you click the Move option, you will see a message "Use arrow keys to move" in the status bar. You can move the window to left, right, bottom or top using the corresponding arrow keys. If you click the Close option, the application will be closed allowing you to save the workbook if you have made any changes.

Going Backstage

Right below the Excel Program button and left to the Home tab in the Ribbon, you will find File button. Once you select the File button, the Backstage view will be opened similar to the one shown in Figure 1-12.

The Info option provides some information about the current workbook file that you are working on. The left of the information panel contains buttons that allow you to change the protection status of the workbook, check the document before publishing, manage its versions and also set options to be viewed on the browser. The right of the panel displays workbook related information including Size, Created, Last Modified, etc. (that you cannot change) and Title, Tags, Categories, Author and so on (that you can change).

Below the Info option, you will find document related commands such as New, Open, Save, Save As, Print, Share, Export and Close. Below the Close option, you will find the Account option that displays user, connection and Microsoft Office account information once selected. The last item in the File tab is the Options item that is used to change the default settings of the program.

You need to click the Back arrow at the top of the File tab to close the Backstage view and to return to the normal worksheet view.

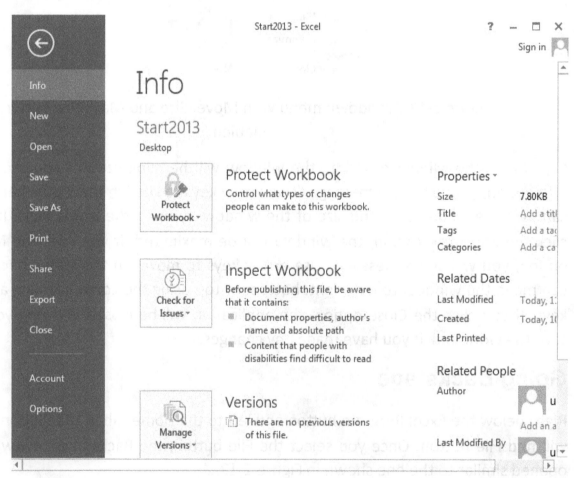

Figure 1-12 The backstage view opened by clicking the File button

Customizing the Quick Access Toolbar

When you start using Excel 2013, you might see only a few buttons in the Quick Access Toolbar such as Save, Undo, Redo and so on. However, you can customize the toolbar to have any Excel command you want so that it becomes easily accessible.

Adding Commands in the Customize Quick Access Toolbar Menu

When you click the Customize Quick Access Toolbar menu (the drop down button at the right of the Quick Access Toolbar with a horizontal bar above a down-pointing triangle), it displays commands such as New, Open, Save, Email, Quick Print, Print Preview and Print, Spelling, Undo, Redo, Sort Ascending, Sort Descending and Touch/Mouse Mode. You could find that the commands that are currently displaying in the Quick Access Toolbar are checked in the menu. You can select as many commands in the menu that you want to display in the toolbar. All the items checked in the menu will be displayed as buttons in the Quick Access Toolbar. You just have to click the checked commands again to remove them from the Quick Access Toolbar and to make them unchecked in the menu.

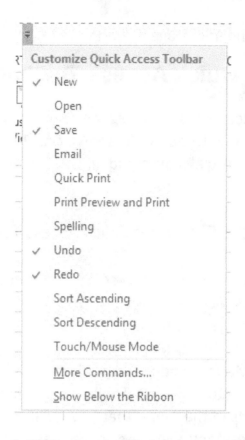

Figure 1-13 Customize Quick Access Toolbar menu

Adding Ribbon Commands to the Quick Access Toolbar

To add a command that is there in the Ribbon and not in the Customize Quick Access Toolbar menu, right click the corresponding command in the Ribbon. You will get a menu as shown in Figure 1-14.

Figure 1-14 Menu to add ribbon commands to the toolbar

You just have to select the option Add to Quick Access Toolbar and it will be added to the toolbar. To remove the item from the toolbar, right click the item added on the Quick Access Toolbar and you will get a menu as shown in the

Figure 1-15. You have to select the option "Remove" from Quick Access Toolbar which will remove the item from the Quick Access Toolbar.

Figure 1-15 Menu to remove commands from the toolbar

Rearranging the Buttons in the Quick Access Toolbar

You can change the order of the buttons in the Quick Access Toolbar. Select the option More Commands from the Customize Quick Access Toolbar menu (Figure 1-13) which will open the Excel Options dialog box with Quick Access Toolbar tab selected as in Figure 1-16.

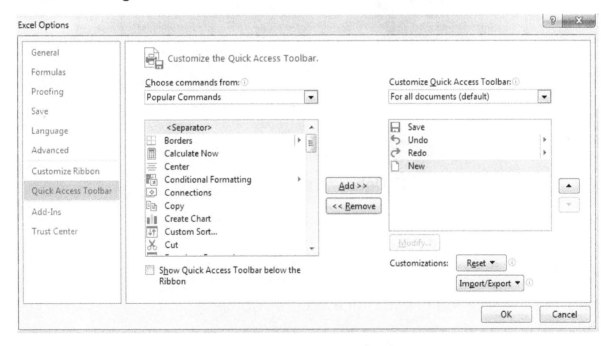

Figure 1-16 Excel Options dialog box

The box at the right hand side displays the buttons in the same order they appear in the Quick Access Toolbar. Using the Move Up and Move Down buttons (two triangles displayed at the right of the window), you can change the order of the buttons.

Adding Non-Ribbon Commands to the Quick Access Toolbar

You can add commands that are not in the Ribbon to the Quick Access Toolbar using the Quick Access Toolbar tab of the Excel Options dialog box (Figure 1-16).

Select the option "Commands not in the Ribbon" from the "Choose commands from:" dropdown menu (circled in red in Figure 1-17).

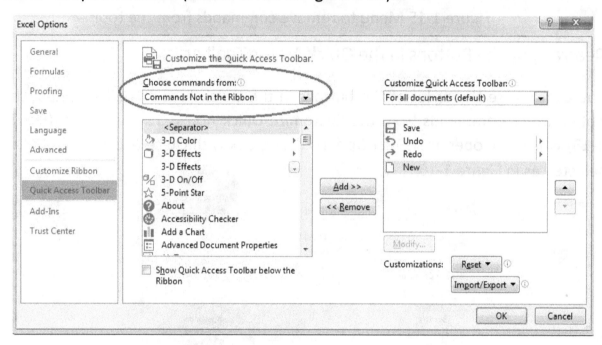

Figure 1-17 Option to select non-ribbon commands

Then you can select the required command from the available list and click the Add button to add it into the Quick Access Toolbar. Click OK to close the Excel Options dialog box.

Changing the Position of the Quick Access Toolbar

You can change the position of Quick Access Toolbar easily. By default, it is positioned just right to the Excel Program button. You need to click the drop down button at the right of the toolbar (a horizontal bar above a down-pointing triangle) and select the option "Show Below the Ribbon" to display the toolbar below the ribbon (circled in red in Figure 1-18).

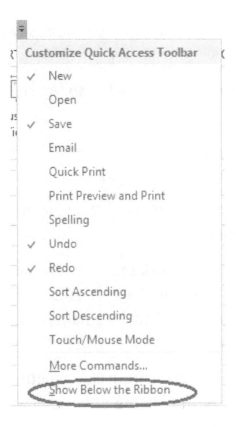

Figure 1-18 Option to change the position of the Quick Access Toolbar

Using the Excel Ribbon

As we proceed, the main part that we deal with in an Excel worksheet would be the wonderful Excel Ribbon that includes the most commonly used Excel commands.

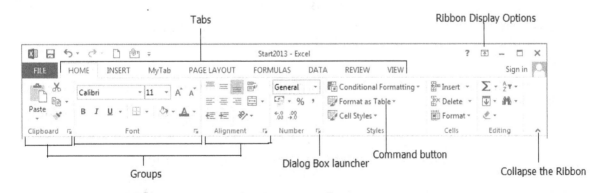

Figure 1-19 The Excel Ribbon

The Excel Ribbon has the following components:

1. **Tabs**: The Excel commands are grouped logically and displayed in different tabs.

2. **Groups**: Excel commands in each tab is classified into subtasks and displayed as groups.

3. **Command buttons**: The command buttons perform a specific action or open a gallery for you to click a thumbnail.

4. **Dialog box launcher**: Once clicked, the launcher opens a dialog box with some additional options.

5. **Ribbon collapse**: Once you click the angle symbol at the right bottom of the ribbon, the entire ribbon will be collapsed and you will only see the tab names. Once you click any of the tab name, you will see the option to pin the ribbon back at the right bottom of the ribbon.

6. **Ribbon display options**: You can decide whether to auto hide the ribbon, display only the tabs or display the tabs along with commands by choosing the appropriate options.

Different Tabs

Different tabs you would see when a new workbook is opened in Excel 2013, from left to right, are:

1. **Home**: The Home tab includes the basic commands that are used when creating, formatting and editing a worksheet. These commands are classified into different groups such as Clipboard, Font, Paragraph, Styles and Editing.

2. **Insert**: The Insert tab includes commands to add new elements such as tables, images, shapes, charts, links, reports and so on. These commands are classified into different groups such as Tables, Illustrations, Apps, Charts, Reports, Sparklines, Filters, Links, Text and Symbols.

3. **Page Layout**: The Page Layout tab includes commands used to prepare the worksheet for printing or to rearrange the graphics on the worksheet. These commands are classified into groups such as Themes, Page Setup, Scale to Fit, Sheet Options and Arrange.

4. **Formulas**: The Formulas tab includes commands to add formulas and functions and to check errors in formulas. Different groups in this tab are Function Library, Defined Names, Formula Auditing and Calculation.

5. **Data**: The Data tab includes commands for managing data from internal and external sources. Different groups in the Data tab are Get External Data, Connections, Sort & Filter, Data Tools and Outline.

6. **Review**: The Review tab includes commands for proofing and protecting the spreadsheet. Different groups are Proofing, Language, Comments and Changes.

7. **View**: The View tab includes commands to manage the display of the Worksheet area arranged into the Workbook Views, Show, Zoom, Window and Macros groups.

In addition to these tabs, there are few optional tabs such as Developer, Design and Format. These tabs will be added after the View tab based on the item you are working on. For example, if you include a chart in your workbook, the Design and Format tabs will be added that helps you manage the design and format of your chart easily. If you create macros, you could find the Developer tab after the View tab. These tabs will be displayed only when you select the item to be managed. In short, Excel adds contextual tabs with their own groups and commands based on the objects you add in your workbook.

Having Fun with the Formula Bar

The Formula Bar displays the address of the current cell as a combination of letters and numbers and its contents. The Formula Bar has three sections. The first section is the Name Box that displays the address of the current cell. The middle section includes Formula Bar buttons such as Cancel (a cross mark), Enter (a check mark) and Insert Function (labeled fx) buttons. The last section displays the contents of the current cell.

Figure 1-20 The Formula Bar

Deal with the Worksheet Area

The Worksheet area consists of the cells where a great deal of Excel activities take place.

How to Select a Particular Cell?

To enter data in a particular cell, you need to select that cell so that you will see that cell's address in the Name Box in the Formula Bar. There are different ways to select a particular cell:

1. You can click the required cell.

2. You can directly enter the address in the Name Box and press the Enter key.

3. You can press F5 which will open Go To dialog box. You just have to enter the address of the required cell in the Reference textbox and click OK.

4. You can use the keystroke shortcuts (shown in Table 1-1) appropriately to select the required cell.

Keystroke	Where the Cell Cursor Moves
→ or Tab	Cell to the immediate right
← or Shift+Tab	Cell to the immediate left
↑	Cell up one row
↓	Cell down one row
Page Up	Cell one full screen up in the same column
Page Down	Cell one full screen down in the same column
Home	Cell in Column A of the current row
Ctrl + Home	Cell A1 of the worksheet

Table 1-1 Keyboard shortcuts to move to different cells

Surfing the Sheets in a Workbook

Though a new workbook contains only a single worksheet, you might need more worksheets to logically group your data. You can add more worksheets in your workbook by just clicking the New Sheet button (plus sign in a circle) or by selecting Shift + F11.

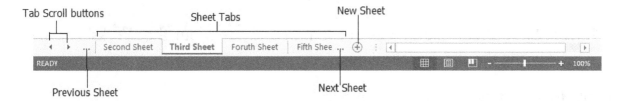

Figure 1-21 Options to surf the worksheets in a workbook

You can select a worksheet for editing by clicking the name of the required worksheet from the Sheet tabs. The name of the active worksheet will be bolded and underlined among the Sheet tabs.

If there are too many worksheets in your workbook, you can use the Sheet Tab Scroll buttons to bring the required tab into view. You can bring the previous worksheet into view by clicking the Previous Sheet button (three periods to the left of the Sheet tabs) and the next worksheet into view by clicking the Next Sheet button (three periods to the right of the Sheet tabs).

Showing Off the Status bar

The Status bar is positioned at the bottom of the screen. There are four components in the Status bar.

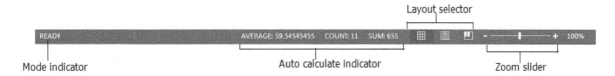

Figure 1-22 The status bar

1. The **Mode indicator** on the left shows the current status of the Excel program such as Ready, Edit, Enter and so on.

2. The **Auto Calculate indicator** displays the average, count and sum of the numerical entries in the selected cells.

3. The **Layout selector** allows you to select between three layouts for the Worksheet area: Normal, Page Layout and Page Break Preview. The Normal layout displays the Worksheet area including cells with column and row headings. The Page Layout displays Worksheet area with rulers, page margins and page breaks. The Page Break Preview allows you to adjust the paging of a report.

4. The **Zoom slider** allows you to zoom in and zoom out the Worksheet area by moving the slider accordingly.

Help is on the Way

You can get Excel 2013 help online any time using Excel 2013. You just need to click the Help button (question mark icon to the left of Ribbon Display Options icon) or press F1 to open an Excel help window. Of course, you need to be connected to the Internet to get online help. You can enter the topic, keyword or phrase that you are looking for inside the search box. Once you press Enter key or search icon, all the related links will be displayed so that you can get the required information. The Excel Help window also provides the option to print the help topic.

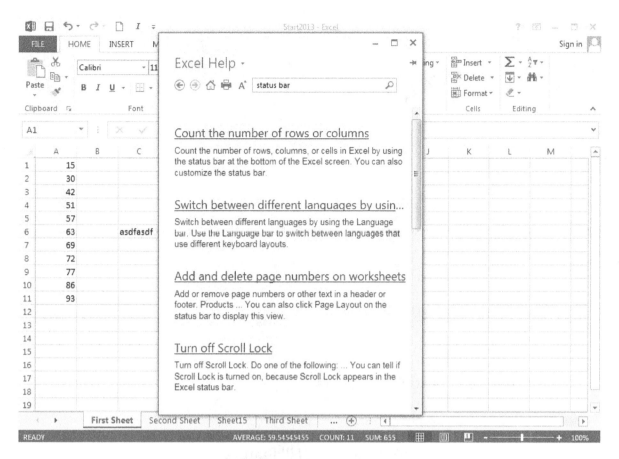

Figure 1-23 The Excel Help window

New Great Excel Features

The Excel 2013 user interface provides a number of graphical elements that make Excel more user friendly as well as easier and faster to work with. The first and foremost is Live Preview. As the name indicates, it helps you preview a change before actually making it. For example, you could see how the data appear in a different font, size, color etc with the help of Live Preview. The happy news is that you can even see the changes in Pivot Tables and Charts using Live Preview.

Page Layout View is another new feature that allows you see headers and footers along with margins and rulers for every worksheet. You will also find a Zoom slider at the bottom right of the screen that allows you zoom in and zoom out on the data.

2. Creating a Spreadsheet from Scratch

Introduction

In this chapter, we will learn how to

- ➢ Start a new workbook
- ➢ Enter three different types of data
- ➢ Create simple formulas
- ➢ Use AutoCorrect, AutoFill and Flash Fill features
- ➢ Enter and edit formulas that contain functions
- ➢ Save and recover your workbooks

We have already seen how to launch Excel 2013 in the previous chapter. In this chapter, we are going to see how to actually add data into the Worksheet area to have real magic. We will get familiar with a number of excellent Excel 2013 features that are really helpful in adding error-less data quickly.

Which Workbook do You Want?

When you launch Excel 2013, you will get a start screen similar to the one shown in Figure 2-1. The information is displayed in two panes where the left pane includes the names of recently opened workbooks (if any) and also a link to open other workbooks that are not listed already. Once you click the Open Other Workbooks link, you will have the chance to browse the required workbook from your computer.

On the right pane, you could find thumbnails of different templates that you can use for your work. A template will create a new workbook that is in a specific format with ready-made data which will help you do your work easier and faster. You just need to make the required changes to the available data and save it as you want. Thus, the burden of creating data from scratch can be avoided.

The thumbnails start with a Blank workbook immediately followed by a "Take a tour template". It is a great idea to open the Take a tour template to explore some of the wonderful features of Excel 2013 quickly. After the Take a tour template, you could find a number of templates for commonly used workbooks ranging from daily work schedule through budgets. You can look for a template that matches your needs from the available list.

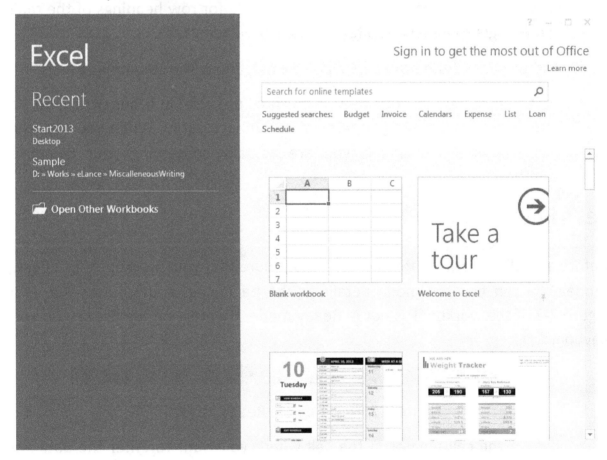

Figure 2-1 Excel 2013 Start Screen

If you could not find a matching one in the provided list, you can even look for online templates with the help of "Search for online templates" search box seen at the top of the Start screen's right panel. If you need a workbook without any data or labels, you need to select the Blank workbook template which opens a new workbook named Book1. The Book1 will have a single worksheet named Sheet1 that you can use to enter data.

Data Entry Etiquette

- Whenever you enter data, make sure that you start from the cell in the upper left corner of your worksheet. It is better to organize data from top to bottom instead of having it across the sheet.

- Whenever possible, organize your data in tables that use adjacent rows and columns.

- Leave a single column at the left of the table for row headings of the table and a single row at the top for the column headings.

- Add the title of the table (if any) in the row above the column headings.

- Try to enter data in close cells as much as possible. In other words, do not spread out the data in your worksheet unnecessarily. When you conserve space in your worksheet, you are actually conserving your computer memory.

Let's Enter Data

Before actually entering data into cells, make sure that your workbook is in Ready mode. You can find the mode details at the beginning of the Status bar as in Figure 2-2. If the workbook is not in Ready mode, try pressing the Esc key on your keyboard.

Figure 2-2 Workbook in Ready Mode

Now position the cell pointer in the cell where you want to enter the data and begin typing the entry. Once you start entering the data in the active cell (current cell), the mode in the Status bar will become Enter instead of Ready as in Figure 2-3.

Figure 2-3 Workbook in Enter Mode

As you enter data in a cell, you could find that the same character you enter in the active cell appears simultaneously on the Formula bar though the cursor (insertion point) appears at the end of the characters in the cell only as in Figure 2-4. You could also find that the Formula bar buttons including Cancel (a cross mark) and Enter (a check mark) also become enabled as you enter data in a cell. You can press the Cancel button to clear the data you entered.

Figure 2-4 Data being displayed in cell and on Formula bar simultaneously

Once you finish entering the data in a particular cell, you need to press the Enter key on your keyboard or click Enter button (check mark) on the formula bar or click another cell to let Excel know that you are done with the active cell. You can also press the Tab key or Shift + Tab keys or one of the arrow keys (↑, ↓, →, ←) to complete a cell entry. Then the mode will become again Ready back from Enter on the Status bar.

- If you press Enter button on the Formula bar, the entered text goes into the cell and the cursor remains in the same cell.

- If you press any of the keyboard keys, the neighboring cell in the direction of the arrow will become the active cell automatically.

- If you press the Enter key on the keyboard, the cell below in the next row will become the active cell automatically.

- If you press the Tab or Shift + Tab, the cell pointer moves to the adjacent cell in the immediate right or left column.

Different Types of Data: Text, Value and Formula

You can enter a text, value or a formula into an Excel cell. Data other than formulas can be classified as either text or value. The text entries will be aligned to the left of the cell and values will be aligned to the right of the cell. A formula can be easily identified because any formula starts with an equal sign (=).

Tremendous Text

A text entry could be a combination of letters, numbers and punctuations. Text entry is mainly used for headings, titles and notes in a worksheet. It is easy to identify whether an entry is text or not. If the entry is left aligned, it means that the entry is a text entry. If the text entry is too wide to be accommodated in a cell, the text spills over the empty neighboring cell(s) on the right. When data is entered in a cell that contains spillover text from a cell to its left, Excel cuts off the long text to make space for the new entry as in Figure 2-5.

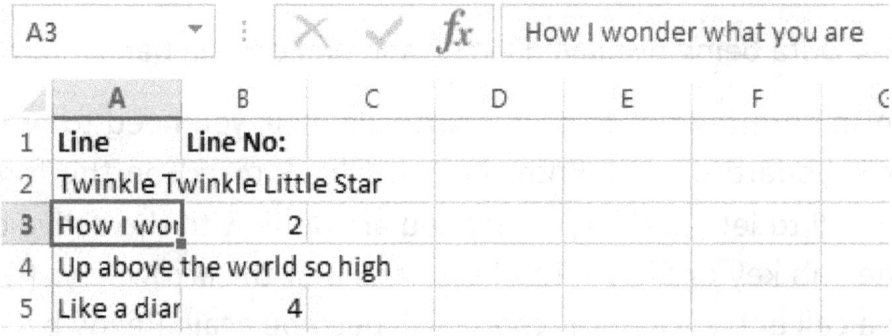

Figure 2-5 Entries in cells to the right cut off the spillover text in cells on the left.

However, the long entry will not be lost. Once you widen the column that contains the cell with long entry, you can see the complete data.

Magic of Values

Values are the building blocks of most of the Excel formulas. Values are mainly of two types: numbers that represent quantities (50 or $50000) and numbers that represent date or time (April 20, 1990 or 2 a.m.). You can easily differentiate a value from a text because values are right aligned. If the value is too wide to accommodate in a cell, it gets converted to scientific notation as in Figure 2-6. Just widening the column that contains the cell with large value will display the number as usual.

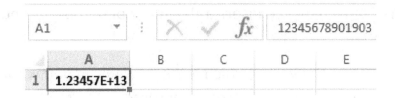

Figure 2-6 Long number displayed in scientific notation

To enter a positive number, you just have to type the number and complete the entry by pressing Enter key or any of the other keys allowed. To enter a negative number, you first need to enter the minus sign (hyphen) followed by the number and then complete the entry. You can even enter a number enclosed in parentheses to make it negative. That is (200) is equal to -200.

To enter decimal numbers, you have to enter period (.) as the decimal point. If you have to enter hundreds of financial figures with decimal places, say for accounting purposes, you can decide in prior to the number of decimal places you want for each number. To set this,

1. Go to File → Options and select the Advanced tab of the opened Excel Options dialog box to get a screen as in Figure 2-7.

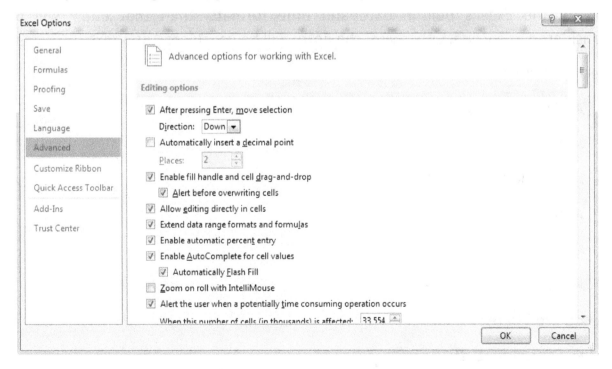

Figure 2-7 Excel Options dialog box with Advanced Tab opened

2. Check the "Automatically insert a decimal point" option under the Editing options section.

3. Make changes to the value (which is 2 by default) if you want to have more than or less than 2 decimal places. Otherwise, do not make any changes.

4. Click the OK button or press the Enter key on your keyboard.

Now if you enter 56789, it will be automatically changed to 567.89 (if you have not changed the default value 2). After making the Fixed Decimal setting on, if you want to enter 56789 itself (not 567.89), you have to enter the period by yourself, that is you need to enter the data as "56789." (without double quotes). Once you are done with the financial figures, do not forget to go the Advanced tab of the Excel Options dialog box and uncheck the Automatically insert a decimal point option.

It is better to enter dates and times as values rather than text because dates and times entered as values can be used in formulas, whereas dates and times entered as text cannot be. Based on the format you enter the date and time in, Excel decides whether the data is value or text. If you enter date or time following any of the Excel's built-in date and time formats, then that entry will be considered as a value. Otherwise, the entry will be considered as a text.

Recognized Time Formats

> 5 AM or 5 PM

> 5 A or 5 P

> 5:40 AM or 5:40 PM

> 5:40:10 AM or 5:40:10 PM

> 17:40

> 17:40:10

Recognized Date Formats

> February 21, 2010

> February 21, 10

- 21/2/ 10
- 21-2-10
- 21-Feb-10
- 21/ Feb/ 10
- 21Feb10
- 21/ 2
- 21-Feb
- 21/ Feb
- 21Feb
- Feb-21
- Feb/ 21
- Feb21

While entering an amount of money in dollars or rupees, you can add the symbol of currency as well as commas to make the data more readable. If you want to enter a value that contains a fraction, make sure that you add a space between the integer and fraction. To make it clearer, if you want to enter 3 ¼ (3 and ¼) make sure that you enter it as "3 1/4" (with a space between 3 and 1) and not "31/4" (without a space between 3 and 1). Now you will see the value 3 ¼ in the cell and whereas its corresponding decimal value on the Formula bar as in Figure 2-8.

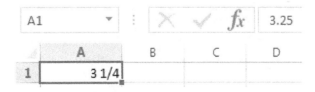

Figure 2-8 Data (value containing fraction) in the cell and formula bar

If you want to enter a simple fraction, make sure that you enter a zero (0) followed by the fraction. Otherwise, the fraction will be considered as a Date value. For example, if you just enter 3/5 and press the Enter key, the data will be automatically converted as 03-May as in Figure 2-9. On the other hand, if you enter 0 3/5, then the data will be considered as 0.6.

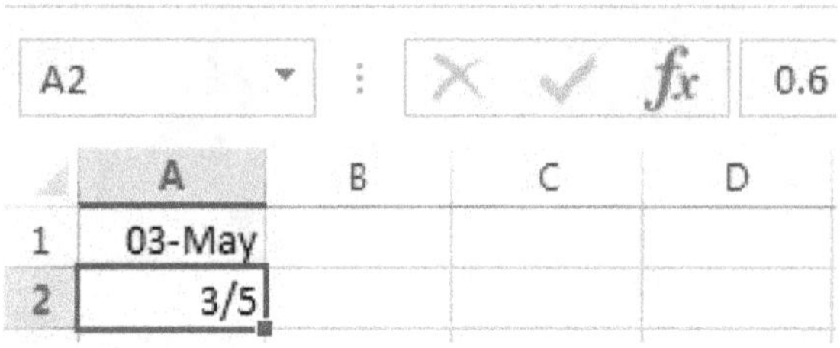

Figure 2-9 Simple fraction as a mixed number and as simple fraction itself

You can enter a percentage value either as a decimal number (.25) or as a number with percent sign (25%).

Fabulous Formulas

Formulas are actually making Excel really powerful and magical. If you enter a formula in a cell, Excel automatically calculates the formula and displays the result in the cell. However, you will see the formula itself (not the result) on the Formula bar. Once the formula is entered correctly, the result in the cell will be automatically recalculated whenever the data used in the formula changes.

You can use a series of values, cell references (A1 or B10), cell ranges (A1:A10), mathematical operators (+, -, *, / and ^) and built-in functions inside a formula. To create a formula in cell C1 that subtracts the value in cell B1 from the value in cell A1,

Select cell C1, enter the formula =A1-B1 and press the Enter key.

OR

Select cell C1, enter the = sign, select cell A1, enter – sign, select cell B1 and then press the Enter key.

The method of selecting the referencing cells (second method) instead of manually entering the cell address (first method) is faster and error-less especially when you have many cell references in your formula. This method is known as pointing.

If you have values in the cells A1 and B1, once you finish entering the formula in cell C1, you will see the calculated result in cell C1 and the formula on the formula bar as in Figure 2-10.

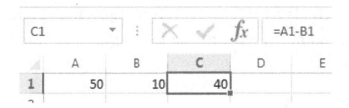

Figure 2-10 Formula subtracting value in cell B1 from value in cell A1

The power of Excel formulas is that Excel automatically recalculates the result as soon as the value in any of the referencing cells (A1 and B1 here) is changed. Change the value in cell A1 to 100 and the value in cell B1 to 50. You will get the result as in Figure 2-11.

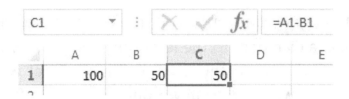

Figure 2-11 Result recalculated automatically when value in the referencing cell changed

Operator Precedence

Most of the Excel formulas contain different mathematical operators such as + (addition), - (subtraction), * (multiplication), / (division) and ^ (to the power of). The order in which different operations are performed is known as operator precedence. Excel normally calculates the formula from left to right. As per this order, multiplication and division operators have more precedence than addition and subtraction operators. That is, multiplication and division will be executed first before addition and subtraction even though multiplication and division operators do not come first in the formula.

For example, the result of the formula =10-2*3 is 4 and not 24 because 2*3 is calculated first and the result (6) is subtracted from 10. It does not happen in the way 10-2 first and then multiplying the result (8) by 3. This is because that * (multiplication) operator has more precedence than – (subtraction) operator.

If you want to change the normal operator precedence, then you have to enclose the operation that needs to happen first in parenthesis. In the previous example, if you want the subtraction operation to happen before multiplication, then you need to enter the formula as =(10-2)*3. This will give the result 24. While creating complex formulas, you might have to change the normal operator precedence by using the parentheses wisely.

Clumsy Formulas

When you create formulas, especially complex ones with lots of parentheses, operators and cell references, you might get unexpected strange messages or results. If you get a message in uppercase beginning with # (number sign) and ending with ! (exclamation) or ? (question mark), then do not panic. It is an error value that helps you know that there are some errors in your formula that is preventing Excel from calculating the result.

If your formula has some kind of error, you will also see an alert indicator (exclamation mark in a diamond) to the left of the cell that contains the formula. When you place the cursor on this alert indicator, Excel will display a brief description of the error with a drop-down button to the right of the box. Once clicked, the drop-down will display options to access online help and suggestions on how to get rid of the error. Table 2-1 includes some of the common errors and their causes.

Error Description	Possible Reason for the Error
#DIV/0!	When the divisor in the formula is either 0 or empty
#NAME!	When the formula refers to a range name that does not exist in the worksheet
#REF!	When the formula contains an invalid cell reference
#VALUE!	When you reference a text in a formula instead of a value

Table 2-1 Excel common errors and their possible reasons

Formulas become Fantastic with Functions

We have created a simple mathematical formula that performs some mathematical operations. In fact, Excel offers a variety functions that we can use in our formulas instead of creating formulas from scratch. A function is nothing but a predefined formula that performs some computation. To use a function, we need to specify the name of the function and pass the inputs required for computation, called as arguments, in the order Excel expects.

Just as in a formula, the inputs can be text, value, cell reference or cell range. You need to start a function also with an equal sign. Once you enter the first few letters of the name of the function, Excel will display all functions that start with the letters you entered. You just have to double-click the function name you want so that Excel will finish the name of the function along with left parentheses. This makes it really easy for you to choose the function you want.

You will also see the arguments that the function expects to complete the computation. Thus, you do not have to remember each function's arguments and their order. Excel helps you create functions you want as simple as that.

 You need to separate the arguments using comma. Once all the arguments are entered, you should close the arguments list with a right parentheses. Now you will see the function name along with the arguments on the Formula bar. Once you click the Enter key, you will see the result of calculation inside the cell that contains the particular function.

If you use the AVERAGE function to find the average of five numbers in cells A1 to A5 and display the result in cell C1, then you will get a screen similar to Figure 2-12.

C1		⋮	✕	✓	*fx*	=AVERAGE(A1:A5)

	A	B	C	D	E
1	1256		3169.2		
2	4356				
3	1345				
4	2498				
5	6391				

Figure 2-12 Average calculated using AVERAGE function

You can also use the Insert command button marked with fx on the Formula bar to insert a function directly. Once you click the Insert command button, it opens an Insert Function dialog box as shown in Figure 2-13. You can select the function you want from the Select a function: list. Using the Or select a category: dropdown, you can select a category and get functions of different types. If you are not sure of the name of the function, you can look for a function that matches your needs using Search for a function: textbox.

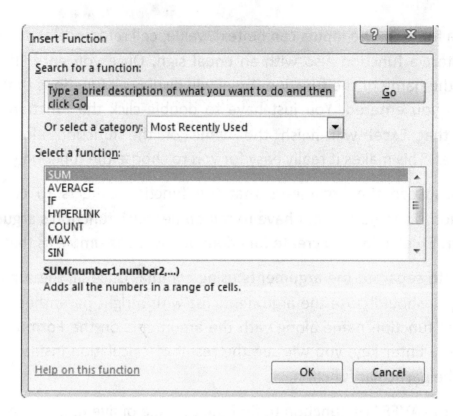

Figure 2-13 Insert Function dialog box

Once you select your function and click OK, Excel inserts the function name in the active cell and opens Function Arguments dialog box where you can enter the function arguments. The Function Arguments dialog box is really a blessing when you deal with functions that you are not familiar with. You can easily complete the arguments making use of the help offered by Excel. This dialog box displays both required and optional arguments.

Suppose you select AVERAGE function and click OK, you will get the Function Arguments dialog box as shown in Figure 2-14. As shown in the figure, you can calculate the average of up to 255 numbers in the dialog box if you want. You can either enter values or cell references in the space provided. You can also enter a cell range (A1:A10) if the values are in continuous cells. Every time you enter arguments, you could find the updated result on the bottom left of the dialog box as shown in Figure 2-15.

You can also edit a function with the Insert Function button. After selecting the cell that contains the function, click the Insert Function button on the formula bar. This will open the Function Arguments dialog box with the already existing arguments. You can modify it and click OK to make the changes.

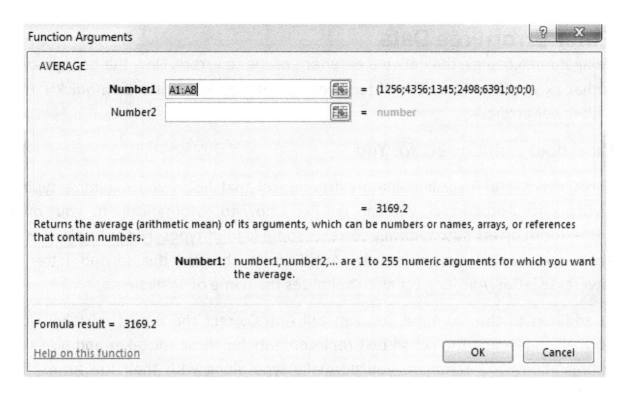

Figure 2-14 Function Arguments dialog box opened for AVERAGE function

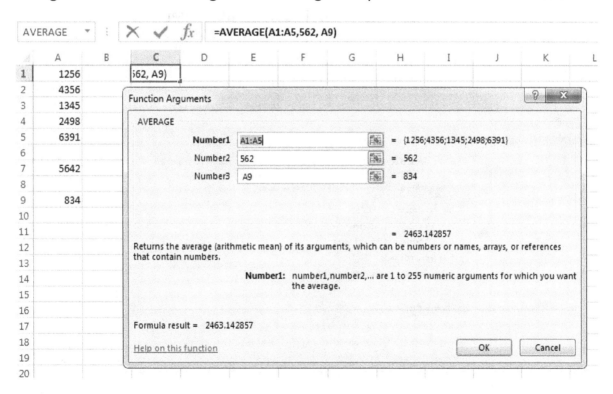

Figure 2-15 Function Arguments dialog box with arguments entered

Enter Error-Free Data

Being human beings, the data we enter are prone to errors. Now the happy news is that Excel offers a number of techniques that help you enter data quickly and with fewer errors.

Excel does AutoCorrect for You

AutoCorrect is an excellent feature from Excel that helps you minimize typing errors. With AutoCorrect, you can tell Excel how to automatically fix your own typos. AutoCorrect automatically corrects some kind of typos. For example, if you enter two capital letters initially, AutoCorrect changes the second letter a lowercase letter. AutoCorrect also capitalizes the name of weekdays.

In addition to this, anytime you can tell AutoCorrect the typing mistakes you normally make and the actual text replacements for those mistakes and also the abbreviations and acronyms you normally type along with their full forms. To create or add the text replacements,

1. Go to File → Options and open the Proofing tab to get a screen as in Figure 2-16.

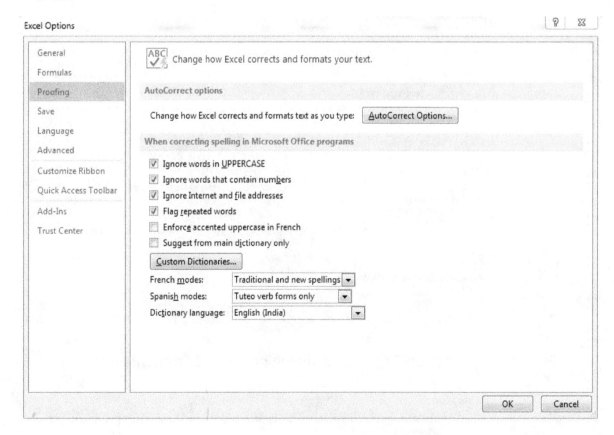

Figure 2-16 Excel Options dialog box with Proofing Tab opened

2. Click the AutoCorrect Options button.

3. In the AutoCorrect tab, enter the typo or abbreviation in the Replace: textbox and the actual replacement in the Width: textbox as in Figure 2-17.

4. Click the Add button or press Enter key on your keyboard to add a new item to the Autocorrect list.

5. Click the OK button twice, once to close the AutoCorrect dialog box and to close the Excel Options dialog box.

Figure 2-17 Acronym entered in Replace: textbox and text replacement entered in With: textbox

Excel is not Complete without AutoComplete

AutoComplete feature attempts to cut down your typing load doing some kind of mind reading. This feature starts its magic only when you enter text entries in a column (not when you enter values or formulas and not when you enter text entries in a row). AutoComplete analyzes the entries you make in a column and then automatically suggests what you might want to enter when you start a new entry with the same letter that of an existing entry.

For example, I enter Great in cell A1 and Wonderful in cell A2. Then, as soon as I enter G in cell A3, the AutoComplete feature displays Great in cell A3 next to the letter G as in Figure 2-18.

Figure 2-18 AutoComplete suggests an entry

Now if you wish to enter Great in cell A3, you just need to press the Enter key which will enter Great in A3 for you. Now if you want to enter Game in A3, you also have the freedom to do it. But later on, if you type G in any of the cells, AutoComplete does not come up suggesting Great or Game as you expect. In other words, by typing on your own without accepting the suggestions offered by AutoComplete, you effectively shut down its capability to supply anymore suggestions for that particular letter, which is G here. Again if you type Ga, in another cell in the same column, AutoCorrect will enter me (making it Game).

If you find AutoComplete feature is actually disturbing you instead of being a help, then you can turn off the AutoComplete feature.

1. Go to File → Options and open the Advanced tab.

2. Uncheck the Enable Autocomplete for cell values under the Editing options as in Figure 2-19 (circled in red).

3. Click the OK button.

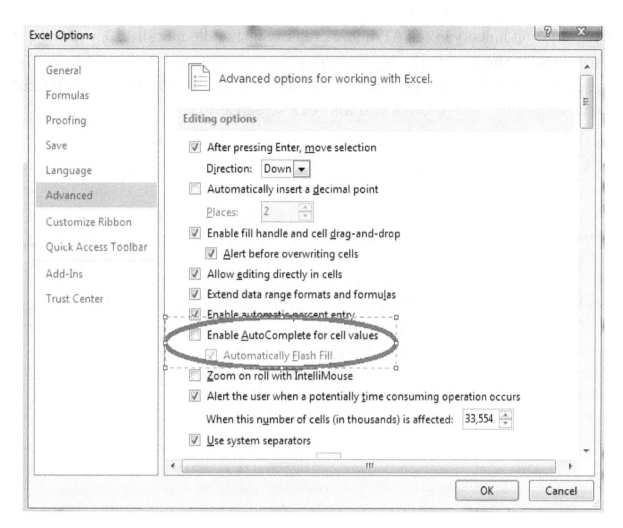

Figure 2-19 Excel Options dialog box with AutoComplete feature off

Excel's AutoFill is just Awesome

You might have to enter sequential dates or numbers normally in worksheets. For example, you might have to enter months from January through December or numbers from 1 to 100. Here comes AutoFill to help you. You just enter the starting value for the series and Excel is smart enough to fill out the series for you. You just have to drag the fill handle, the plus sign which appears as shown in Figure 2-20, to the right if you want the series in a row or to the bottom if you want the series in a column.

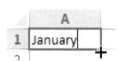

Figure 2-20 Fill handle

After entering January in cell A1, if you drag the fill handle till cell A10, you will get a screen that shows months from January through October. To the right of the last entry in the filled series, you will see a dropdown button that is a shortcut menu of options. Once clicked, you will get a screen as in Figure 2-21.

Figure 2-21 AutoFill Options drop down

Using these different options, you can copy the cell values (making January in cells A1 to A10), fill series, fill data with and without formatting and fill months and flash fill.

Working with a Spaced Series

Instead of having continuous numbers, dates or months, you can even have different patterns filled. Suppose you want only even numbers between 100 and 120 displayed in a row. You just need to enter two sample values 102 and 104 and then drag the fill handle after selecting those two entries as in Figure 2-22.

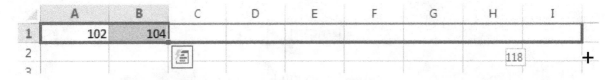

Figure 2-22 Fill handle dragged to get a spaced series of values

Once you release the mouse, you will get a screen as in Figure 2-23.

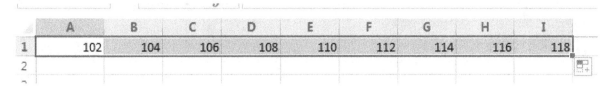

Figure 2-23 Even numbers series filled using AutoFill

Custom Lists for AutoFill

In addition to creating normal or spaced series, you can even have your own custom series. Suppose you want to have a list of rankings in each new worksheet of your workbook. The entries you need are:

- Distinction

- First Class

- Second Class

- Third Class

- Failed

To create the custom series,

1. Go to File → Options and select the Advanced tab.

2. Scroll down and click the Edit Custom Lists button to open Custom Lists dialog box. If you have already entered the list manually in your current worksheet and want to add it as a customs series, skip to Step 4. If you want to enter a new fresh list, go to step 3.

3. Enter the custom series you want in the List entries: area. Do not forget to press the Enter key each time you enter a new item in the series. Click the Add button once you are done with the series so that the series would be added to the Custom lists: area on the left hand side as in Figure 2-24. Skip to Step 6.

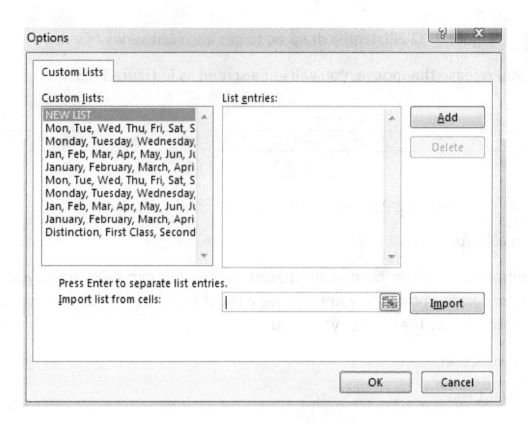

Figure 2-24 New custom List added using Custom Lists dialog box

4. Click inside the Import list from cells: textbox and enter the cell range where you have already entered the custom list in your worksheet. You can even click the icon at the right of the textbox to directly click and select the range of cells. (If you have entered the series in cells A1 to A5, after entering the cell range, your screen will look as in Figure 2-25).

5. Click the Import button to add this list into the List Entries list box.

6. Click the OK button twice, first to close the Options dialog box and second to close the Excel Options dialog box.

Now you are ready with the custom list and if you enter Distinction in cell A1 and drag the fill handle towards the right, you can get the full list.

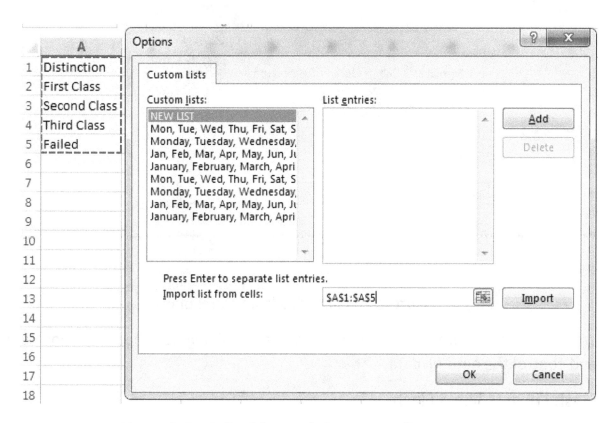

Figure 2-25 Cell address of the custom list to import

AutoFill from Ribbon

You can do the AutoFill directly from the ribbon, especially if you do not have a mouse or touchpad.

1. After entering the initial item(s) of the series, select the cell range where the series is to be created.

2. Go to Home → Fill (under the Editing group) and click Fill with Series selected as in Figure 2-26.

3. From the opened Series dialog box, select AutoFill under the Type section and click OK.

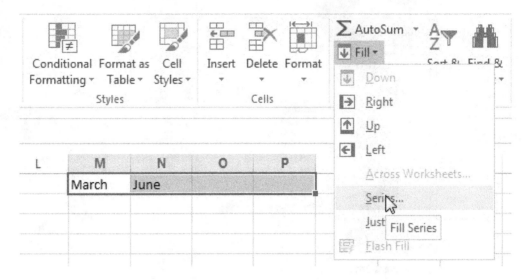

Figure 2-26 Fill Series from the Ribbon

You could find a number of options in the Series dialog box that helps you refine and control the auto fill data.

Flash Fill acts like a Flash

Flash Fill is a brand new feature that helps you enter the required data from one column into another column in the blink of an eye. For example, if you have a column that contains the full name of students. You want to separate their first name, middle name and last name into three separate columns for further processing. You can accomplish this with a couple of keystrokes using Flash Fill feature.

Suppose you have a worksheet as shown in Figure 2-27.

	A	B	C	D
1	Full Name	First Name	Middle Name	Last Name
2	Aaron John Smith			
3	Sarah Maria Young			
4	Emma Rose Turner			
5	Hannah M Arnold			
6	John George Smith			
7	Jane Sarah Harper			

Figure 2-27 Table containing full names which need to be split using Flash Fill

1. Enter name Aaron in cell B2 and press the Enter key.

2. Once you enter S in cell B3, Flash Fill displays a dropdown suggesting all the remaining first names as in Figure 2-28 so that you can select the correct name using arrow key. Hence, you can add all the first names in the remaining cells just with a few keystrokes.

	A	B	C	D
1	Full Name	First Name	Middle Name	Last Name
2	Aaron John Smith	Aaron		
3	Sarah Maria Young	Sarah		
4	Emma Rose Turner	Emma		
5	Hannah M Arnold	Hannah		
6	John George Smith	John		
7	Jane Sarah Harper	Jane		

Figure 2-28 Flash Fill suggesting the first names

3. Enter John in cell C1 and complete the remaining second names and enter Smith in cell D1 and complete the remaining last names.

Data Editing Etiquette

Even after making use of the AutoCorrect feature, some mistakes cannot be avoided. You might notice the mistake either as and when you enter it or after completing a cell entry.

➤ If you identify the mistake before you complete the cell entry, you can just remove it by pressing Backspace key or by double-clicking the mistake entry and pressing the Delete key. Then you can make the correct entry.

➤ If you identify the mistake only after completing the cell entry, you need to go back to the particular cell that contains errors. You can then replace the whole thing or edit just the mistakes.

➤ To replace the whole thing, you can click the cell and press the Delete key or double-click the entry and press the Delete key.

➤ To correct a part of the entry, position the cursor at the appropriate position and delete the part using Del or Backspace keys appropriately.

➤ You can do the same kind of editing you do in a cell on the Formula bar as well.

➢ When you try correcting the mistake after completing the cell entry and going back to the cell, then the mode indicator in the Status bar becomes Edit instead of Enter or Ready as in Figure 2-29.

➢ While Excel is in Edit mode, you need to press the Enter button on the Formula bar or the Enter key on your keyboard to complete entry. You cannot use arrow keys to complete the entry when you are in Edit mode.

Figure 2-29 Workbook in Edit Mode

Insert Something Special

You might have to enter special symbols and characters that are not on the keyboard. For example, you might need foreign currency symbols, mathematical symbols, copyright symbols and so on into your cells. To insert a special symbol or character, go to Insert → Symbol (under the Symbols group) to open a window as shown in Figure 2-30.

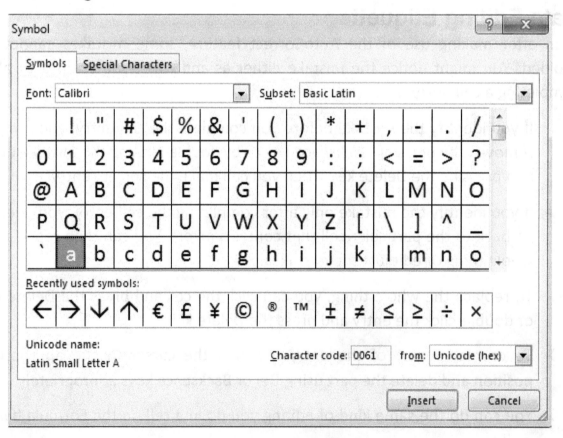

Figure 2-30 Symbols dialog box

You can look for the required symbol in the Symbols tab or Special Characters tab. You just need to select the symbol and click the Insert button to add it in the active cell. You could find the recently used symbols from the Recently used symbols: group under Symbols tab.

Make Sure that Your Data is Safe

Until and unless you save your workbook that contains your valuable data, your data is at risk. If your computer gets shut down unexpectedly or if your computer crashes for any reason, all data that is not saved will be gone. To avoid this, save your work anytime you enter more information than you could bear to lose.

You can save a workbook by clicking the Save button in the Quick Access toolbar or by going to File → Save option or by clicking Alt + F + S. When you try to save a file for the first time, Excel displays the Save As screen and the Documents folder on your Windows Live; SkyDrive would be selected as the place to save the workbook by default. You can change the location by clicking the Browse button if you want to store the workbook locally on your computer.

Once you select the folder where you want to store the workbook, the Save As dialog box will be opened where you need to specify a name for your workbook in the File name: textbox and click the Save button. By default, the name will be Book1 as shown in Figure 2-31.

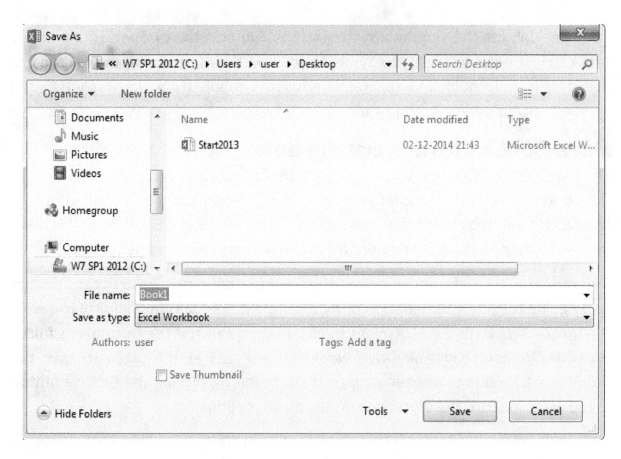

Figure 2-31 Save As Dialog box

Save the Workbook as a PDF File

You can save your workbook as a PDF file in Excel 2013. You just need to select PDF in the Save as type: dropdown of Save As dialog box as shown in Figure 2-32.

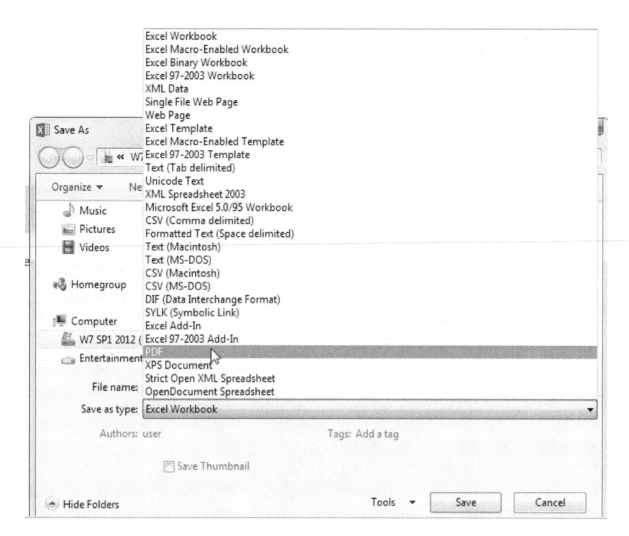

Figure 2-32 Option to save workbook in PDF format

AutoRecover does the Save for You

Excel 2013 offers a document recovery feature which reduces the chances of making you lose everything in case of a system crash or shutdown. The AutoRecover feature saves your workbooks at regular interval (ten minutes by default). You can shorten or lengthen this interval as you want. To accomplish this,

Go to File → Options and select the Save tab.

Change the value in Save Autorecover information every ---- minutes textbox as in Figure 2-33.

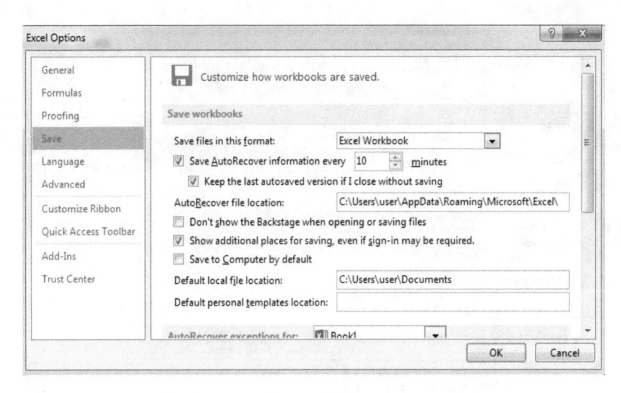

Figure 2-33 Option to change the auto recovery frequency

This AutoRecover feature will work only on workbooks that are saved at least once. Once you re-launch Excel 2013 after a system shutdown or crash, you will find a Document Recovery task pane on the left of the screen showing the available versions of the workbook files that were open. You can find the version you want and get it back by just clicking it.

3. Making it All Look Pretty

Introduction

In this chapter, we will learn how to

- ➤ Select the cells to format
- ➤ Format data tables using the Format as Table command button
- ➤ Adjust column width and row height
- ➤ Hide columns and rows in a worksheet
- ➤ Format cell ranges from Home tab of the Ribbon
- ➤ Use different number formats on cells containing values
- ➤ Format cells using Styles gallery and the Format Painter
- ➤ Format cells under certain conditions

Until you complete entering the data, you might not feel that your cells are not that beautiful. But once you are ready with the data and made it safe, you might feel that data would have been clearer and easier-to-understand if you change the color, size or font of the data appropriately. You don't have to worry at all. Excel has come up with a bunch of tools and techniques to format your data the way you want. Once the formatting is applied to the cells, the existing, edited or newly added data in those cells get that particular format.

Selecting a Group of Cells

A cell selection or the cell range is the collection of cells you choose to format or edit. You have the freedom to apply formatting only to the active cell or to a portion of the worksheet or even to the entire worksheet. You can differentiate the selected cells from other cells because Excel highlights the selected cells in color within the extended cell cursor, except for the active cell that keeps its original color as in Figure 3-1 (cell H13 is the active cell).

You can select different cell ranges at the same time and this is known as noncontiguous selection. Though we see different cell selections in Figure 3-1, it is actually one big noncontiguous cell selection with H13:I13 being the last selection made.

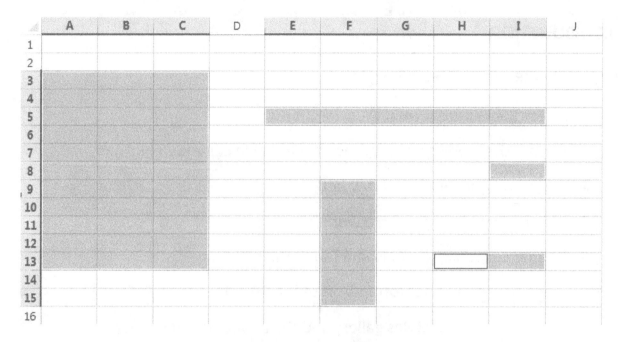

Figure 3-1 Worksheet with several cells selected

Point-and-Click Cells to Select

Selecting the cells using mouse is the most natural and easier way of doing it. You just have to place the mouse, which appears as a white thick cross, on the first cell and just click and drag it in the direction that you want to extend the selection. If you want to select cells in a row, drag your mouse to the right and if you want to select cells in a column, drag your mouse down. If you want to select cells that span in adjacent cells and columns, then drag your mouse diagonally. Once you release the mouse, all the cells highlighted during dragging will be selected.

Shifty Cell Selections

You can speed up the cell selection using Shift + click method. Shift key acts like an extend key that extends selection from the first cell through the last cell you select. To do this,

1. Click the first cell in the selection.

2. Just position the mouse in the last cell in the selection.

3. Hold the Shift key and click the mouse button which will select the cells you want whether cells in the same row, same column or different rows and columns.

Noncontiguous Cell Selections

To make noncontiguous cell selection, select the first group of cells using any of the methods specified above and before selecting the second group of cells, hold down the Ctrl key. As long as you hold down the Ctrl key, Excel does not deselect any of the previous selections because it acts like an add key to include multiple objects in Excel.

Making "big" Selections

You can select an entire row, column or even the whole worksheet easily and quickly.

* To select all the cells in a particular row, click its row number at the left of the row.

* To select all the cells in a particular column, click its column letter at the top of the column.

* To select the entire worksheet, press Ctrl + A or click the Select All button. The Select All button, which is a triangle pointing downwards, is situated below the Formula bar at the left where the row numbers and column names intersect (circled in Figure 3-2).

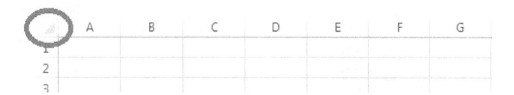

Figure 3-2 Select All button

AutoSelect selects Cells in a Table of Data

Excel's AutoSelect feature allows you to select all the cells in a table of data. To use AutoSelect:

1. Click the first cell of the table to select it.

2. Hold down the Shift key and double-click the right or bottom edge of the active cell with the arrowhead mouse pointer as in Figure 3-3. If you double-clicked the bottom edge of the active cell, then all the cells in the first column of the table would have been selected as in Figure 3-4 and go to Step 3a. If you double-clicked the right edge of the active cell, then all the cells in the first row of the table would have seen selected as in Figure 3-5 and go to Step 3b.

	A	B	C	D
1	Full Name	First Name	Last Name	Grade
2	Aaron Turner	Aaron	Turner	A
3	John Smith	John	Smith	C
4	Hannah Miller	Hannah	Miller	B+
5	Elizabeth Young	Elizabeth	Young	A+
6	Mary Smith	Mary	Smith	B
7	Abel Wright	Abel	Wright	A
8	Janet Arnold	Janet	Arnold	C+
9	Kevin Harper	Kevin	Harper	B+
10	Sarah Smith	Sarah	Smith	A+
11				

Figure 3-3 Arrowhead mouse pointer at the bottom edge of the first cell

3a. Double-click somewhere on the right edge of the cell selection (See Figure 3-6) to select the entire table.

	A	B	C	D
1	Full Name	First Name	Last Name	Grade
2	Aaron Turner	Aaron	Turner	A
3	John Smith	John	Smith	C
4	Hannah Miller	Hannah	Miller	B+
5	Elizabeth Young	Elizabeth	Young	A+
6	Mary Smith	Mary	Smith	B
7	Abel Wright	Abel	Wright	A
8	Janet Arnold	Janet	Arnold	C+
9	Kevin Harper	Kevin	Harper	B+
10	Sarah Smith	Sarah	Smith	A+

Figure 3-4 The entire column of the data table is selected by double-clicking the mouse pointer at the bottom edge of the first cell

3b. Double-click somewhere on the bottom edge of the cell selection to select the entire table.

4. Once selected, the table of data will look like as in Figure 3-7.

	A	B	C	D
1	Full Name	First Name	Last Name	Grade
2	Aaron Turner	Aaron	Turner	A
3	John Smith	John	Smith	C
4	Hannah Miller	Hannah	Miller	B+
5	Elizabeth Young	Elizabeth	Young	A+
6	Mary Smith	Mary	Smith	B
7	Abel Wright	Abel	Wright	A
8	Janet Arnold	Janet	Arnold	C+
9	Kevin Harper	Kevin	Harper	B+
10	Sarah Smith	Sarah	Smith	A+

Figure 3-5 The entire row of the data table is selected by double-clicking the mouse pointer at the right edge of the first cell

	A	B	C	D
1	Full Name	First Name	Last Name	Grade
2	Aaron Turner	Aaron	Turner	A
3	John Smith	John	Smith	C
4	Hannah Miller	Hannah	Miller	B+
5	Elizabeth Young	Elizabeth	Young	A+
6	Mary Smith	Mary	Smith	B
7	Abel Wright	Abel	Wright	A
8	Janet Arnold	Janet	Arnold	C+
9	Kevin Harper	Kevin	Harper	B+
10	Sarah Smith	Sarah	Smith	A+

Figure 3-6 Arrow head mouse pointer at the right edge of the currently selected column before double-clicking and selecting the entire table

	A	B	C	D
1	Full Name	First Name	Last Name	Grade
2	Aaron Turner	Aaron	Turner	A
3	John Smith	John	Smith	C
4	Hannah Miller	Hannah	Miller	B+
5	Elizabeth Young	Elizabeth	Young	A+
6	Mary Smith	Mary	Smith	B
7	Abel Wright	Abel	Wright	A
8	Janet Arnold	Janet	Arnold	C+
9	Kevin Harper	Kevin	Harper	B+
10	Sarah Smith	Sarah	Smith	A+

Figure 3-7 The completely selected table of data

Keyboard Cell Selections

You can use keyboard also to select cells especially if you are more comfortable in using keyboard than mouse. Holding down the Shift key, you need to click arrow keys, PgUp or PgDn keys to move the cell cursor and highlight the cells as it goes.

Extend Cell Selections

If you find it difficult to hold the Shift key while clicking other keys that move the cursor, then there is an easy alternative technique. Just press the F8 key to change the workbook to Extend Selection mode before pressing any cell-pointer movement key. You could see the status as Extend Selection on the Status bar as soon as you release the F8 key as in Figure 3-8. Now Excel will select all the cells when you move the cell cursor as if you were holding down the Shift key.

Figure 3-8 Excel in Extend Mode

Once you are done with the cell selection, do not forget to turn off Extend mode by clicking Esc key or F8 key.

Go to Select Cells

If you are finding it difficult to use the cell-pointer movement keys to select cells, you can make use of the "Go To" feature of Excel. First position the cursor in the first cell of the range and press the F8 key to change Excel to Extend Selection mode. Now press F5 key or Ctrl + G to open the "Go To" dialog box as shown in Figure 3-9. Enter the address of the last cell in the range in the Reference: textbox. Click OK or press Enter to select the specified cell range.

Figure 3-9 Go To dialog box

Noncontiguous Cell Selections

It is a bit complicated to select more than one cell range using keyboard compared to doing it with mouse. You need to alternate between F8 and Shift +F8 to select different cell ranges.

1. Move the cell cursor to the first cell of the first cell range that you want to select.

2. Press F8 to change to Extend mode.

3. Move the cell cursor in the required direction and select the cell range.

4. Press Shift + F8 to switch from Extend mode to Add to Selection mode and you could see the mode information on the Status bar as in Figure 3-10.

5. Move the cell cursor to the first cell of the next cell range that you want.

6. Repeat steps 2 to 5 to select another cell range.

Figure 3-10 Excel in Add to Selection Mode

AutoSelect with Keyboard

You can select all the cells in a table of data using keyboard as well. You have to use the F8 key or Shift key along with Ctrl + arrow keys or End + arrow keys to move the cell cursor from one end to other and to select all the cells in that path. To select an entire table of data,

1. Position the cell cursor in the first cell.

2. Hold the Shift key (or press F8 key).

3. Press Ctrl + →to extend the selection to the cells in the same row.

4. Press Ctrl + ↓ to extend the selection to the cells in the row below.

You can even change the order of the third and fourth steps if you want. Only thing you need to take care is that you should not release the Shift key unless you select all the required cells in the table of data. If you have pressed the F8 key, you should press it again once you are done with the selection.

Format as Table without Selecting Cells

You can apply styles to a table of data without even selecting the cells. If you click the Format as Table button in the Styles group on the Home tab (circled in red in Figure 3-11) when the cell cursor is somewhere within the table of data, the styles selected will be applied to all the cells in that table of data.

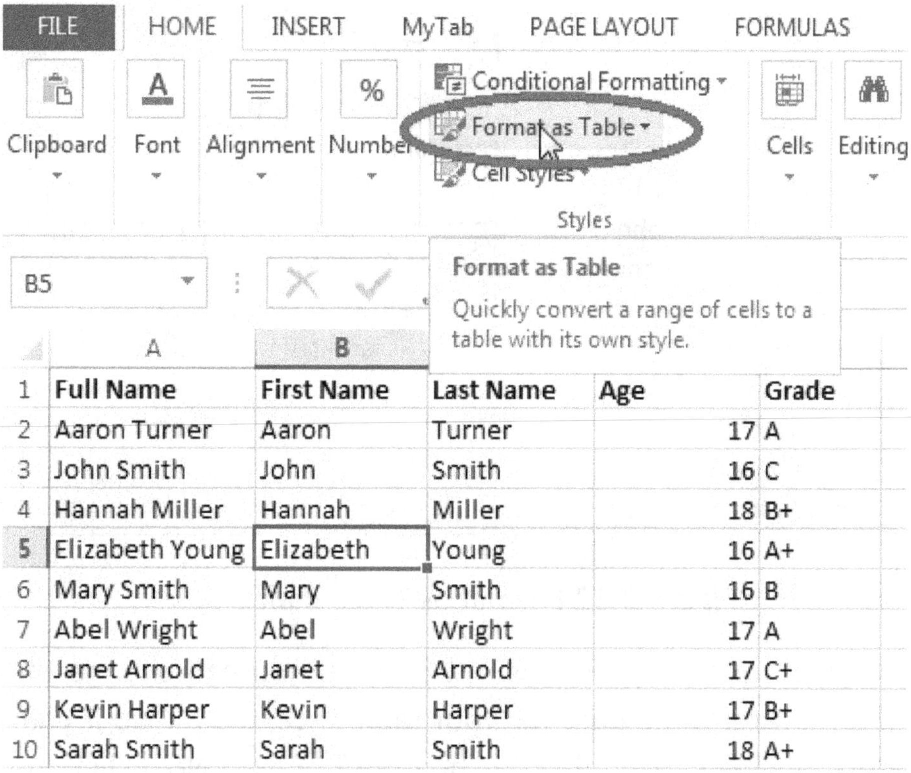

Figure 3-11 Format as Table command button in Styles group

Once you click the Format as Table button, you could find an extensive Table Styles gallery with a number of thumbnails classified in three sections- Light, Medium and Dark. As soon as you click any of the thumbnails, Excel opens a dialog box with address of the data table automatically added as in in Figure 3-12. You could find that Excel tries its best to guess the cell range of the data table to apply the style to.

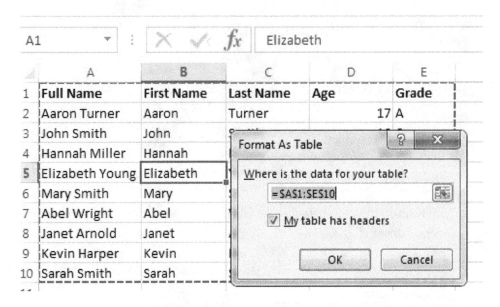

Figure 3-12 Format as Table dialog box

If the cell range assumed by Excel is not correct, you can change the cell range address in the "Where is the data for your table?" textbox. Also if your data table has no headers, uncheck "My table has headers" option. Now click the OK button or press Enter so that Excel applies the selected style to all the cells in the table of data. You could also find a new DESIGN tab (circled in in Figure 3-13) added after the view tab and also a Quick Analysis Tool icon at the right bottom of the table.

The Design tab allows you to see how your table would appear while applying different styles. Just select any of the thumbnails provided in the Table Styles group on the Design tab as shown in Figure 3-14. You can have a Live Preview of these different styles. Click the triangle pointing upwards or downwards to scroll up or down and get more style thumbnails.

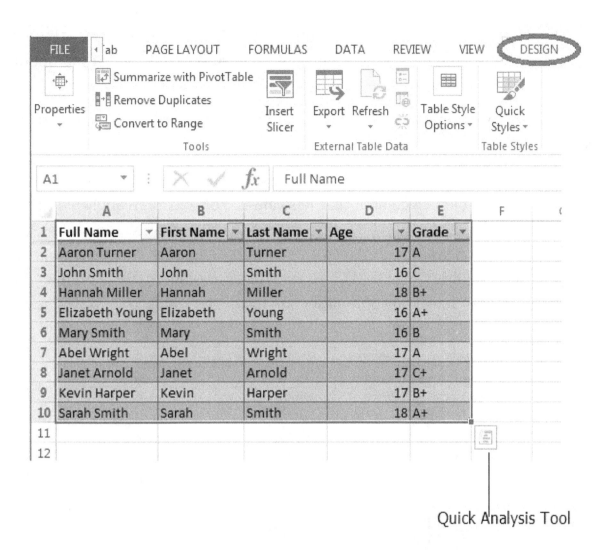

Figure 3-13 Table of data formatted using Format as Table option

Figure 3-14 Live Preview of styles on table of data

You could check or uncheck the options in the Table Style Options group to customize the appearance of the table of data even more. Different options include:

Header Row: Once checked, it adds special formatting and filter buttons to the column headings in the first row of the table.

Total Row: Once checked, it adds a new row at the bottom of the table that displays the sums of each column that has values. You can even apply a different statistical function other than SUM. If you click the cell in the column's Total Row, a dropdown button will be displayed as in Figure 3-15 with functions Average, Count, Count Numbers, Max, Min, Sum, StdDev (Standard Deviation) or Var (Variance). You can select any of the function to get the result.

	A	B	C	D	E
1	Full Name ▾	First Name ▾	Last Name ▾	Age ▾	Grade ▾
2	Aaron Turner	Aaron	Turner	17	A
3	John Smith	John	Smith	16	C
4	Hannah Miller	Hannah	Miller	18	B+
5	Elizabeth Young	Elizabeth	Young	16	A+
6	Mary Smith	Mary	Smith	16	B
7	Abel Wright	Abel	Wright	17	A
8	Janet Arnold	Janet	Arnold	17	C+
9	Kevin Harper	Kevin	Harper	17	B+
10	Sarah Smith	Sarah	Smith	18	A+
11	Total			▾	9
12				None	
13				Average	
14				Count	
15				Count Numbers	
16				Max	
17				Min	
18				Sum	
				StdDev	
				Var	
				More Functions...	

Figure 3-15 Dropdown with different statistical functions

Banded Rows: Once clicked, borders will be added to every row.

Banded Columns: Once clicked, borders will be added to every column.

First Column: Once clicked, the data in the first column of the table is displayed in bold.

Last Column: Once clicked, the data in the last column of the table is displayed in bold.

Once you are done with customizing the table, you have to click a cell outside the table of data which will remove the Design tab from the Ribbon. Whenever you want to format the table, you can click a cell inside the table to add the Design tab automatically.

Have Best-Fit Column with AutoFit

If you are not satisfied the way Excel adjusts the width of your columns, you can do it on your own. It is so simple to do a best-fit using the AutoFit feature. With this method, Excel automatically determines how much to adjust the width to fit the current longest entry in the column. To get the best fit for a column using AutoFit:

1. Position the mouse pointer on the right border of the column title of the column you want to adjust the width of (Figure 3-16).

2. Double click the mouse button which will adjust the width automatically.

Figure 3-16 Mouse pointer on the right border of the column title to adjust the width of the column to best fit

You can apply AutoFit to multiple columns simultaneously. Select all the columns (pressing Ctrl key if columns are not neighboring) and double click any of the right borders.

Changing Column Width

You can adjust the width of the columns by clicking the Format button in the Cells group on the Home tab. The Format dropdown has the following options under the Cell Size section to adjust the width of columns as in Figure 3-17:

Column Width: Once clicked, opens the Column Width dialog box where you can enter the number of characters that you want for the column width and click OK.

AutoFit Column Width: Excel applies AutoFit feature to adjust the width of the columns.

Default Width: Once clicked, opens the Standard Width dialog box displaying the standard column width of 8.43 characters. If you change the value, the specified width will be applied to all columns.

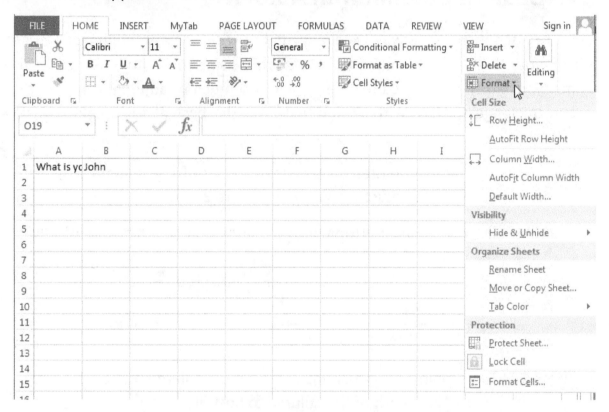

Figure 3-17 Cell Size section in the dropdown opened by clicking the Format button with options to adjust the column width

Rambling Rows

You can adjust the height of the rows almost in the same way as adjusting the width of the columns. But the fact is that as Excel automatically adjusts the height of the rows to accommodate larger entries, you might not have to do it on your own quite often. To adjust the row height, you have to drag the bottom border of the row until the row gets the required height. You can also use the AutoFit feature to adjust the row by double clicking the bottom border of the row number of the column you want to adjust the height of.

As with columns, you can adjust the row height using the height options in the Cell Size section of the Format button's dropdown on the Home tab. The Format dropdown has the following options under the Cell Size section to adjust the height of rows:

Row Height: Once clicked, opens the Row Height dialog box where you can enter the number of points that you want and click OK.

AutoFit Row Height: Excel applies AutoFit feature to adjust the height of the rows.

Vanishing Columns and Rows

Though you can hide worksheet columns and rows by adjusting the width and height, Excel offers an easy method: Hide & Unhide button under the Visibility section on the Format button's dropdown in the Cells group on the Home tab.

To hide a column,

1. Select any cell in the column that you want to hide.

2. Click the Format button in the Cells group on the Home tab.

3. Click Hide & Unhide under the Visibility section.

4. Click the Hide Columns option from the newly opened dropdown menu.

Boom!!! The column is vanished.

To unhide the hidden column,

1. Position the mouse pointer on the previous column heading (if you have hidden column D, position the mouse pointer on C).

2. Drag the mouse pointer right to select both previous column and next column of the hidden column (In this case, to select columns C and E).

3. Click the Format button in the Cells group on the Home tab.

4. Click Hide & Unhide under the Visibility section.

5. Click the Unhide Columns option from the newly opened dropdown menu.

Excel brings back the column.

The procedure for hiding and unhiding rows is exactly the same as that of columns. The only difference is that to hide a row, you need to click the Hide Rows option (Step 4 in hiding the column) and to unhide a row, you need to click the Unhide Rows option (Step 5 in in unhiding column).

Format Cells from Home

Sometimes, you might have to apply some simple cell formatting instead of what the heavy Format as Table feature offers. For example, if you just want to make the column headings bold, you do not have to go for Format as Table option. You could find a number of formatting options on the Home tab under the Font, Alignment and Number groups that allows you to perform this kind of simple and targeted cell formatting. Table 3-1 provides the complete list of formatting options on the Home tab.

Group	Button Name	Function
Font	Font	Displays a dropdown with a list of fonts from which you can select a font of your choice
Font	Font Size	Displays a dropdown with a list of font sizes from which you can a select a font size. You can also enter a font size after clicking the textbox if the font size you prefer is not available in the dropdown
Font	Increase Font Size	Increases the font size by one point
Font	Decrease Font Size	Decreases the font size by one point
Font	Bold	Makes the entries in the cell bold
Font	Italic	Makes the entries in the cell italic
Font	Underline	Makes the entries in the cell underlines
Font	Borders	Displays a dropdown from which you can select the border style for your active cell(s)
Font	Fill Color	Displays a color palette from which you can select a color for the background of the cell
Font	Font Color	Displays a color palette from which you can select a color for the font of the data in the cell

Alignment	Top Align	Vertically align the entries in the cell with the top border of their cells
Alignment	Middle Align	Vertically centers the entries in the cell between the top and bottom borders of their cells
Alignment	Bottom Align	Vertically align the entries in the cell with the bottom border of their cells
Alignment	Align Left	Horizontally align the entries in the cell with the left edge of their cells
Alignment	Center	Horizontally centers the entries in the cell between the left and right edges of their cells
Alignment	Align Right	Horizontally align the entries in the cell with the right edge of their cells
Alignment	Orientation	Displays a dropdown from which you can select options to change the angle and direction of entries in the cell
Alignment	Increase Indent	Increases the margin between the entries in the cell selection and their left cell borders by one tab stop
Alignment	Decrease Indent	Decreases the margin between the entries in the cell selection and their left cell borders by one tab stop
Alignment	Wrap Text	Wrap entries in the cell that spills over the right borders onto multiple lines within the current column width
Alignment	Merge and Center	Merges the selected cells into a single cell and centers the entry between left and right border
Number	Number Format	Displays a dropdown from which you can select a number format
Number	Accounting Number Format	Displays a dropdown from which you can select an accounting number format
Number	Percent Style	Formats the cell selection using the Percent format that multiplies the value by 100 and adds a percent sign
Number	Comma Style	Formats the cell selection using the Comma format that uses commas to separate thousands
Number	Increase Decimal	Adds a decimal place to the value in the cell

Number	Decrease Decimal	Removes a decimal place from the value in the cell

Table 3-1 Different formatting options on the Home tab

Mini-Bar Makes Formatting Easier

You can apply formatting to the required cells just within the worksheet, not without going to the Ribbon, using a new feature offered by Excel 2013: mini-bar (Yes, it is mini toolbar's nickname). Select the cells that need formatting and right click somewhere in the selection to open the mini-bar (circled in Figure 3-18) along with the context menu.

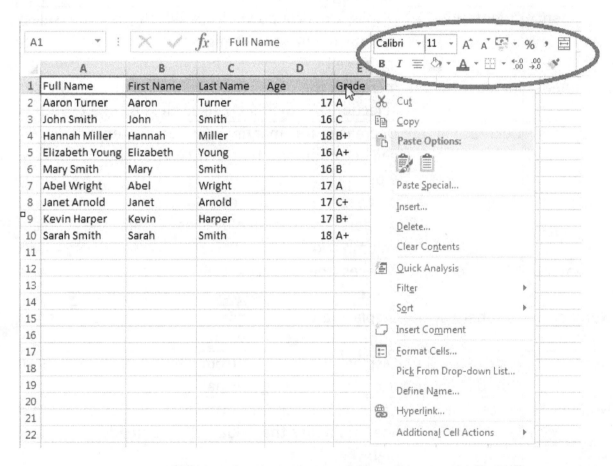

Figure 3-18 Mini-bar displayed along with context menu

You could find that the mini-bar contains many of the formatting options available in Font, Alignment and Number groups on the Home tab. Moreover, mini-bar also contains the Format Painter option from the Clipboard group of the Home tab to copy the formatting. Once you click any of the button, the context menu disappears and the particular formatting gets applied to the selected cells.

Have More Formatting Options with Format Cells Dialog Box

Though Font, Alignment and Number groups of Home tab offers a number of formatting options, all Excel formatting commands are not available there. The Format Cells dialog box provides access to all the formatting commands. To open the Format Cells dialog box, you can follow any of the method give below:

- ✓ Click the Number format dialog box launcher (circled in Figure 3-19) in the Number group of the Home tab.

- ✓ Press Ctrl + 1 (1 is the number key 1 and not F1)

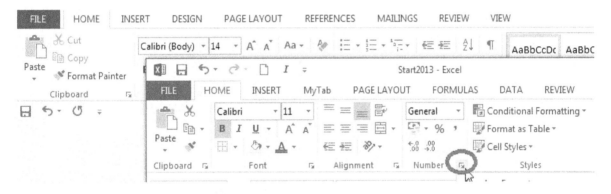

Figure 3-19 Number Format command button to open Format Cells dialog box

The Format Cells dialog box contains six tabs including Number, Alignment, Font, Border, Fill and Protection.

Experiment with the Fonts

When you start a new workbook, the default font assigned to all the entries is the Calibri font in 11 point size. You can change this default font by going to File → Options, opening the General tab, and selecting the font from the Use this as the default font: dropdown under the When creating new workbooks section (circled in Figure 3-20). You can also change the default font size by changing the value in the Font size: dropdown.

You can change the font of the entry in selected cells by selecting the font from the Font button's dropdown menu on the Home tab. You can change the font size by selecting the font size from the Font Size button's dropdown menu or by clicking Increase Font Size or Decrease Font Size buttons in the Font group on the Home tab.

You can also add or remove the styling of bold, italic, underlining, or strikethrough to the font you use. Once you select any of these styling buttons, the particular button becomes shaded whenever you position the cell cursor in the cell(s) that contain that styling as in Figure 3-21.

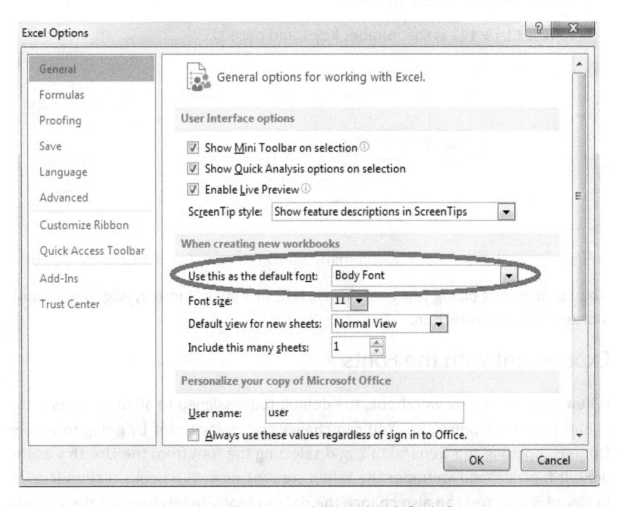

Figure 3-20 Option to change the default font

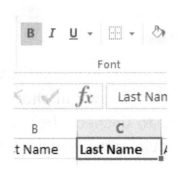

Figure 3-21 Styling button shaded

You can make changes to the font from the Font tab in the Format Cells dialog box which will be opened by clicking Ctrl + 1. You could find all font changing options under one roof if you open the Font tab of the Format Cells dialog box as in Figure 3-22. The advantage of using options with Font tab is that it contains a Preview box where you can see the changes live.

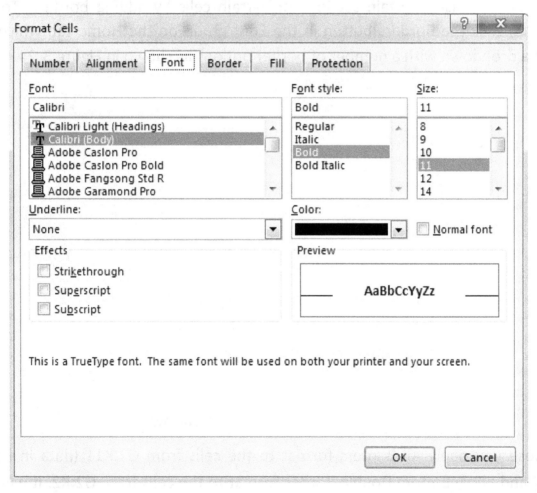

Figure 3-22 Format Cells dialog box with Font tab opened

Bring on the Borders

The gridlines that separate rows and columns in the worksheet are just guidelines that help you see each cell clearly. You can choose to print the sheet without those gridlines even. You need to uncheck the View option under the Gridlines section in the Sheet Options group on the Page Layout tab (circled in Figure 3-23).

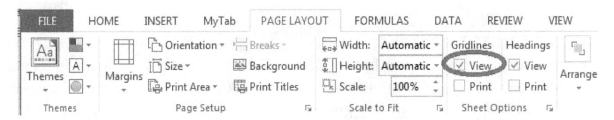

Figure 3-23 View option to hide or show gridlines while printing

You can emphasize certain sections or certain cells by adding borders. To add borders, click the Borders button in the Font group on the Home tab which will open a dropdown with a number of border options as shown in Figure 3-24.

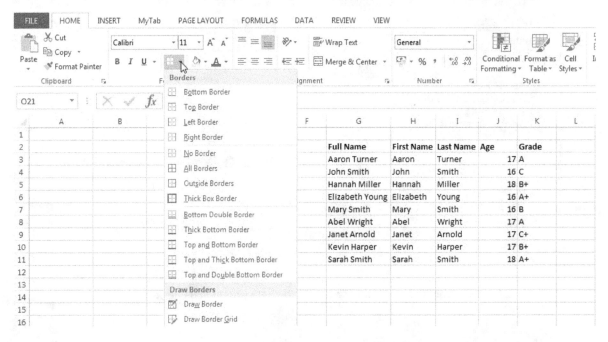

Figure 3-24 The Borders dropdown

Suppose you apply All Borders format to the cells from G2:K11 (data in Figure 3-24) and apply Bottom Double Border format to the cells from G2:K2. It will give a screen as shown in Figure 3-25.

	F	G	H	I	J	K

Full Name	First Name	Last Name	Age	Grade
Aaron Turner	Aaron	Turner	17	A
John Smith	John	Smith	16	C
Hannah Miller	Hannah	Miller	18	B+
Elizabeth Young	Elizabeth	Young	16	A+
Mary Smith	Mary	Smith	16	B
Abel Wright	Abel	Wright	17	A
Janet Arnold	Janet	Arnold	17	C+
Kevin Harper	Kevin	Harper	17	B+
Sarah Smith	Sarah	Smith	18	A+

Figure 3-25 Table of data with borders added

You can change the type, thickness or color of your border from the Border tab of the Format Cells dialog box. To change the thickness or style of the border, select one from the Style: list. To change the color of the border, select the color from the Color: dropdown palette. Click OK to apply the style you selected.

Color the Cell and Font

You can color the selected cell(s) by clicking the Fill Color button in the Font group on the Home tab. It will open a Color palette dropdown from where you can select the required color. Live Preview is available which helps you see how the cell appears in the going-to-select color just by moving the cursor over different colors.

You can even change the color of the text or value entered in a cell by clicking the Font Color button in the Font group on the Home tab. It will open a Color palette dropdown from where you can select the required color.

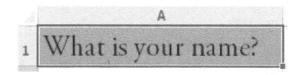

Apply Patterns and Gradient Effects

You can apply a new pattern to your selected cell(s) from the Fill tab of the Format Cells dialog box (Ctrl + 1). Select a pattern from the Pattern Style: dropdown palette. You can also change the background color of the pattern by selecting a color from the Background Color: palette and change the color of the pattern by selecting a color from the Pattern Color: color palette. If you select the Thin Vertical Stripe pattern in the Pattern Style: dropdown, Light Blue in the Pattern Color: and Red in the Background Color: and apply it to an empty cell, you will get a screen as shown in Figure 3-27. The height and width is increased just to have a clearer view.

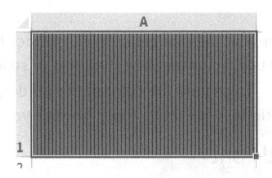

Figure 3-27 A cell with a pattern applied

You can apply a gradient effect that goes from one color to another in a certain direction to the selected cells. Click the Fill Effects button in the Fill tab of the Format Cells dialog box. It will open a Fill Effects dialog box from which you can select colors, shading styles and variants. You can have a preview of your effect in the Sample: section of the Fill Effects dialog box. Once you get the preview as you want, click OK to close the Fill Effects dialog box. The selected effect appears in the Sample area in the Fill tab of the Format Cells dialog box. Click OK to apply the gradient effect to the selected cell(s).

Altering the Alignment

Horizontal Alignment

All text entries are left aligned horizontally and all value entries are right aligned horizontally by default. There are three horizontal alignment options in the Alignment group of the Home tab: Align Left, Center and Align Right that aligns the text left, center or right respectively.

You could also find a special alignment button named Merge & Center in the Alignment group itself. You can use this to center a title or any text across multiple cells. Suppose you have a table of data as in Figure 3-28.

1	Sales (2014-2015)					
2		Half Year - 1		Half Year - 2		
3	Sales Representative	Quarter 1	Quarter 2	Quarter 3	Quarter 4	Full Year
4	Aaron Turner	17,569.25	16,256.00	18,450.50	17,368.00	$ 69,643.75
5	John Smith	8,657.00	8,896.00	6,743.80	7,912.20	$ 32,209.00
6	Hannah Miller	14,699.20	18,900.50	18,090.80	16,231.60	$ 67,922.10
7	Elizabeth Young	12,980.60	11,080.50	13,875.00	12,768.40	$ 50,704.50
8	Mary Smith	10,890.60	11,545.00	12,457.40	9,873.80	$ 44,766.80
9		$ 64,796.65	$ 66,678.00	$ 69,617.50	$ 64,154.00	$ 2,65,246.15

Figure 3-28 Table of data

Suppose you want to center the title "Sales (2014-2015)" entered in cell A1 over the entire table (from cells A1 through F1). To do this, select cells from A1 through F1 and click the Merge & Center button in the Alignment group on the Home tab. Now the title will be centered across the entire table. Similarly, if you want to make the title "Half Year – 1" across B and C columns, you need to select B2 and C2 cells and click the Merge & Center button. Repeat the same after selecting D2 and E2 to center the title "Half Year – 2". After merging and centering, your table of data will look as in Figure 3-29.

	A	B	C	D	E	F
1				Sales (2014-2015)		
2		Half Year - 1		Half Year - 2		
3	Sales Representative	Quarter 1	Quarter 2	Quarter 3	Quarter 4	Full Year
4	Aaron Turner	17,569.25	16,256.00	18,450.50	17,368.00	$ 69,643.75
5	John Smith	8,657.00	8,896.00	6,743.80	7,912.20	$ 32,209.00
6	Hannah Miller	14,699.20	18,900.50	18,090.80	16,231.60	$ 67,922.10
7	Elizabeth Young	12,980.60	11,080.50	13,875.00	12,768.40	$ 50,704.50
8	Mary Smith	10,890.60	11,545.00	12,457.40	9,873.80	$ 44,766.80
9		$ 64,796.65	$ 66,678.00	$ 69,617.50	$ 64,154.00	$ 2,65,246.15

Figure 3-29 Titles centered using Merge & Center button

You can unmerge the cells as before by selecting the merged cell and clicking the Merge & Center button.

Vertical Alignment

The Align Left, Center and Align Right buttons align the entries with respect to the left and right borders of the cell, which is horizontally. You can align the entries with respect to the top and bottom borders if you want, that is vertically. By default, all entries align vertically with the bottom border as in Figure 3-30.

You can change the vertical alignment by clicking the button Top Align or Middle Align in the Alignment group on the Home tab.

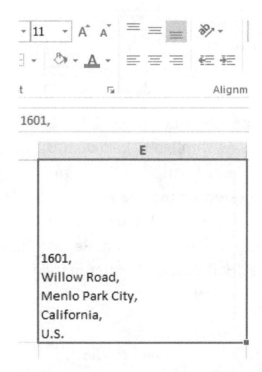

Figure 3-30 Entries aligned vertically with the bottom by default

Intent on Indents

You can increase or decrease the horizontal indent by clicking the Increase Indent button (button with a right pointing arrow) or the Decrease Indent button (button with a left pointing arrow). When you click the Increase Indent button once, Excel indents the entry in the selected cell(s) to the right by three character widths. The Decrease Indent button does the opposite.

Wrap the Text

If you want to see long entries completely in the cell without spilling the text over the right cells and without widening the width of the column, you can use the Wrap Text option in the Alignment group on the Home tab. Suppose you have an entry in cell E1 as shown in Figure 3-31 that is spilled over to the cells in the right.

Figure 3-31 Entry spilled over to the right column

If you use the AutoFit feature to increase the width of the column, the screen will look as shown in Figure 3-32.

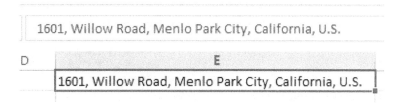

Figure 3-32 The full entry displayed by widening the column using AutoFit feature

If you want to see the full entry without widening the column, you need to click the Wrap Text button in the Alignment group on the Home tab before widening the column and you will get a screen as shown in Figure 3-33.

Figure 3-33 Entry aligned using the Wrap Text option

Now you are able to see the full entry without widening the column.

To enter a long entry in separate lines in the same cell, you need to press Alt + Enter where you want the new line.

Rotate the Entry

Instead of just wrapping the text entries, you can change the orientation of the wrapped entry as you want using any of the options available in Orientation button's dropdown in the Alignment group on the Home tab (Figure 3-34). It will make the entries more readable.

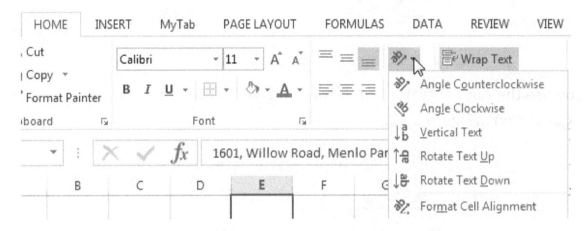

Figure 3-34 Orientation drop down

If you rotate the entry 90 degrees counter clockwise using the Rotate Text Up option, the entry will look as shown in Figure 3-35.

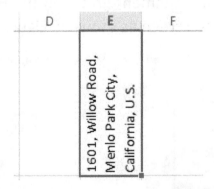

Figure 3-35 Entry rotated counterclockwise

To rotate the entry at a required angle that is not available in the dropdown, click the Format Cell Alignment option in the Orientation's dropdown menu which opens the Format Cells dialog box with Alignment tab opened. You can use the controls in the Orientation section to set the angle.

Shrink to Fit

You can prevent Excel from widening the column, at the same time displaying the full entry using the "Shrink to Fit" option available in the Alignment tab of the Format Cells dialog box. Only thing is that when the entry is shrinked, it could become too small to be legible as shown in Figure 3-36.

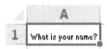

Figure 3-36 Font size reduced when the "Shrink to Fit" formatting is done

Formatting Numbers

You can format the cells that contain numbers (values) before or after you enter values in. Select cells that contain values that need formatting. Select the number format you want to apply from the Number group of the Home tab or from the Number tab of the Format Cells dialog box.

Accounting for Currency

You might have to use the Accounting Number Format option more often whenever you deal with financial data. The Accounting Number Format adds a currency sign, commas between thousands of dollars, and two decimal places to any values in a selected range and also negative values are enclosed in parentheses.

In Figure 3-37, you could find that only the total values (cells B7:E7 and F2:F7) are formatted for accounting. Though all the values can be formatted for accounting, it will make the table too much congested and confusing with lots of $ signs and commas.

A	B	C	D	E	F
1 Sales Representative	Quarter 1	Quarter 2	Quarter 3	Quarter 4	Full Year
2 Aaron Turner	17569.25	16256	18450.5	17368	$ 69,643.75
3 John Smith	8657	8896	6743.8	7912.2	$ 32,209.00
4 Hannah Miller	14699.2	18900.5	18090.8	16231.6	$ 67,922.10
5 Elizabeth Young	12980.6	11080.5	13875	12768.4	$ 50,704.50
6 Mary Smith	10890.6	11545	12457	9873.8	$ 44,766.40
7	$ 64,796.65	$ 66,678.00	$ 69,617.10	$ 64,154.00	$ 2,65,245.75

Figure 3-37 Table of data with total values formatted using Accounting Number format

Clever Comma Style

You can apply the Comma Style format to insert commas in larger numbers to separate thousands, hundred thousands and so on. Though the Comma Style format does not display currency signs, it displays two decimal places and puts negative values in parentheses. Hence, the Comma Style format can be used as an alternative to the Currency format especially when it is so obvious that you are dealing with currency that you do not have to insert currency signs.

If you apply Comma Style format to the cells that contain values except that contains totals (B2:E6), your data will look as shown in Figure 3-38.

A	B	C	D	E	F
1 Sales Representative	Quarter 1	Quarter 2	Quarter 3	Quarter 4	Full Year
2 Aaron Turner	17,569.25	16,256.00	18,450.50	17,368.00	$ 69,643.75
3 John Smith	8,657.00	8,896.00	6,743.80	7,912.20	$ 32,209.00
4 Hannah Miller	14,699.20	18,900.50	18,090.80	16,231.60	$ 67,922.10
5 Elizabeth Young	12,980.60	11,080.50	13,875.00	12,768.40	$ 50,704.50
6 Mary Smith	10,890.60	11,545.00	12,457.00	9,873.80	$ 44,766.40
7	$ 64,796.65	$ 66,678.00	$ 69,617.10	$ 64,154.00	$ 2,65,245.75

Figure 3-38 Table of data with values formatted using Comma Style format

Play with Percent Style

When you want to insert data such as inflation rates, growth rates, interest rates and so on, you might have to insert percent sign in your cells. Of course, you can manually insert percent signs for values that you enter. But there could be many cells that get percent values as a result of formula calculation. In such cases, as it is not practical to insert percent sign on your own, you can apply the Percent Style formatting. You just have to select the cells and click the Percent Style button in the Number group on the Home tab.

Decide the Decimals

You can change the number of decimal places displayed in a number by using the Increase Decimal button (the one with the arrow pointing left) or the Decrease Decimal button (the one with the arrow pointing right). When you click the Increase Decimal button once, Excel adds one more decimal place to the value in the selected cell and the Decrease Decimal button does the opposite.

Excel's Double Play in Formatting Numbers

Excel does a kind of double play and acts like an illusionist when formatting values. Suppose, you enter the value 78.9657 in a cell and you format the value by clicking the Comma Style button. Now you will see the value 78.97 in the cell whereas the value displayed on the Formula bar will still be 78.9657 itself as in Figure 3-39.

E2	▼	:	✕ ✓ f_x	78.9657

	A	B	C	D	E
1					
2					78.97

Figure 3-39 The formatted value and the actual value in the cell is different

If you do some calculation using the value in the cell, you could find that the value on the formula bar is actually taken. For example, if you enter the formula =E2*1000 in cell A1, A1 will contain the value 78,965.70 and not 78,970.00. So, it is obvious that Excel rounds up only the display of the value.

You can match the formatted value and the actual value by following some simple steps and checking an option. But only thing is that you cannot return to the previous state by unchecking the same option. To match the formatted value and the actual value:

1. Go to file → Options and select the Advanced tab.

2. Check Set precision as displayed option (circled in Figure 3-40) under the When calculating this workbook: section.

3. Click OK when you see the message Data will permanently lose accuracy in an alert box. Click OK again to close the Excel Options dialog box.

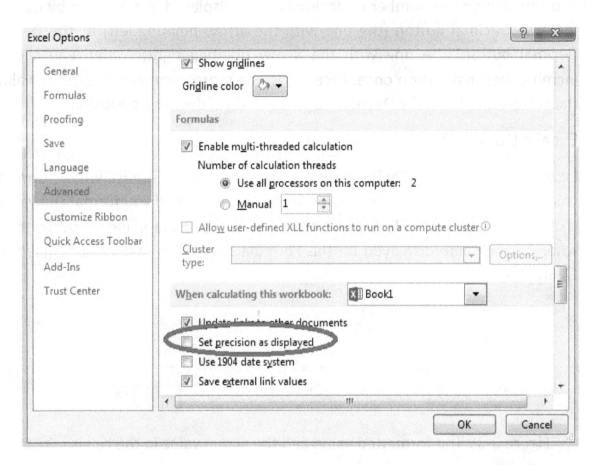

Figure 3-40 Set precision as displayed option to match the display and value

Be Happy to Have More Number Formats

There are many more number formats available in addition to the formats available in the Number group on the Home tab. Open the Format Cells dialog box by clicking Ctrl+1 and inside the Category list box in the Number tab, you could find some special number formats including Fraction, Scientific, Text, Special and Custom. Even the formats existing in the Number group on the Home tab have some additional options here to refine the formatting. By clicking each item in the Category list box, you could find different options available with each of them.

Readymade Styles Make it Easy

You could find a collection of readymade styles that you can immediately apply to the selected cell(s) in the Cell Styles gallery opened by clicking the Cell Styles button in the Styles group on the Home tab as shown in Figure 3-41.

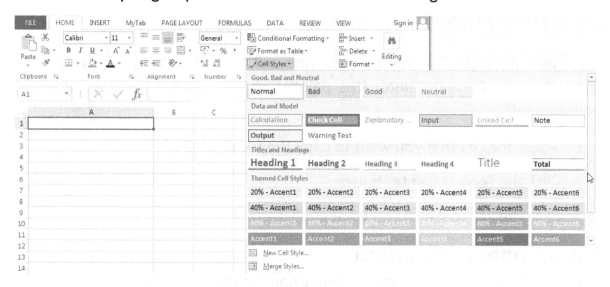

Figure 3-41 Cell Styles gallery opened with readymade styles

You can have a Live Preview each time you select a new style.

Contribute a Custom Style to the Gallery

You can create a new style on your own and add it to the gallery. Manually format a cell with the styles you want including font, font size, color, background color, patterns, borders, alignment and so on. Then click the Cell Styles button in the Styles group on the Home tab followed by the New Cell Style option. It will open a Style dialog box where you can provide a name for your style before clicking OK. Now the style you created is added to the gallery under the Custom section.

Copy Custom Styles from One Workbook into Another

You can easily copy custom styles from one workbook to another.

1. Open the workbook that has the custom style.

2. Open the workbook that needs the custom style added to it.

3. Click the Cell Styles button in the Styles group on the Home tab.

4. Click the Merge Styles option at the bottom which opens the Merge Styles dialog box.

5. Click the name of the open workbook file that contains the custom styles and then click OK.

Copy Formatting using Format Painter

If you want to apply the formatting in one cell to another cell, you can use the wonderful tool: Format Painter (the paintbrush icon) in the Clipboard group on the Home tab.

1. Select the cell that you want to copy the formatting of.

2. Click the Format Painter button.

3. Click the cell to which you want apply formatting.

Conditional Formatting

Conditional formatting is a great formatting option that enables you to apply formatting only if the entry satisfies certain condition. It is a great tool when it comes to data visualization and analysis. Click the Conditional Formatting button in the Styles group on the Home tab and it opens a dropdown menu as shown in Figure 3-42.

You could find the following options in the dropdown:

➢ Highlight Cell Rules: Once clicked, opens a new menu with various options for defining formatting rules that highlight the cells in the cell selection that contain certain values, text, or dates; that have values greater or less than a particular value; or that fall within a certain ranges of values.

➢ Top/Bottom Rules: Opens a new menu with various options for defining formatting rules that highlight the top and bottom values, percentages, and above and below average values in the cell selection.

➢ Data Bars: Opens a palette with different color data bars that you can apply to indicate the cell values relative to each other by clicking the data bar thumbnail.

➢ Color Scales: Opens a palette with different two- and three-colored scales that you can apply to indicate the values relative to each other by clicking the color scale thumbnail.

➢ Icon Sets: Opens a palette with different sets of icons that you can add to the selected cells.

➢ New Rule: Opens the New Formatting Rule dialog box where you define a custom conditional formatting rule to apply to the cell selection.

➢ Clear Rules: Opens a new menu where you can remove conditional formatting rules by clicking the correct option.

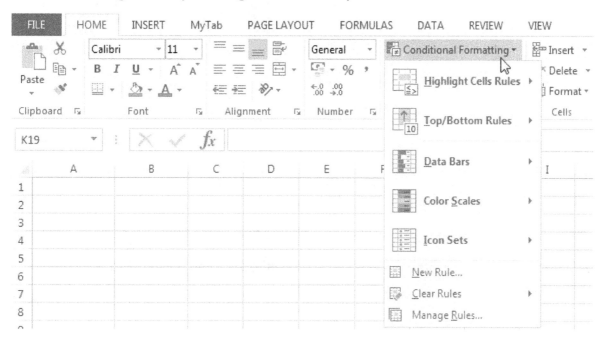

Figure 3-42 Conditional Formatting button's dropdown

Figure 3-43 shows a table of data while being the Greater Than rule is applied. You could find that only the cell that contains a value greater than the specified values gets formatting. This way you could find easily who achieved a specified target (here 18500)

Figure 3-44 shows a table of data where the top 3 items are conditionally formatted and the bottom 3 items are being formatted. This way you could find who are best and worst performers.

Figure 3-45 shows a table of data where the sales data is visualized using data bars.

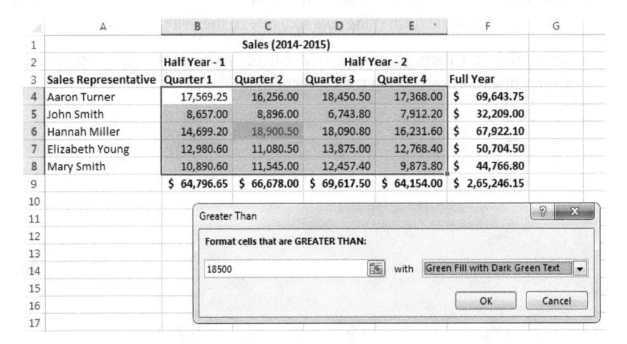

Figure 3-43 Conditional Formatting applied using Highlight Cell Rules

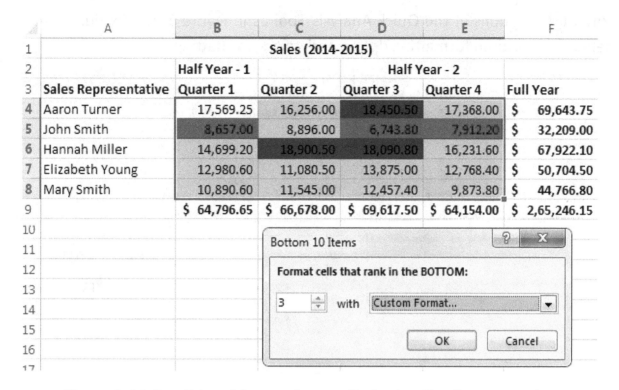

Figure 3-44 Conditional formatting applied using Top/Bottom Rules

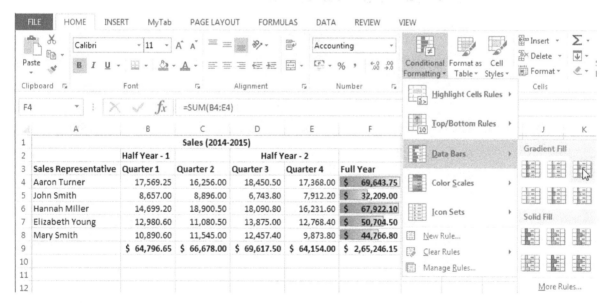

Figure 3-45 Conditional formatting applied using Data Bars Rules

Quick Conditional Formatting with Quick Analysis Tool

The quickest and easiest way to format selected cells based on different conditions is using Quick Analysis Tool. You could find most of the conditional formatting options in the Quick Analysis Tool as in Figure 3-46. You just need to select the required formatting option and do the formatting.

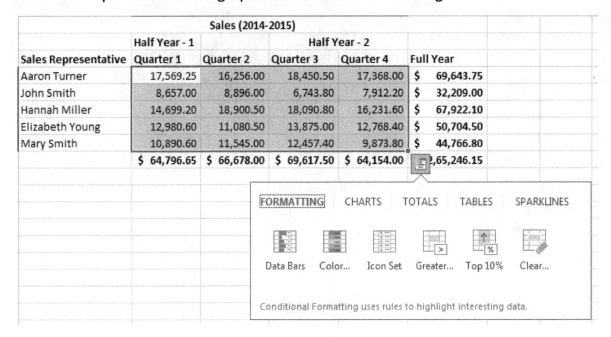

Figure 3-46 Quick Analysis Tool

4. Going Through Changes

Introduction

In this chapter, we will learn how to

- ➤ Open workbooks for editing
- ➤ Undo your boo-boos
- ➤ Move and copy with drag and drop
- ➤ Copy formulas with AutoFill
- ➤ Move and copy with Cut, Copy and Paste
- ➤ Delete or clear cell entries
- ➤ Delete and insert columns and rows
- ➤ Spell-check the worksheet
- ➤ Validate cell entries with the Text to Speech feature

Suppose you are now happily and proudly relaxing after completing a major Excel project. But because of some data changes, your project manager asks you to change values in some of the current cells and also to add a new column. To include a new data analysis table, you are also supposed to add a new worksheet. What will you be thinking in such a situation? Will you be totally upset thinking of how to do the tough and nearly impossible task? Hey, You will be capable of doing any kind of editing to your workbook by the end of this chapter.

When you edit a workbook:

- You might have to make changes that affect the contents of the cells like changing values in some of the cells or copying a table from one worksheet to another.

- You might have to make changes that affect the structure of the worksheet like adding new columns or rows or deleting existing columns or rows.

- You might have to change the number of worksheets in a workbook like adding a worksheet or deleting a worksheet.

In this chapter, we are going to see how to make changes to a workbook safely.

Opening Your Workbooks for Editing

Before making any changes to a workbook, you need to have the workbook opened in Excel. If you have not launched Excel 2013 yet, then launch it and you can select your workbook for editing by selecting the file you want from the list of files under the Recent heading displayed in the left pane of the Start screen as shown in Figure 4-1.

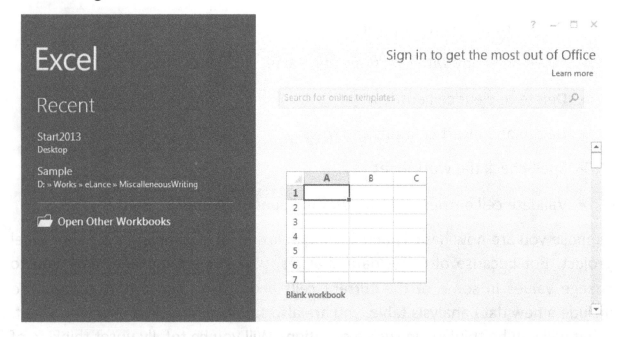

Figure 4-1 Excel's Start screen with option to open workbook for editing

If you could not find the file that you want to edit under the Recent heading, then you can click the link Open Other Workbooks displayed at the bottom of the left pane and browse for your workbook from the Open screen.

Opening Files in the Open Screen

If you are already within Excel, then to open a workbook in Excel, go to File →Open or press Alt + FO. It will open the Open screen in the Excel 2013 Backstage with the Recent Workbooks option selected as shown in Figure 4-2.

If you could not find the file that you want to edit among the names of files displayed in the right-hand pane, then you need to select one of the following Place options on the left-hand pane:

OneDrive: You could open files saved to the cloud using OneDrive. OneDrive was previously called SkyDrive.

Computer: You could open files that you have saved locally on your computer or a network drive by selecting this option. Once clicked, you could find the folders that you accessed recently on your local and network drives, the Documents folder and the Desktop along with the Browse button which allows you to browse for your file locally.

Add a Place: The Add a Place option allows you to designate add access to a SharePoint site or your SkyDrive account. When you select this option, you could find an Office365 SharePoint and OneDrive button on the right-hand pane. You can log into a SharePoint site for which you have a user ID and password to add its folders to the Open screen under the Computer option by clicking the Office365 SharePoint button. You can select the OneDrive option to log into your Windows Live account (if you have) and add your space in the cloud to the Open screen under the OneDrive option.

Figure 4-2 The Open screen with Recent Workbooks option selected

Opening Files from the Open Dialog Box

Once you select a folder from the Open screen, the program opens an Open dialog box as shown in Figure 4-3. The Open dialog box has two panes. The left pane is a Navigation pane where you can select a new folder if you want and the right pane is the main pane showing the icons for all the Excel files and subfolders in the currently selected folder. If you want to see all the files (not only the Excel files), then click the dropdown to the right of the File name: textbox which currently displays All Excel Files and select the option All Files.

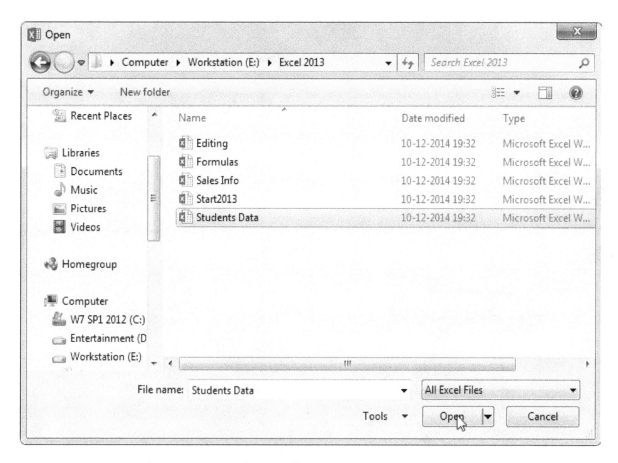

Figure 4-3 The Open dialog box

Once you find the icon of the workbook that you want to edit in the Open dialog box, open it by either double clicking the icon or clicking it and then clicking the Open button.

Find Your Workbook Easily

Are you finding it difficult to get your workbook that you need to edit? You could solve this problem if you take a bit of care while saving your workbook for the first time. When you save your workbook for the first time, check the Save Thumbnail option in the Save As dialog box (circled in Figure 4-4).

When you browse for your workbook that you want to edit, after reaching the folder that contains your workbook, click "Change your view." icon (Figure 4-5) and select Extra Large Icons or Large Icons option. It will display a preview of the data of all Excel files that are saved by checking the Save Thumbnail option which helps you identify your workbook file easily and quickly as in Figure 4-5.

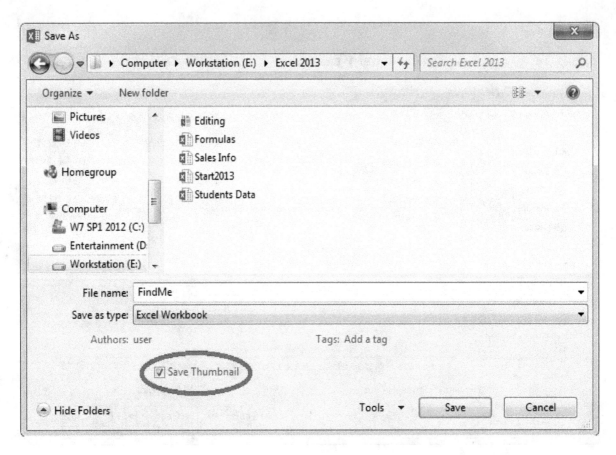

Figure 4-4 Save Thumbnail option in the Save As dialog box

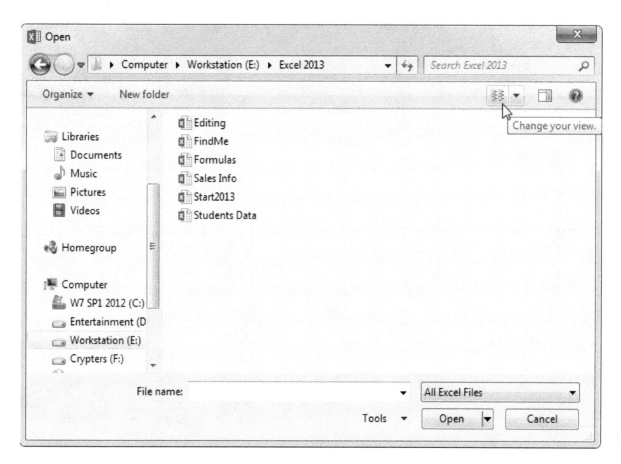

Figure 4-5 Change your view option

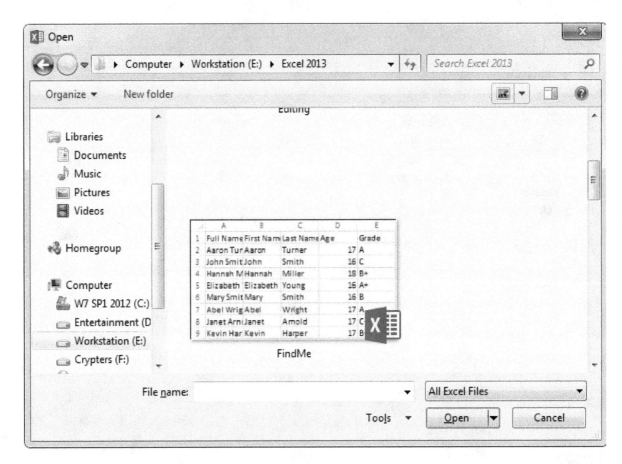

Figure 4-6 The preview feature that helps you select the workbook for editing easily

Changing the Recent Files Settings

Excel 2013 automatically keeps a list of last 25 files you opened and you could find them when you click the Recent Workbooks list on the Open screen. If you want to display more than or less than 25 files, you have the freedom to change it. To change the number of recently opened files that displayed,

1. Go to File → Options and open the Advanced tab of the Excel Options dialog box.

2. Change the value in the Show this number of Recent Workbooks: under the Display section (circled in Figure 4-7) from 25 to the number you want.

3. Click OK or press Enter to close the dialog box.

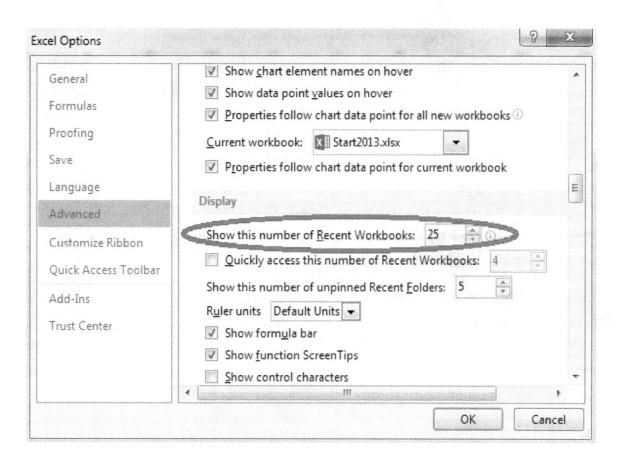

Figure 4-7 The Show this number of Recent Workbooks: option under the Display section

You can display a few of the most recently opened workbooks as menu items itself at the bottom of the File menu in the Backstage view. Hence, you can open them even without opening the Open screen just by clicking the File menu. To have Excel display a few of the most recently opened workbooks as menu items,

1. Go to File → Options and open the Advanced tab of the Excel Options dialog box.

2. Check the Quickly access this number of Recent Workbooks: under the Display section and change the number to the number of workbooks you want as menu items.

3. Click OK or press Enter to close the dialog box.

Opening Multiple Workbooks

If you plan to edit more than one workbook, then you can select all the workbooks you want to edit and open all of them. To select multiple files that appear sequentially in the Open dialog box or browse window, you click the first workbook name and then click the last workbook name holding down the Shift key. If the files do not appear sequentially, you need to click the workbook names holding down the Ctrl key.

Finding Workbook Files

If you know where you have saved your workbook (name of the folder), it is really easy to open the workbook from the Open dialog box. But normally it might be difficult to remember the name of the folder especially when you have lots of workbook files in different folders.

The Search Documents textbox in the upper right corner of the Open dialog box can help you in such situations. You just need to enter some of the characters used in the workbook's filename or contained in the workbook itself. Once Windows finds any matches, the names of the workbooks appear in the Open dialog box and you just need to open the file you want to edit.

Using the Open file options

The options available in the dropdown button attached to the Open command button at the bottom of the Open dialog box (Figure 4-8) enables you to open the selected workbook in a special way such as:

✓ Open Read-Only: This opens the workbook file(s) as read-only but not editable.

✓ Open as Copy: This opens a copy of the workbook file(s) so that you will have the original file untouched even if you mess up the copy.

✓ Open in Browser: This opens workbook file as webpages in your browser. This option is available only if the program identifies that the selected file(s) were saved as web pages rather than plain old Excel workbook files.

✓ Open in Protected View: This opens the workbook file in Protected View mode so that you will be able to edit the workbook only after you click the Enable Editing button.

✓ Open and Repair: This tries to repair corrupted workbook(s) before opening them in Excel.

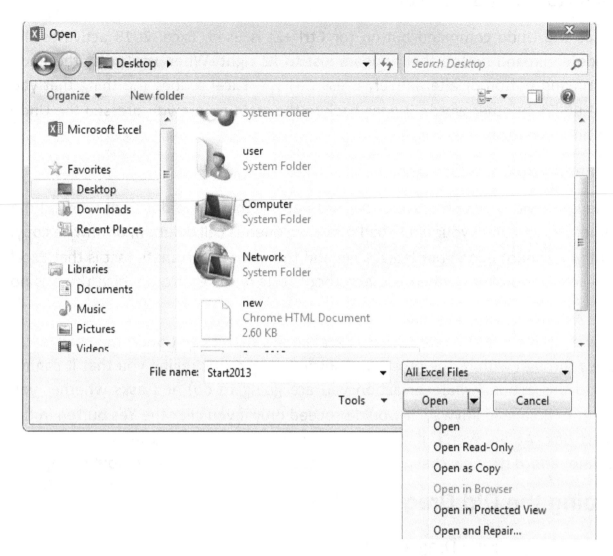

Figure 4-8 Different options to open the workbook file

Undo Your Boo-Boos

Excel's Undo feature is a great bliss to correct many of your mistakes that you made unknowingly and could have inadvertently messed up your worksheet. You could find the Undo command button on the Quick Access Toolbar with an arrow pointing towards left. The Undo feature is really smart to display proper Screen Tip based on your action. For example, once you enter some content in a cell, then Undo button's Screen Tip reads Undo Type. When you delete some entry in a cell, then it reads Undo Clear. You could press Ctrl + Z as well instead of clicking the Undo command button.

Undo to Activate the Redo

Once the Undo command button (or Ctrl +Z) is used, Excel 2013 activates the Redo command button that appears just to its right. When you press the Redo command button or alternatively press Ctrl + Y, Excel redoes the thing that you just undid. In other words, it goes back to the state before you pressed the Undo command button.

What if You Can't Undo?

Though Undo is a great feature, the sad news is that Undo does not work all the time. You can undo your latest bad move, erroneous cell deletion, or unwise copy. But you cannot undo your latest save and the most unfortunate fact is that Excel doesn't let you know when you are about to take a step from which there is no return.

However in some situations where Excel knows that it can't undo the change if it goes through with it, the program displays an alert box telling you that it cannot undo this action (whatever action you are going to do) and asks whether you want to go ahead anyway. It would proceed only if you click the Yes button in the alert box. At the worst, if you cannot undo the change and at the same time cannot afford the new change, then better close the workbook without saving it.

Doing the Old Drag and Drop

Move Cell(s) using Drag and Drop

You can make editing lot easier if you know the drag and drop technique. With this technique, you can pick up a cell selection and drop it into a new place on the worksheet. To drag a range of cell entries and drop to a new location,

1. Select a cell range.

2. Position the mouse pointer on an edge of the extended cell cursor that surrounds the entire cell range.

3. Drag your selection to the new destination as in Figure 4-9.

4. Release the mouse button to have the data in the new location as in Figure 4-10.

	A	B	C	D	E	F
1		Sales (2014-2015)				
2		Half Year - 1		Half Year - 2		
3	Sales Representative	Quarter 1	Quarter 2	Quarter 3	Quarter 4	Full Year
4	Aaron Turner	17,569.25	16,256.00	18,450.50	17,368.00	$ 69,643.75
5	John Smith	8,657.00	8,896.00	6,743.80	7,912.20	$ 32,209.00
6	Hannah Miller	14,699.20	18,900.50	18,090.80	16,231.60	$ 67,922.10
7	Elizabeth Young	12,980.60	11,080.50	13,875.00	12,768.40	$ 50,704.50
8	Mary Smith	10,890.60	11,545.00	12,457.40	9,873.80	$ 44,766.80
9		$ 64,796.65	$ 66,678.00	$ 69,617.50	$ 64,154.00	$ 2,65,246.15
10						
11						
12	B11:F11					
13						

Figure 4-9 The cell range dragging to a new location

	A	B	C	D	E	F
1		Sales (2014-2015)				
2		Half Year - 1		Half Year - 2		
3	Sales Representative	Quarter 1	Quarter 2	Quarter 3	Quarter 4	Full Year
4	Aaron Turner	17,569.25	16,256.00	18,450.50	17,368.00	$ 69,643.75
5	John Smith	8,657.00	8,896.00	6,743.80	7,912.20	$ 32,209.00
6	Hannah Miller	14,699.20	18,900.50	18,090.80	16,231.60	$ 67,922.10
7	Elizabeth Young	12,980.60	11,080.50	13,875.00	12,768.40	$ 50,704.50
8	Mary Smith	10,890.60	11,545.00	12,457.40	9,873.80	$ 44,766.80
9						
10						
11		$ 64,796.65	$ 66,678.00	$ 69,617.50	$ 64,154.00	$ 2,65,246.15

Figure 4-10 The cell content after dropping into a new location

Copy Cell(s) using Drag and Drop

Instead of moving a cell range from one location to another, you can also copy the cell range in one location to another location. To copy the cell range,

1. Select a cell range.

2. Hold down the Ctrl key when you position the mouse pointer on an edge of the extended cell cursor that surrounds the entire cell range.

3. Drag your selection to the new destination.

4. Release the mouse button to have the data in the new location as well as in the old location.

Move or Copy Cell(s) without Wiping Out

When you move or copy cell(s) to a new location, the new entry completely replaces the old entry in that location. If you want to insert the new entry without wiping out the existing entry, you need to hold down the Shift key. If you are copying data to a new location, then you really need to be a skilled "keyboard player" as you have to hold down both Ctrl and Shift keys.

When you drag the cell range holding down the Shift key, you get an I-beam shape (as in Figure 4-11) that shows where the selection will be inserted if you release the mouse button along with the address of the cell range instead of a rectangular outline of the cell range.

	A	B	C	D	E	F
1		Sales (2014-2015)					
2		Half Year - 1		Half Year - 2			
3	Sales Representative	Quarter 1	Quarter 2	Quarter 3	Quarter 4	Full Year
4	Aaron Turner	17,569.25	16,256.00	18,450.50	17,368.00	$ 69,643.75
5	John Smith	8,657.00	8,896.00	6,743.80	7,912.20	$ 32,209.00
6	Hannah Miller	14,699.20	18,900.50	18,090.80	16,231.60	$ 67,922.10
7	Elizabeth Young	12,980.60	11,080.50	13,875.00	12,768.40	$ 50,704.50
8	Mary Smith	10,890.60	11,545.00	12,457.40	9,873.80	$ 44,766.80
9		$ 64,796.65	$ 66,678.00	$ 69,617.50	$ 64,154.00	$ 2,65,246.15
10						
11		B10:F10				

Figure 4-11 The I – beam displayed that shows where the selection will be inserted

Once you release the mouse button at the required location, Excel inserts the cell range moving the existing entries to neighboring blank cells. Suppose you release the cell range in B7:F7, the screen will appear as in Figure 4-12.

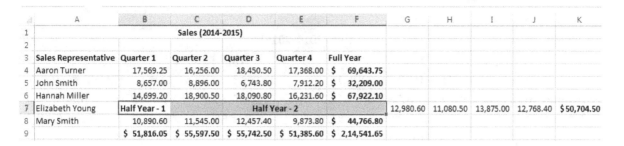

	A	B	C	D	E	F	G	H	I	J	K
1			Sales (2014-2015)								
2											
3	Sales Representative	Quarter 1	Quarter 2	Quarter 3	Quarter 4	Full Year					
4	Aaron Turner	17,569.25	16,256.00	18,450.50	17,368.00	$ 69,643.75					
5	John Smith	8,657.00	8,896.00	6,743.80	7,912.20	$ 32,209.00					
6	Hannah Miller	14,699.20	18,900.50	18,090.80	16,231.60	$ 67,922.10					
7	Elizabeth Young	Half Year - 1			Half Year - 2		12,980.60	11,080.50	13,875.00	12,768.40	$ 50,704.50
8	Mary Smith	10,890.60	11,545.00	12,457.40	9,873.80	$ 44,766.80					
9		$ 51,816.05	$ 55,597.50	$ 55,742.50	$ 51,385.60	$ 2,14,541.65					

Figure 4-12 Cell range moved without wiping out the existing entries

Copying Formulas with AutoFill

Drag and drop technique is useful when you need to copy a bunch of neighboring cells to another location on the worksheet. But you cannot use the drag and drop technique to copy a single formula to a bunch of neighboring cells that need to do the same calculation with different data. You can use the AutoFill feature or the Copy (Ctrl + C) and Paste (Ctrl + V) commands to achieve this.

When using the AutoFill feature select the cell that contains the formula that needs to be copied to other cells and then drag the fill handle to the cells to where you want to copy the formula as in Figure 4-13. This will copy the formula to those cells and do the calculation then and there itself and you will get a screen as shown in Figure 4-14.

	A	B	C	D	E	F
1		Sales (2014-2015)				
2		Half Year - 1		Half Year - 2		
3	Sales Representative	Quarter 1	Quarter 2	Quarter 3	Quarter 4	Full Year
4	Aaron Turner	17,569.25	16,256.00	18,450.50	17,368.00	$ 69,643.75
5	John Smith	8,657.00	8,896.00	6,743.80	7,912.20	$ 32,209.00
6	Hannah Miller	14,699.20	18,900.50	18,090.80	16,231.60	$ 67,922.10
7	Elizabeth Young	12,980.60	11,080.50	13,875.00	12,768.40	$ 50,704.50
8	Mary Smith	10,890.60	11,545.00	12,457.40	9,873.80	$ 44,766.80
9		$ 64,796.65				

Figure 4-13 Fill handle dragged to copy the formula in B9 to cells B10:F10

	A	B	C	D	E	F
1		Sales (2014-2015)				
2		Half Year - 1		Half Year - 2		
3	Sales Representative	Quarter 1	Quarter 2	Quarter 3	Quarter 4	Full Year
4	Aaron Turner	17,569.25	16,256.00	18,450.50	17,368.00	$ 69,643.75
5	John Smith	8,657.00	8,896.00	6,743.80	7,912.20	$ 32,209.00
6	Hannah Miller	14,699.20	18,900.50	18,090.80	16,231.60	$ 67,922.10
7	Elizabeth Young	12,980.60	11,080.50	13,875.00	12,768.40	$ 50,704.50
8	Mary Smith	10,890.60	11,545.00	12,457.40	9,873.80	$ 44,766.80
9		$ 64,796.65	$ 66,678.00	$ 69,617.50	$ 64,154.00	$ 2,65,246.15

Figure 4-14 Formula copied using AutoFill feature

Excel is Smart Enough to Make Relative Changes to the Formula

When you copy formula in one cell to other cells, Excel actually plays smartly to handle the copied formulas relatively. The formula in cell B9 (Figure 4-14) is =SUM (B4:B8). Now if you check the formula in cell C9 to F9 that is just copies from cell B9, you could find that they are not exactly the same. Cell C9 contains the formula =SUM (C4:C8), cell D9 contains the formula =SUM(D4:D8) and so on. Who made those changes?

In fact, Excel adjusts the column reference, changing it from B to C, B to D and so on. Excel adjust the column reference (column letter) and row reference (row number) based on the direction of the cells to which you copied the formula. A formula =SUM (B3:B7) in cell C4 will be changed to =SUM (C3:C7) if you copy it to cell D4. The same formula =SUM (B3:B7) in cell C4 will be changed to =SUM (B5:B9) if you copy it to cell C6. The process of adjusting the cell references in copies of a formula relative to the direction of copying is known as relative cell referencing.

Make Cell References Absolute

You might have to make your cell references absolute in some rare cases. Suppose you want to compare the sales with a target value to promote the sales person who achieved the target. In that case, if the cell reference in the formula changes relatively, it will create problems. You can make a cell reference absolute by adding dollar signs in front of the column letter and row number.

Consider the data in Figure 4-15.

	B16		fx	=IF(B4>I3,"Achieved","Not Achieved")

	A	B	C	D	E	F	G	H	I
1				Sales (2014-2015)					
2		Half Year - 1		Half Year - 2				Target	
3	Sales Representative	Quarter 1	Quarter 2	Quarter 3	Quarter 4	Full Year		Quarter 1	13,000.00
4	Aaron Turner	17,569.25	16,256.00	18,450.50	17,368.00	$ 69,643.75		Quarter 2	11,500.00
5	John Smith	8,657.00	8,896.00	6,743.80	7,912.20	$ 32,209.00		Quarter 3	15,000.00
6	Hannah Miller	14,699.20	18,900.50	18,090.80	16,231.60	$ 67,922.10		Quarter 4	16,000.00
7	Elizabeth Young	12,980.60	11,080.50	13,875.00	12,768.40	$ 50,704.50			
8	Mary Smith	10,890.60	11,545.00	12,457.40	9,873.80	$ 44,766.80			
9		$ 64,796.65	$ 66,678.00	$ 69,617.50	$ 64,154.00	$ 2,65,246.15			
10									
11									
12									
13				Sales (2014-2015)					
14		Half Year - 1		Half Year - 2					
15	Sales Representative	Quarter 1	Quarter 2	Quarter 3	Quarter 4				
16	Aaron Turner	Achieved	16,256.00	18,450.50	17,368.00				
17	John Smith	8,657.00	8,896.00	6,743.80	7,912.20				
18	Hannah Miller	14,699.20	18,900.50	18,090.80	16,231.60				
19	Elizabeth Young	12,980.60	11,080.50	13,875.00	12,768.40				
20	Mary Smith	10,890.60	11,545.00	12,457.40	9,873.80				

Figure 4-15 Tables of data

You could see that I have written a formula in cell B16 (=IF(B4>I3,"Achieved","Not Achieved")) which enters the text "Achieved" if the target is achieved and "Not Achieved" if the target is not achieved. It is obvious that the target for Quarter 1 is 13,000 (in cell I3). Suppose you copy the formula in cell B16 to cells B17:B20 and check the result. You will get a screen as shown in Figure 4-16.

B17		fx	=IF(B5>I4,"Achieved","Not Achieved")					

	A	B	C	D	E	F	G	H	I
1			Sales (2014-2015)						
2		Half Year - 1			Half Year - 2			Target	
3	Sales Representative	Quarter 1	Quarter 2	Quarter 3	Quarter 4	Full Year		Quarter 1	13,000.00
4	Aaron Turner	17,569.25	16,256.00	18,450.50	17,368.00	$ 69,643.75		Quarter 2	11,500.00
5	John Smith	8,657.00	8,896.00	6,743.80	7,912.20	$ 32,209.00		Quarter 3	15,000.00
6	Hannah Miller	14,699.20	18,900.50	18,090.80	16,231.60	$ 67,922.10		Quarter 4	16,000.00
7	Elizabeth Young	12,980.60	11,080.50	13,875.00	12,768.40	$ 50,704.50			
8	Mary Smith	10,890.60	11,545.00	12,457.40	9,873.80	$ 44,766.80			
9		$ 64,796.65	$ 66,678.00	$ 69,617.50	$ 64,154.00	$ 2,65,246.15			
10									
11									
12									
13			Sales (2014-2015)						
14		Half Year - 1			Half Year - 2				
15	Sales Representative	Quarter 1	Quarter 2	Quarter 3	Quarter 4				
16	Aaron Turner	Achieved	16,256.00	18,450.50	17,368.00				
17	John Smith	Not Achieved	8,896.00	6,743.80	7,912.20				
18	Hannah Miller	Not Achieved	18,900.50	18,090.80	16,231.60				
19	Elizabeth Young	Not Achieved	11,080.50	13,875.00	12,768.40				
20	Mary Smith	Achieved	11,545.00	12,457.40	9,873.80				

Figure 4-16 Formula in cell B16 is copied into cells B17:B20

Just check the result. Is it correct? If you do the check on your own (hey, do not look at the second table), you could see that the sales persons who achieved the target are Aaron Turner and Hannah Miller. But as per the second table, Aaron Turner and Mary Smith achieved the target. How it happened? Is Excel wrong in its calculations? No, it is because that we have used the relative cell references. If you see the formula bar, you could find that instead of checking B5>I3, it is checking B5>I4. So, the sales value of John Smith is checked against the value in cell I4, which is actually the target of Quarter 2. Similarly, the sales value of Mary Smith is checked against the value in cell I7, which is 0 (empty).

To make the cell reference absolute, click cell B16 and add dollar signs before the column letter and row number in I3 as we do not want to make it relative. Hence the formula in cell B16 becomes =IF(B4>I3,"Achieved","Not Achieved"). Now if you copy the formula in cell B16 to cells B17:B20, you will get a screen as in Figure 4-17. If you check the formula in cells B17 to B20, you could find that I3 remains as such in all formulas.

112

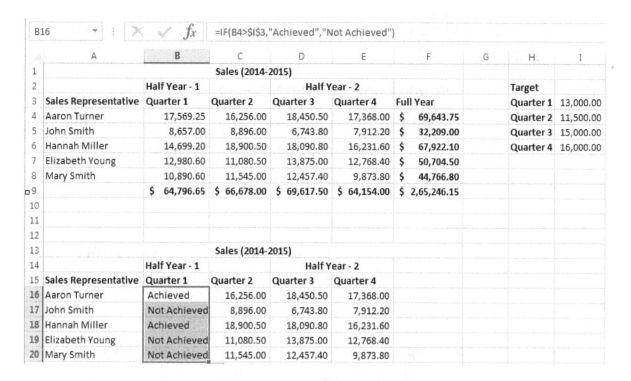

Figure 4-17 Formula with absolute cell reference

Instead of adding dollar signs manually,

1. Double-click the cell with the formula.

2. Position the insertion point somewhere on the reference you want to convert to absolute.

3. Press F4 which adds dollar signs automatically and click Enter.

Cut, Copy and Paste – The Digital Style

You do not have to depend on the drag and drop or AutoFill always to move or copy information. The Cut, Copy and Paste commands make it lot easier by using the Office Clipboard as a temporary storage place. The data you cut or copy reside in Clipboard until you paste it somewhere. Clipboard makes it possible to move or copy data to other worksheets and workbooks and even to other programs such as Word.

To move a cell selection with Cut and Paste,

1. Select the cells you want to move.

2. Click the Cut command button in the Clipboard group on the Home tab or press Ctrl + X.

3. Click the cell where you want the information to move to.

4. Press Enter to complete the operation. You can also click the Paste command button in the Clipboard group or even press Ctrl + V.

To copy a cell selection with Copy and Paste,

1. Select the cells you want to move.

2. Click the Copy command button in the Clipboard group on the Home tab or press Ctrl + C

3. Click the cell where you want the information to copy to.

4. Press Enter to complete the operation. You can also click the Paste command button in the Clipboard group or even press Ctrl + V.

Paste, Paste and Paste

When you copy data using the Copy button and paste it using Paste button or pressing Ctrl + V (not by pressing the Enter key), the greatest advantage is that you can paste the same data repeatedly. You can do the last copy by pressing the Enter key if you want.

Paste Options to Paste

Once you click the Paste button on the Home tab or press Ctrl + V to paste cell entries that you copy (not cut), Excel displays a Paste Option button with the label (Ctrl) as in Figure 4-18.

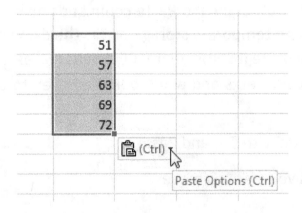

Figure 4-18 Paste Options button

When you click the dropdown button or press Ctrl key, a palette similar to the one shown in Figure 4-19 appears with three group of buttons: Paste, Paste Values and Other Paste Options. You can control or restrict the type of content and formatting of the pasting data using these different options.

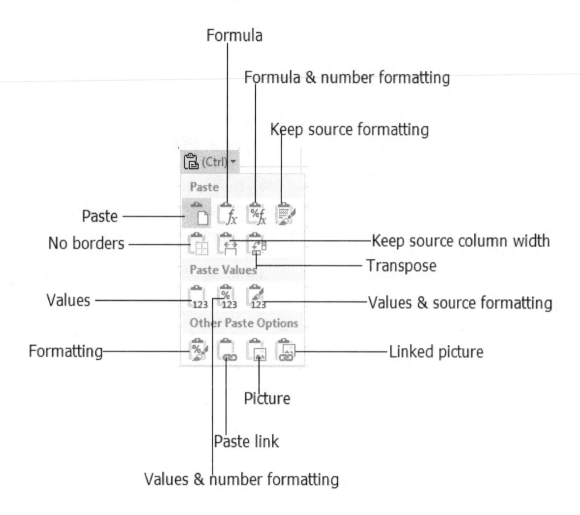

Figure 4-19 Paste Options palette

Different options on the Paste Options palette include:

✓ Paste (P): Excel copies everything from the original cells including data and formatting and pastes this into the destination cells.

✓ Formulas (F): Excel copies only the data from the original cells, without the formatting and pastes this into the destination cells.

✓ Formulas & Number Formatting (O): Excel copies the number formats assigned to the values along with their formulas and pastes this into the destination cells.

✓ Keep Source Formatting (K): Excel copies the formatting from the original cells and pastes this into the destination cells along with the data.

✓ No Borders (B): Excel copies data and formatting without borders (if any) from the original cells and pastes this into the destination cells.

✓ Keep Source Column Widths (W): Excel copies the cell entries with formatting from the original cells and paste this into the destination cells, keeping the width of the columns in the destination range the same as those in the source range.

✓ Transpose (T): Excel changes the orientation of the pasted entries. The entries in a row will be displayed in a column and vice versa.

✓ Values (V): Excel pastes only the calculated results of formulas and not the formulas.

✓ Values & Number Formatting (A): Excel pastes the calculated results of any formulas along with all the formatting.

✓ Values & Source Formatting (E): Excel pastes the calculated results of any formulas along with all formatting assigned to the source cell range.

✓ Formatting (R): Excel pastes only the formatting and not the entries from the source cell range to the destination range.

✓ Paste Link (N): Excel creates linking formulas in the destination range so that any changes that you make to the entries in cells in the source range are immediately brought forward and reflected in the corresponding cells of the destination range.

✓ Picture (U): Excel pastes only the pictures in the copied cell selection.

✓ Linked Picture (I): Excel pastes a link to the pictures in the copied cell selection.

Paste from the Clipboard Task Pane

The Clipboard does not have only the copied or cut content from Excel. Instead, it is a common temporary storage place for all programs running under Windows. So you can paste stuff from the Clipboard even after finishing a move or copy operation.

To open the Clipboard in its own task pane to the immediate left of the Worksheet area as in Figure 4-20, click the Dialog box launcher in the lower right corner (circled in Figure 4-20) of the Clipboard group on the Home tab.

To paste an item other than the last cut or copied data from the Clipboard into a worksheet, click the cell where you want to copy the item on the worksheet and then click the item to be copied in the Clipboard task pane and the item is now on your worksheet. To paste all the items in the Clipboard on your worksheet, click the Paste All button on the top of the Clipboard task pane. To remove all the items in the Clipboard, click the Clear All button on the top of the Clipboard task pane. To remove a specific item in the Clipboard, position the mouse pointer over the item in the Clipboard task pane to see its dropdown and then click the Delete option from the dropdown.

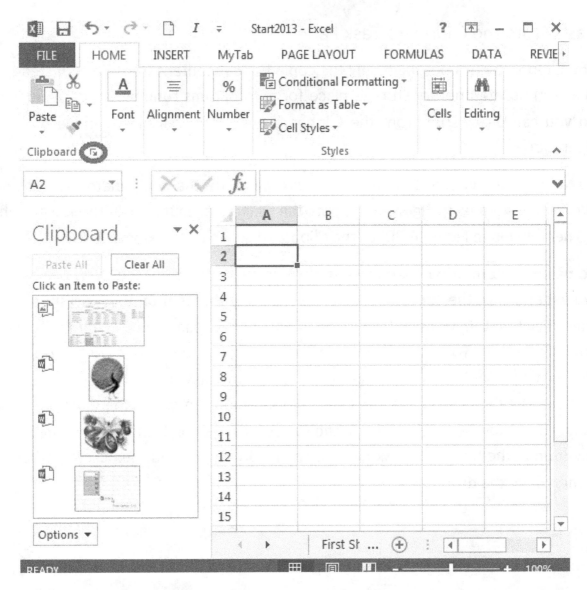

Figure 4-20 The Clipboard task pane appears on the left side of the Excel Worksheet area.

You can manage the display of the Clipboard task pane by trying different options that appear when you click the Options dropdown at the bottom of the Clipboard task pane.

Paste Special is So Special

Excel copies all the information including data, formatting and formulas from the original cells unless you use the special options available with Paste Options. You can set which data, formatting or formulas need to be used in the current paste

118

operation by using the Paste Special command. You could find most of the Paste Special options on the Paste Options palette as well (Figure 4-19).

Click the dropdown button displayed at the bottom of the Paste command in the Clipboard group on the Home tab to open the Paste Special dialog box shown in Figure 4-21.

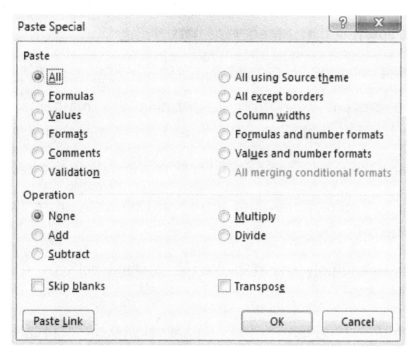

Figure 4-21 Paste Special dialog box

The options in the Paste Special dialog box include:

✓ All: to paste everything.

✓ Formulas: to paste all the entries without formatting.

✓ Values: to paste only the calculated values of formulas without formulas.

✓ Formats: to paste only the formatting.

✓ Comments: to paste only the notes attached to the cell.

✓ Validation: to paste only the data validation rules.

✓ All Using Source Theme: to paste all the information and cell styles.

✓ All Except Borders: to copy everything except borders.

- ✓ Column Widths: to apply the column width of the original cells to the destination cells.

- ✓ Formulas and Number Formats: to apply the number formats to the pasted values and formulas.

- ✓ Values and Number Formats: to paste only the calculated values of formulas applying their number formats.

- ✓ All Merging Conditional Formats: to paste Conditional Formatting.

- ✓ None: to prevent Excel from performing any mathematical operation between the data in the original cells and destination cells.

- ✓ Add: to add the data in the original cells to the data in the destination cells.

- ✓ Subtract: to subtract the data in the original cells from the data in the destination cells.

- ✓ Multiply: to multiply the data in the original cells by the data in the destination cells.

- ✓ Divide: to divide the data in the original cells by the data in the destination cells.

- ✓ Skip Blanks: to paste the data everywhere except in blank cells.

- ✓ Transpose: to change the orientation of the pasted entries.

- ✓ Paste Link: to paste a link between copies of data in original cells and destination cells so that changes in the original cells get updated in the destination cells automatically.

Are Delete and Clear the Same?

You can get rid of the stuff you put into cells in two ways: clear and delete. When you clear a cell, Excel just removes the contents of the cell without actually removing the cell from the worksheet. When you delete a cell, Excel deletes the cell structure along with all its contents and formatting. In other words, when you delete a cell, Excel has to shuffle the position of entries in the surrounding cells to plug up any gaps made by the action.

Clear the Cell(s)

To clear a cell, that is just to remove the contents, select the cells you want to clear and simply press the Delete key. If you want to clear more than just the contents of selected cell(s), click the Clear button in the Editing group on the Home tab and then click any of the following options you see on the dropdown.

- ✓ Clear All: Deletes all formatting and notes as well the content.

- ✓ Clear Formats: Deletes only the formatting.

- ✓ Clear Contents: Deletes only the content.

- ✓ Clear Comments: Removes the notes.

- ✓ Clear Hyperlinks: Removes the hyperlinks leaving its descriptive text.

- ✓ Remove Hyperlinks: Removes the hyperlinks along with the formatting.

Delete the Cell(s)

To delete the cell(s), that is the whole structure of the selected cell(s), select the cell range and click the Delete command button in the Cells group on the Home tab to open a dropdown. Click Delete Cells on the dropdown which opens a Delete dialog box with the following options:

- ✓ Shift Cells Left: moves entries from neighboring columns on the right to the left to fill in gaps created by deleting cells.

- ✓ Shift Cells Up: moves entries from neighboring columns on the bottom to the top to fill in gaps created by deleting cells.

- ✓ Entire row: Removes all the rows in the current cell selection.

- ✓ Entire column: Removes all the columns in the current cell selection.

Inserting New Columns and Rows

You might need to insert new data into an already setup table of data anytime. In such cases, instead of moving existing data to new columns or rows and making space, you can just insert rows or columns at the required position and then enter the new data as simple as that. To insert a new cell range, select the cells where you want the new cells to appear and then click the drop-down button on the Insert command button in the Cells group on the Home tab. Click Insert Cells on the drop-down menu which opens the Insert dialog box with the following option buttons:

- ✓ Shift Cells Right: Shifts existing cells to the right to make space for the new cells.

- ✓ Shift Cells Down: Shifts existing cells to the down to make space for the new cells.

- ✓ Entire Row: Inserts complete rows.

- ✓ Entire Column: Inserts complete columns.

Stamping Out Your Spelling Errors

You can now be happily relieved to know that Excel 2013 has a built-in spell checker that can find and remove all your spelling errors. To check the spelling in a worksheet, you can do any of the following:

- ✓ Click the Spelling command button on the Review tab.

- ✓ Press F7

- ✓ Press Alt + RS

When you select any of the above options, Excel checks the spelling of all text entries in the worksheet and when it finds an unknown word, it displays the Spelling dialog box (Figure 4-22) with some suggestions. You can choose any one of the suggestions and proceed.

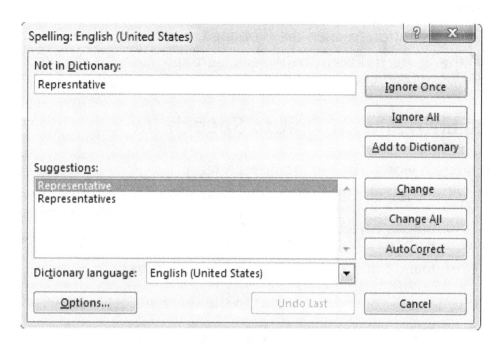

Figure 4-22 Spelling dialog box

Spelling dialog box has the following options:

Ignore Once and Ignore All: When Excel's spell check comes across a word its dictionary finds suspicious but you know is viable, click the Ignore Once button. If you don't want the spell checker to check this word again, click the Ignore All button.

Add to Dictionary: Click this button to add the unknown word to a custom dictionary so that Excel won't flag it again when you check the spelling in the worksheet later on.

Change: Click this button to replace the word listed in the Not in Dictionary text box with the word Excel offers in the Suggestions list box.

Change All: Click this button to change all occurrences of this misspelled word in the worksheet to the word Excel displays in the Suggestions list box.

AutoCorrect: Click this button to have Excel automatically correct this spelling error with the suggestion displayed in the Suggestions list box.

Dictionary Language: To switch to another dictionary, click this dropdown and select the name of the desired language.

Options: Click this button to open the Proofing tab in the Excel Options dialog box to modify the current Excel spell-check settings such as Ignore Words in Uppercase, Ignore Words with Numbers, etc.

Validate Entries with Text to Speech

Excel introduces a wonderful Text to Speech feature which allows your computer to read aloud entries in the worksheet. Thus, you can find and correct errors easily just listening to the voice. You could not find the Text to Speech command button anywhere on the ribbon even if you search thoroughly. You should add the Speak Cells command buttons on the Quick Access Toolbar.

To add Text to Speech command buttons to the Quick Access toolbar:

1. Click Customize Quick Access Toolbar button at the end of the toolbar.

2. Click the More Commands on the Customize Quick Access toolbar's dropdown menu which opens the Excel Options dialog box.

3. Click Commands Not in the Ribbon option from the Choose commands from: dropdown and scroll down the list until you see the Speak Cells commands.

4. Click the Speak Cells from the list box on the left and then click the Add button to add it to the Quick Access toolbar.

5. Repeat Step 4 for Speak Cells – Stop Speaking Cells, Speak Cells by Columns, Speak Cells by Rows and Speak Cells on Enter.

6. Click the OK button to close the Excel Options dialog box and now your Quick Access Toolbar appears as shown in Figure 4-23.

Figure 4-23 Speak Cells buttons on Quick Access Toolbar

Once you are ready with the Text to Speech commands, you can use them to validate text entries as follows:

1. Select the cells whose contents you want read aloud by Text to Speech.

2. Click the Speak Cells button on the Quick Access toolbar to have the computer read the entries in the selected cells.

3. To have the Text to Speech feature read each cell entry while you press the Enter key, click the Speak Cells on Enter button.

4. To stop the reading, click the Stop Speaking button.

5. Printing the Masterpiece

Introduction

In this chapter, we will learn how to

- ➤ Preview pages in Page Layout view
- ➤ Print from the Backstage
- ➤ Quick print from the Quick Access Toolbar
- ➤ Setup a Print Area
- ➤ Setup the pages correctly
- ➤ Adjust the margins of pages
- ➤ Change the page orientation
- ➤ Print column and row headings as print titles on pages
- ➤ Add a header and/or footer to the pages
- ➤ Adjust page breaks
- ➤ Print formulas in your worksheet

You can print anything and everything on your worksheet including data, formatting and formulas easily and quickly. The main thing to consider while printing a worksheet is that many of the worksheets are longer and wider than one printed page. So, Excel 2013 might have to break up them both horizontally and vertically to fit correctly into different pages. By the end of this chapter, you will realize how easy it is to print reports with Excel 2013.

Previewing Pages in Page Layout View

Excel 2013's Page Layout view gives you instant access to the paging of the current worksheet. You can have a Page Layout view by clicking the Page Layout button (the center one among three buttons) to the left of the Zoom slider on the Status bar (circled in Figure 5-1) or by clicking the Page Layout View command button in the Workbook Views group on the View tab (circled in Figure 5-2).

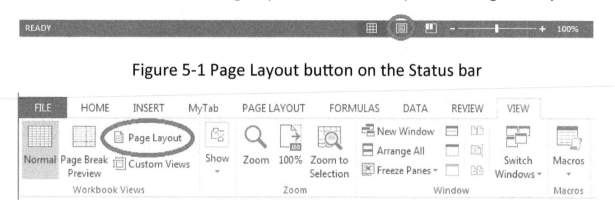

Figure 5-1 Page Layout button on the Status bar

Figure 5-2 Page Layout button on the View tab

When your worksheet is in Page Layout view, you could see horizontal and vertical rulers on the column letter and row number headings as in Figure 5-3. You could also see margins for each printed page, any headers and footers and also the breaks between each page.

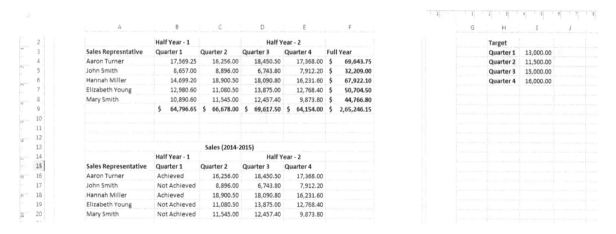

Figure 5-3 Worksheet in Page Layout view with horizontal and vertical rulers

You could see all the pages in your worksheet, if you drag the Zoom slider on the Status bar to the left until you see all the pages. You could decide whether or not to see the horizontal and vertical rulers by checking the Ruler option in the Show group on the View tab. When you uncheck this option, rulers will be removed and when you check it, rulers will be added.

Printing from the Backstage

You can print your worksheet directly from the Backstage view by going to File →
Print to open a Print screen as in Figure 5-4. The Print screen displays your current
print settings along with a preview of the first page of the report.

As worksheets are divided into different pages, checking the page breaks and
ensuring that you will get the prints exactly as you need is really a great practice.
The print preview area in the Print screen helps you know how exactly your data
will appear in different pages when you take printouts. If required, you can
change the page settings from the Page Layout tab and make sure that everything
appears as you need before sending the worksheet for printing.

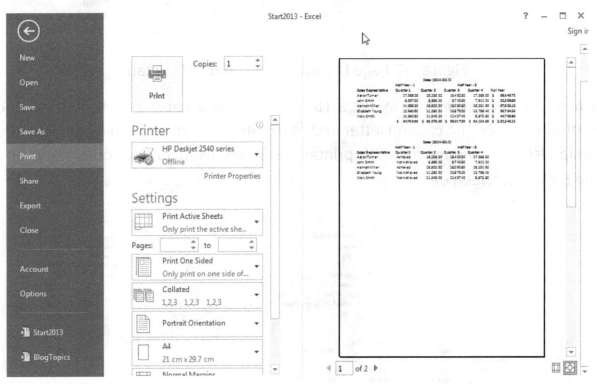

Figure 5-4 The Print screen in Backstage view

It is really difficult to see the data in the pages clearly in the print preview area. If
you want to verify some of the data before printing, you can see the pages in their
actual size by clicking the Zoom to Page button in the lower right corner of the
Print screen (circled in Figure 5-5).

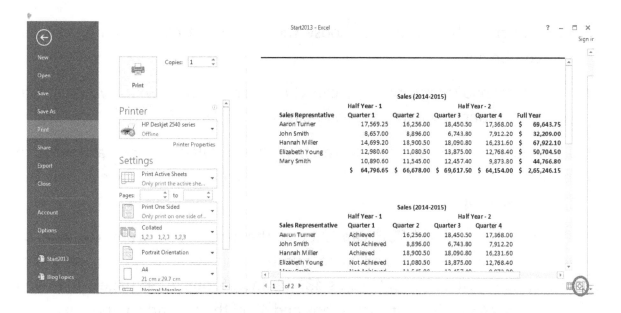

Figure 5-5 The Zoom to Page button to see the page in actual size in the print preview area

You could see the difference in the size of the pages in Figure 5-4 and Figure 5-5. You might have to use scrollbars to see some of the parts of the page when it is in zoomed state. Once you click the Zoom to Page button (deselect the button) a second time, it will be return to the full page view (Figure 5-4).

You could see the total number of pages at the bottom of the print preview area. To see different pages, you can use the Previous Page button displayed to the left of the first page number and the Next Page button displayed to the right of the last page number correctly. The Previous Page button will not be clickable when you are in the first page and the Next Page button will not be clickable when you are in the last page.

You can click the Show Margins button displayed to the left of the Zoom to Page button if you want to see markers indicating the left, right, top and bottom margins along with the column widths. You can adjust column widths as well as margins by dragging the appropriate markers.

Once you are ready with the page settings, you can change any of the following print settings before you send it to a printer.

✓ Print button: You can use this button to print the worksheet using the current settings.

✓ Copies combo box: You can choose the number of copies you want from this combo box.

✓ Printer dropdown button: You can choose the printer which you want to use for printing when more than one device is installed.

✓ Print What dropdown button: You can choose what you actually want to print, whether only the active worksheet, the entire workbook or only the current selection.

✓ Pages combo boxes: You can choose the pages you want to print by entering the start and end page number you want to get printed. For example, if you only want pages 43, 44 and 45 out of 50 pages, then you can specify 43 in the first combo box and 45 in the second combo box.

Beneath the Pages combo boxes, you find dropdown list buttons to print on both sides of each page, collate the pages of the report, switch the page orientation from Portrait to Landscape, select a paper size and customize the size of the margins.

Printing the Current Worksheet

Printing in Excel 2013 is so easy if you want to print the current worksheet without changing any default print settings. You can add the Quick Print button to the Quick Access Toolbar which is already available in the Customize Quick Access Toolbar's dropdown. You can print a single copy of all the information in the current worksheet, except comments, by clicking this button.

When you click the Quick Print button, Excel sends the print job to the Windows print queue which then sends the job to the printer. You will see a Printing dialog box when Excel sends the print job to the print queue which informs you of the print progress like Print 100% Complete or Printing Page 3 of 3 etc. Once this dialog box disappears, you can continue your Excel work. If you want to stop the printing, you can click the Cancel button in the Printing dialog box.

Setting the Print Area

Excel provides options to print only a specific area on the worksheet. Select the cell range that you want to set as print area and click the Print Area command button in the Page Setup group on the Page Layout tab. Click the Set Print Area option from the dropdown shown in Figure 5-6. The selected cell range will be set as print area. You can add more areas to the existing print area by clicking the Add to Print Area option from the dropdown after you select the new cell range. You can clear the print are by just clicking the Clear Print Area option.

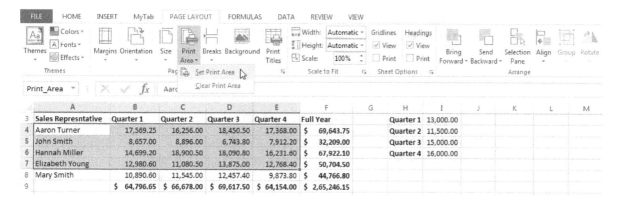

Figure 5-6 Setting Print Area

There is another method to set and clear the print area.

1. Click the Dialog Box launcher in the Page Setup group on the Page Layout tab.

2. Click Sheet tab from the opened Page Setup dialog box to get a window as shown in Figure 5-7.

3. Click the Print area: textbox and then select the cell range or ranges in the worksheet.

4. Click OK which sets the print area.

To clear the print area from this dialog box, clear the content in the Print area: textbox and click OK.

Figure 5-7 Page Setup dialog box

If you click the Quick Print button on the Quick Access Toolbar after setting the print area anytime, Excel prints the cell range you set as Print Area. Again, if you print from the Print screen on the Backstage, the same Print Area will be printed regardless of the Print What option you select in the Settings section. But if you have already cleared the print area or you click the Ignore Print Area option at the very bottom of the Print What dropdown list, then it will not print the Print Area.

Setting Up Your Pages

Once you set up your pages correctly, taking prints in Excel 2013 is a breeze. The Page Layout tab offers different command buttons in the Page Setup group, Scale to Fit group and Sheet Options group that help you set your page exactly as you need them. If you want to see the effect of changes instantaneously, put the worksheet into Page Layout view by clicking the Page Layout button on the Status bar (Figure 5-1) before working with the command buttons on the Page Layout tab.

Using Buttons in the Page Setup Group

The Page Setup group contains the following buttons:

- ✓ Margins: You can select one of three preset margins or create custom margins by clicking Custom Margins (last option in the dropdown) and changing different margins from the Margins tab of the newly opened Page Setup dialog box.

- ✓ Orientation: You can select either Portrait or Landscape orientation for printing.

- ✓ Size: You can select the size of your printing paper from one of the preset paper size. You can also change the printing resolution or page number from the Page tab of the Page Setup dialog box which can be opened by clicking More Paper Sizes (last option in the dropdown).

- ✓ Print Area: You can set and clear print area.

- ✓ Breaks: You can insert or remove page breaks.

- ✓ Background: You can set an image or photo as the background of your current worksheet from the Sheet Background dialog box. The button becomes Delete Background once you set a background image.

- ✓ Print Titles: You can define rows of the worksheet to repeat at the top and columns of the worksheet to repeat at the left as print titles from the Sheet tab of the Page Setup dialog box opened.

Manipulating the Margins

When you create a new worksheet, Excel applies normal margin settings to it. That is, the top and bottom margins are of ¾ inches and left and right margins are of 0.7 inch with 0.3 inch separating the header and footer from the top and bottom margin respectively.

You could select two other standard margins, Wide and Narrow, from the Margin command button's dropdown.

✓ Wide: Top, bottom, left and right margins are of 1 inch with ½ inch separating the header and footer from the top and bottom margin respectively.

✓ Narrow: Top and bottom margins are of ¾ inch and left and right margins are of ¼ inch with 0.3 inch separating the header and footer from the top and bottom margin respectively.

If you find none of the standard margins make your page as you want to be, you could create a custom margin from the Margins tab of the Page Setup dialog box (Figure 5-8) which can be opened by clicking the Custom Margins option (the last item in the Margins command button's dropdown). You need to enter values for Top, Bottom, Left and Right textboxes or adjust the values in the textboxes using the respective spinner buttons. You can center the data between current margins either horizontally or vertically by selecting the Horizontally or Vertically options under the Center on page section.

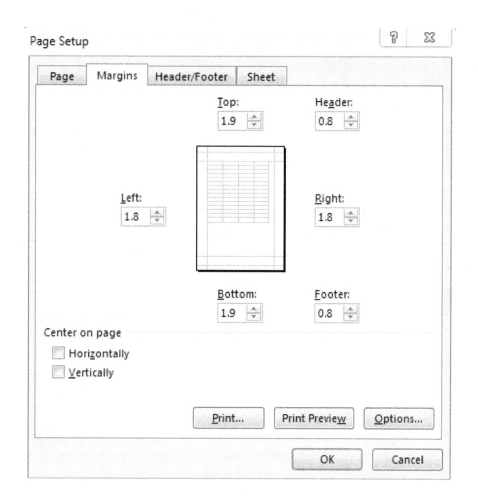

Figure 5-8 Margins tab in the Page Setup dialog box to create custom margins

You could also adjust the margins manually by dragging the margin markers in the preview area of the Print screen in the Backstage view. Click the Show Margins button (circled in Figure 5-9) in the Print screen and then drag the margin marker with your mouse after positioning the mouse pointer on the desired margin marker. You could also adjust the width of the columns similarly by dragging the column marker to the required side. If you want to include more columns on a page, then you should reduce the left and right margins. To include more rows on a page, try reducing the top and bottom margins.

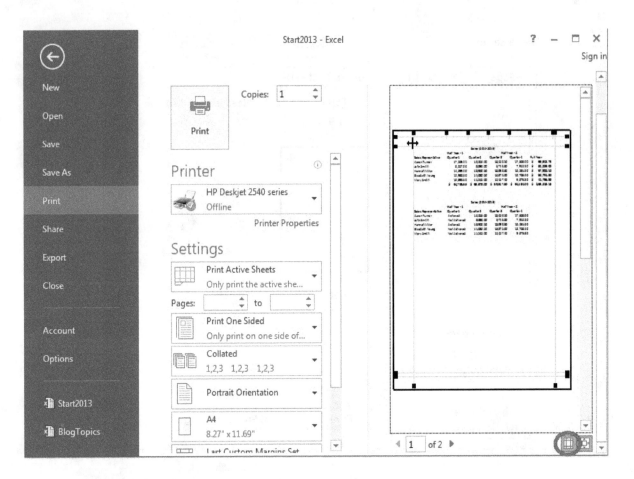

Figure 5-9 Margin markers to adjust the margins manually

Alter the Orientation

You can setup your page in such a way that it accommodates either fewer columns or fewer rows. This is possible by setting the orientation of your page to either Portrait or Landscape. You need to click the Orientation button in the Page Setup group on the Page Layout tab (Figure 5-10) which opens a dropdown with the following two options:

✓ Portrait: This is the default view which accommodates fewer columns and printing runs parallel to the short edge of the paper.

✓ Landscape: This view accommodates fewer rows and printing runs parallel to the long edge of the paper.

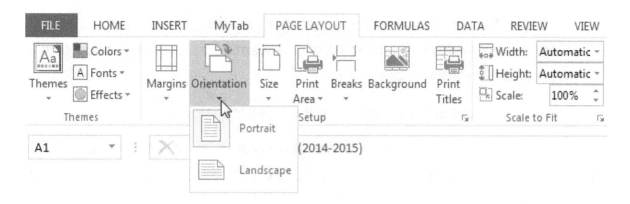

Figure 5-10 Orientation command button in the Page Setup group on the Page Layout tab

If your worksheets are wider than they are tall, you could find that your pages will look more beautiful when you change the page orientation from Portrait to Landscape. Similarly, Portrait orientation will be more suitable for taller worksheets.

Putting Out the Print Titles

You can print particular row and column headings on each page of the report with Excel's Print Title feature. Print titles become important in case of multipage reports where the rows and columns of related data spill over to other pages. Print titles are not at all same as headers. Of course, both headers and print titles are printed on each page. But, headers appear in the top margin of the report whereas print titles appear in the body of the report, which is at the top in case of rows used as print titles and on the left in case of columns.

To set rows and/or columns as print titles:

1. Click the Print Titles button in the Page Setup group on the Page Layout tab to open the Page Setup dialog box with the Sheet tab selected as in Figure 5-11. To set columns as print titles go to Step 2 and to set rows as print titles go to Step 3.

2. Click in the Columns to repeat at left: textbox and then select the range of columns with the information you want to appear at the left of each page of the printed report. Go to Step 4.

3. Click in the Rows to repeat at top: textbox and then select the range of rows with the information you want to appear at the top of each page of the printed report.

4. Click OK or press Enter to close the Page Setup dialog box.

To clear the print titles, delete the row and column ranges from the Rows to repeat at top: and the Columns to repeat at left: textboxes in the Sheet tab of the Page Setup dialog box.

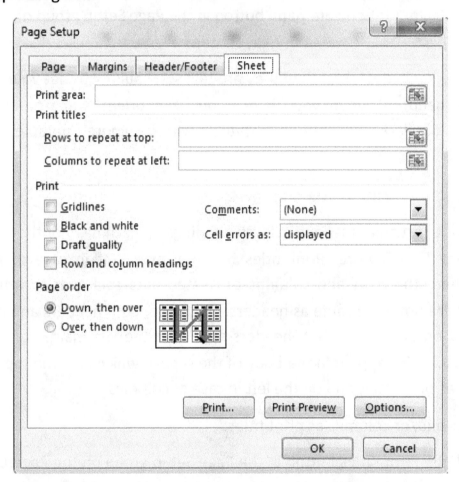

Figure 5-11 Page Setup dialog box with Sheet tab opened

Using Buttons in the Scale to Fit Group

You can get your worksheet correctly fit on a single page by selecting the option "1 Page" on the Width as well as Height dropdown menus in the Scale to Fit group on the Page Layout tab (Figure 5-12). When you select these options, Excel calculates how much to reduce the size of the data on your worksheet to fit it all on one page.

After clicking the Page Break Preview button on the Status bar, if you find that the printing is too small to read comfortably, then press Esc to go back to the Normal worksheet view, select the Page Layout tab and select some other option instead or "1 Page" in the Width and Height drop-down menus in the Scale to Fit group.

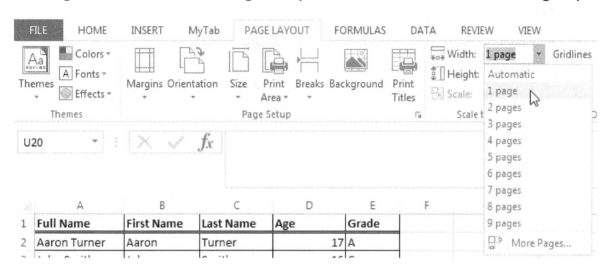

Figure 5-12 Values of Width and Height dropdowns set to "1 Page" to fit the worksheet on a single page

Using Print Buttons in the Sheet Options Group

The Sheet Options group contains two Print checkboxes as in Figure 5-13: first one in the Gridlines column and the second in the Headings column.

Figure 5-13 Print checkboxes in Sheet Options group

Print check box in the Gridlines column: Select it to print the column and row gridlines on each page.

Print check box in the Headings column: Select it to print the row headings with the row numbers and the column headings with the column letters on each page.

From Header to Footer

Headers and footers are nothing but text that appear on every page of the report. A header appears in the top margin of the page and a footer appears in the bottom margin of the page. Excel does not add headers and footers to a new workbook automatically, you should do it if you want.

Your worksheet needs to be in Page Layout view to add headers and/or footers. Click the Page Layout button on the Status bar (Figure 5-1) or click the Page Layout button in the Workbook Views group on the View tab (Figure 5-2) to switch to the Page Layout view. Once your worksheet is in the Page Layout view, position the mouse pointer over the section in the top margin of the first page marked Click to Add Header (Figure 5-14) or in the bottom margin of the first page marked Click to Add Footer.

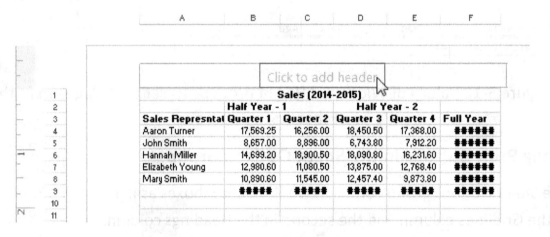

Figure 5-14 Worksheet in Page Layout view to add a centered header

You can create a left aligned, centered or right aligned header or footer. You just have to click in the required section of the header or footer area to set the insertion point. After setting the insertion point, you just have to enter the text for the header or footer. Once you set the insertion point, Excel adds a Header & Footer Tools contextual tab with its own Design tab as in Figure 5-15. The contextual Design tab is divided into Header & Footer, Header & Footer Elements, Navigation, and Options groups.

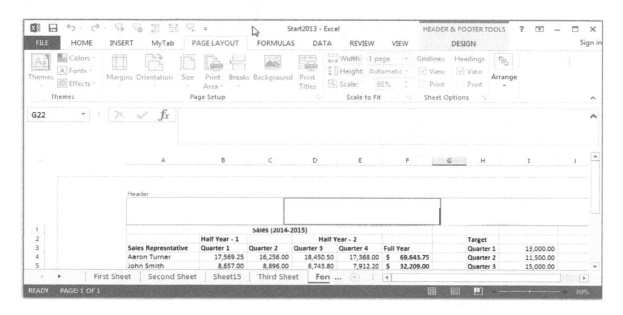

Figure 5-15 Design tab of the Header & Footer Tools contextual tab

Adding an Auto Header or Footer

You can easily add header and footer which is already in stock using the Header and Footer command buttons (circled in Figure 5-16) in the Header & Footer section on the contextual Design tab. You just have to click the command button and select the header or footer example you want to use from the dropdown menu that appears.

Figure 5-16 Header and Footer buttons to add stock header or footer

To create an auto header and footer as shown in Figure 5-17, I selected Fourth Sheet, Confidential, Page 1 from the Header command button's dropdown. Here, Fourth Sheet is the name of the worksheet, Confidential is stock text which can be changed if you want and Page 1 is the current page number. I also selected Page 1 of ? From the Footer command button's dropdown menu. Figure 5-17 displays both the pages in the fourth worksheet. You could find that the page number is displayed appropriately in both the header and the footer.

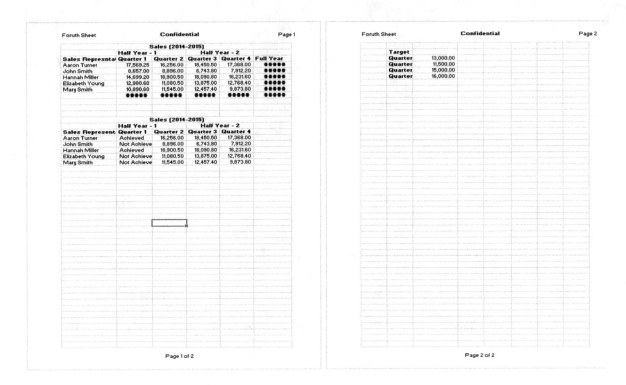

Figure 5-17 Auto header and footer added from the stock list

You can clear the header and footer added from the stock list at any point of time. You just need to select the None option (the first option) from the Header or Footer command button's dropdown.

Creating a Custom Header or Footer

If you feel that the readymade headers or footers are not sufficient for your report printing needs, you can create a header or footer that is customized for your needs. You need to use the command buttons in the Header & Footer Elements group on the contextual Design tab. You can combine the information you want and display on the header or footer using the following command buttons in the Header & Footer Elements group.

✓ Page Number: Click this button to insert the current page number.

✓ Number of Pages: Click this button to insert the total number of pages.

✓ Current Date: Click this button to insert the current date.

✓ Current Time: Click this button to insert the current time.

- ✓ File Path: Click this button to insert the directory path along with the name of the workbook file.

- ✓ File Name: Click this button to insert the name of the workbook file.

- ✓ Sheet Name: Click this button to insert the name of the worksheet.

- ✓ Picture: Click this button to insert an image from online collection or your computer.

- ✓ Format Picture: Click this button to apply formatting to the inserted picture.

Once your worksheet is in Page Layout view, set the insertion point by clicking the mouse pointer in the left, center or right sections of the header or footer. You then need to click the required command button in the Header & Footer Elements group based on the information you need to display. You can also add your own text at the insertion point if you want. For example, if you want to display "My Data" as the header, you just need to enter it.

You can also format the header and footer exactly as you format the cell content, which is using the command buttons in the Home tab. Once you create and format the header or footer, click any cell in the worksheet to deselect the header or footer area. You could now find the created header and footer on all the pages of your worksheet.

Creating First-Page Headers or Footers

Excel 2013 allows you to create a header and footer for the first page that is different from the header and footer of the rest of the pages. In some cases, you will not require header and footer for your very first page. So to make a different (even empty) header and footer for the first page, you need to click the Different First Page check box in the Options group on the contextual Design tab and then define the header and/or footer for the first page.

If you have already defined the header and footer for your worksheet, you could find that the header and footer of the first page is different from the header and footer of the rest of the pages. If you have not created header and footer for the rest of the pages, you can do it anytime making the header and footer of the first page different from the rest of the pages.

Creating Even and Odd Page Headers or Footers

Excel 2013 also allows you to create one header and footer for the even pages and another for the odd pages. This becomes really useful if you plan to do two sided printing. To create different header and footer for odd and even pages, click the Different Odd & Even Pages checkbox in the Options group on the contextual Design tab. Then create a header or footer on the first page of the report and then create another header or footer on the second page.

Breaking Your Pages

Excel's Page Break Preview feature helps you identify and solve page break problems quickly. If you click the Page Break Preview button (circled in Figure 5-18) on the Status bar or click the Page Break Preview command button in the Workbook Views group on the View tab, you could find the page breaks as shown in Figure 5-19.

Figure 5-18 Page Break Preview button

In Figure 5-19, you could find that the data in the second table is split where the Full Name column appears in Page 1 and the remaining columns appear in Page 3. You can adjust the page breaks as you want so that the data appears in a more logical manner.

To adjust the page breaks, click the Page Break Preview button on the Status bar. Then, position the mouse pointer somewhere on the page break indicator (the heavy dotted blue line) and when the pointer changes to a double-headed arrow, drag the page break indicator to the desired column or row and release the mouse button. You could find the worksheet in Page Break Preview mode after adjusting the page breaks in Figure 5-20. Once you are done with the page breaks, you need to click the Normal button (second button to the left of Page Break

Preview button) on the Status bar or click the Normal command button in the Workbook Views group on the View tab to return the worksheet to its normal view.

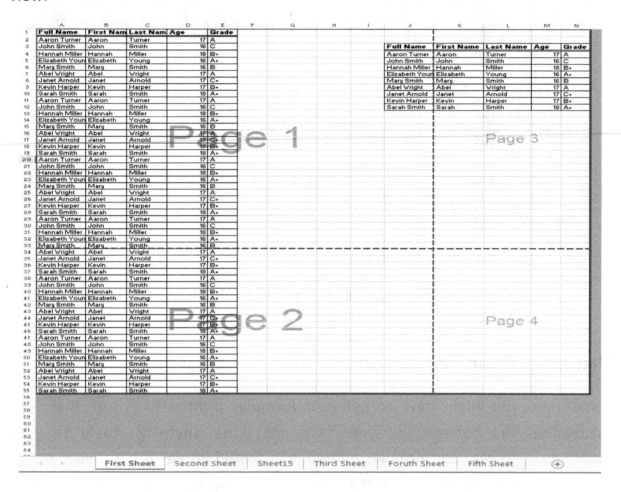

Figure 5-19 Worksheet in Page Break Preview mode

	Full Name	First Nam	Last Nam	Age		Grade					Full Name	First Name	Last Name	Age		Grade
1	Full Name	First Nam	Last Nam	Age		Grade										
2	Aaron Turner	Aaron	Turner	17		A										
3	John Smith	John	Smith	16		C					Full Name	First Name	Last Name	Age		Grade
4	Hannah Miller	Hannah	Miller	18		B+					Aaron Turner	Aaron	Turner	17		A
5	Elizabeth Youn	Elizabeth	Young	16		A+					John Smith	John	Smith	16		C
6	Mary Smith	Mary	Smith	16		B					Hannah Miller	Hannah	Miller	18		B+
7	Abel Wright	Abel	Wright	17		A					Elizabeth Youn	Elizabeth	Young	16		A+
8	Janet Arnold	Janet	Arnold	17		C+					Mary Smith	Mary	Smith	16		B
9	Kevin Harper	Kevin	Harper	17		B+					Abel Wright	Abel	Wright	17		A
10	Sarah Smith	Sarah	Smith	18		A+					Janet Arnold	Janet	Arnold	17		C+
11	Aaron Turner	Aaron	Turner	17		A					Kevin Harper	Kevin	Harper	17		B+
12	John Smith	John	Smith	16		C					Sarah Smith	Sarah	Smith	18		A+
13	Hannah Miller	Hannah	Miller	18		B+										
14	Elizabeth Youn	Elizabeth	Young	16		A+										
15	Mary Smith	Mary	Smith	16		B										
16	Abel Wright	Abel	Wright	17		A										
17	Janet Arnold	Janet	Arnold	17		C+										
18	Kevin Harper	Kevin	Harper	17		B+										
19	Sarah Smith	Sarah	Smith	18		A+										
20	Aaron Turner	Aaron	Turner	17		A										
21	John Smith	John	Smith	16		C										
22	Hannah Miller	Hannah	Miller	18		B+										
23	Elizabeth Youn	Elizabeth	Young	16		A+										
24	Mary Smith	Mary	Smith	16		B										
25	Abel Wright	Abel	Wright	17		A										
26	Janet Arnold	Janet	Arnold	17		C+										
27	Kevin Harper	Kevin	Harper	17		B+										
28	Sarah Smith	Sarah	Smith	18		A+										
29	Aaron Turner	Aaron	Turner	17		A										
30	John Smith	John	Smith	16		C										
31	Hannah Miller	Hannah	Miller	18		B+										
32	Elizabeth Youn	Elizabeth	Young	16		A+										
33	Mary Smith	Mary	Smith	16		B										
34	Abel Wright	Abel	Wright	17		A										
35	Janet Arnold	Janet	Arnold	17		C+										

Figure 5-20 Worksheet in Page Break Preview mode after adjusting the page breaks

Printing Your Formulas

Sometimes, you might have to get your formulas printed to ensure that your calculations are correct and you have not done anything stupid in your worksheets. To get your formulas printed, you should display the formulas rather than the calculated results in the cells. To display formulas, click the Show Formulas button in the Formula Auditing group on the Formula tab (circled in Figure 5-21).

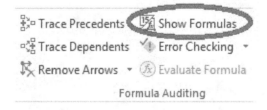

Figure 5-21 Show Formulas button in the Formula Auditing group

Excel then displays the contents of each cell in the worksheet the way it appears in the Formula bar. Moreover, value entries lose their number formatting, formulas appear in their cells and long text entries no longer spill into neighboring blank cells. Now if you print your worksheet, you will get your formulas printed.

You can print your worksheet with column and row headings (put a check mark in the Print check box in the Headings column on the Sheet Options group of the Page Layout tab) so that if you do spot an error, you can easily identify the cell that contains the particular formula. After you print your formulas, return the worksheet to normal by clicking the Show Formulas button on the Formulas tab again.

6. Maintaining the Worksheet

Introduction

In this chapter, we will learn how to

- ➤ Zoom in and out on a worksheet

- ➤ Split the workbook window into different panes

- ➤ Freeze columns and rows for worksheet titles

- ➤ Add comments to cells

- ➤ Name your cells or cell ranges

- ➤ Find and/or replace data in your worksheet

- ➤ Look up data using online resources in the Research task pane

- ➤ Protect your worksheets

You can store huge amounts of data in each worksheet in an Excel 2013 workbook. But the fact is that you are able to see only a small part of the worksheet even with your computer screen at a specific time. It makes the issue of keeping on top of information a necessity. By the end of this chapter, you will realize how easy it is to see the data you want wherever and however it exists on a worksheet, whether it is in the cell IV88 or it is too small to read.

Zooming In and Out

Will you be able to find the data that you need from an Excel worksheet easily if you are accessing it with your favorite tablet that of course has a small screen compared to your computer screen? Are your eyes that powerful or will you strain your eyes throughout trying to read that important data lying in those tiny cells? You do not have to worry at all because you can make the best use of the Zoom feature which is available in the form of Zoom slider on the Status bar.

Just slide the Zoom slider (Figure 6-1) towards the right to zoom in a part of the worksheet or towards the left to shrink it down to the tiniest size. If you drag the slider button to the left or right, you can zoom in or zoom out the worksheet to any percentage you want at a stretch with 10% magnification being the lowest percentage and 400% being the highest percentage. You can even click the Zoom In button (the plus sign) or the Zoom Out button (the minus sign) so that the worksheet zooms in or zooms out by 10% per every click.

You could see a part of a worksheet zoomed into 150% in Figure 6-2 and the same worksheet zoomed out to 50% in Figure 6-3.

Figure 6-1 The Zoom slider on the Status bar

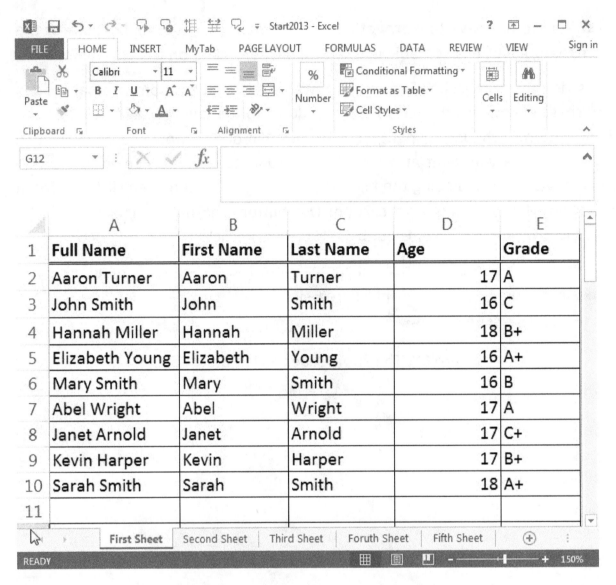

Figure 6-2 Worksheet zoomed in to 150%

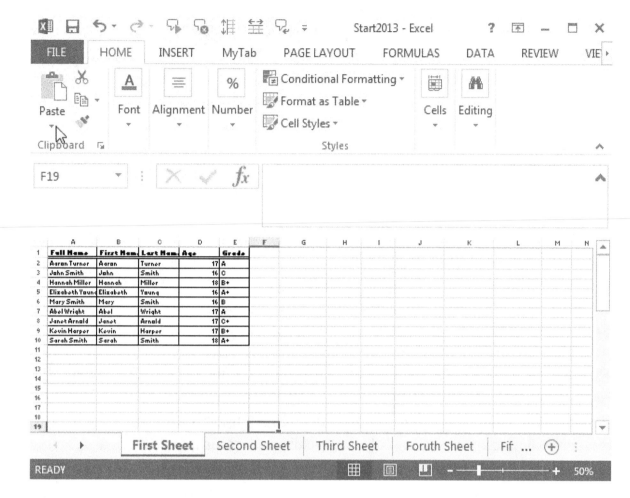

Figure 6-3 Worksheet zoomed out to 50%

There is another technique to zoom in and zoom out the worksheet other than using the Zoom slider on the Status bar. You can use any of the command buttons in the Zoom group on the View tab (Figure 6-4).

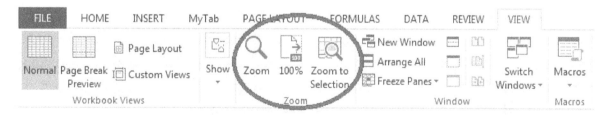

Figure 6-4 The Zoom buttons on the View tab

If you click the Zoom command button, a Zoom dialog box (Figure 6-5) will be opened. If the magnification percentage you want is already available in the dialog box (200%, 100%, 75%, 50% or 25%), then you just need to select it and click OK. If you want to use other percentages besides those, then click the

Custom: option and then enter the magnification percentage you want in the provided textbox.

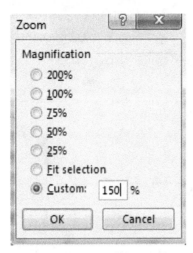

Figure 6-5 The Zoom dialog box

If you want to magnify the worksheet to 100%, you can quickly do it by clicking the 100% command button in the View group. If you click the Zoom to Selection command button in the View group, then Excel figures out the percentage necessary to fill your screen with just the selected cell range. This is extremely useful if you don't know what percentage to enter in order to display a particular cell range on the screen.

Splitting the Worksheet into Windows

How easy it would be if we could bring together two separate sections of a worksheet so that we can compare data on both the sections easily and quickly? Yes, it will make data comparison a breeze and the happy news is that Excel allows you to do it. You can split the worksheet area into separate panes so that you can scroll each pane separately to display the parts you want to compare. When you split a worksheet into different panes, each pane will have its own scroll bar so that you can scroll each pane as you want.

To split a worksheet into two horizontal panes, just select the cell in column A of the row where you want to split the worksheet and then click the Split button in the Window group on the View tab. To split a worksheet into two vertical panes, select the cell in row 1 of the column where you want to split the worksheet and then click the Split button. To split the worksheet into four panes, two horizontal and two vertical, select an intermediate cell and then click the Split button.

You can see a Sales Analysis worksheet for three financial years 2012-2013, 2013-2014 and 2014-2015 in Figure 6-6.

	Sales (2012-2013)				
	Half Year - 1		Half Year - 2		
Sales Represntative	Quarter 1	Quarter 2	Quarter 3	Quarter 4	Full Year
Aaron Turner	10,545.20	9,635.10	14,320.20	17,250.80	$ 51,751.30
John Smith	589.25	10,258.50	7,548.30	9,602.30	$ 27,998.35
Hannah Miller	9,632.40	11,560.80	14,597.60	12,500.00	$ 48,290.80
Elizabeth Young	8,569.00	10,253.00	13,540.50	8,596.20	$ 40,958.70
Mary Smith	10,251.75	10,236.10	8,974.25	6,580.00	$ 36,042.10
	$ 39,587.60	$ 51,943.50	$ 58,980.85	$ 54,529.30	$ 2,05,041.25
	Sales (2013-2014)				
	Half Year - 1		Half Year - 2		
Sales Represntative	Quarter 1	Quarter 2	Quarter 3	Quarter 4	Full Year
Aaron Turner	18,231.95	8,530.40	15,500.45	16,452.60	$ 58,715.40
John Smith	4,387.00	9,873.80	8,365.10	8,000.00	$ 30,625.90
Hannah Miller	10,800.60	13,655.90	20,120.00	14,230.90	$ 58,807.40
Elizabeth Young	7,809.00	10,105.70	12,680.15	11,800.40	$ 42,395.25
Mary Smith	13,150.50	9,547.25	9,631.00	8,536.50	$ 40,865.25
	$ 54,379.05	$ 51,713.05	$ 66,296.70	$ 59,020.40	$ 2,31,409.20
	Sales (2014-2015)				
	Half Year - 1		Half Year - 2		
Sales Represntative	Quarter 1	Quarter 2	Quarter 3	Quarter 4	Full Year
Aaron Turner	17,569.25	16,256.00	18,450.50	17,368.00	$ 69,643.75
John Smith	8,657.00	8,896.00	6,743.80	7,912.20	$ 32,209.00
Hannah Miller	14,699.20	18,900.50	18,090.80	16,231.60	$ 67,922.10
Elizabeth Young	12,980.60	11,080.50	13,875.00	12,768.40	$ 50,704.50
Mary Smith	10,890.60	11,545.00	12,457.40	9,873.80	$ 44,766.80
	$ 64,796.65	$ 66,678.00	$ 69,617.50	$ 64,154.00	$ 2,65,246.15

Figure 6-6 Sales Analysis worksheet

If you want to compare the sales of two years, 2012-2013 and 2014-2015, you can click the cell A12 and then click the Split button. You will get a new window with two different panes and you can scroll the bottom pane to view the sales data of year 2014-2015 clearly as in Figure 6-7.

	A	B	C	D	E	F	G
1				Sales (2012-2013)			
2		Half Year - 1		Half Year - 2			
3	Sales Represntative	Quarter 1	Quarter 2	Quarter 3	Quarter 4	Full Year	
4	Aaron Turner	10,545.20	9,635.10	14,320.20	17,250.80	$ 51,751.30	
5	John Smith	589.25	10,258.50	7,548.30	9,602.30	$ 27,998.35	
6	Hannah Miller	9,632.40	11,560.80	14,597.60	12,500.00	$ 48,290.80	
7	Elizabeth Young	8,569.00	10,253.00	13,540.50	8,596.20	$ 40,958.70	
8	Mary Smith	10,251.75	10,236.10	8,974.25	6,580.00	$ 36,042.10	
9		$ 39,587.60	$ 51,943.50	$ 58,980.85	$ 54,529.30	$ 2,05,041.25	
10							
11							
24							
25				Sales (2014-2015)			
26		Half Year - 1		Half Year - 2			
27	Sales Represntative	Quarter 1	Quarter 2	Quarter 3	Quarter 4	Full Year	
28	Aaron Turner	17,569.25	16,256.00	18,450.50	17,368.00	$ 69,643.75	
29	John Smith	8,657.00	8,896.00	6,743.80	7,912.20	$ 32,209.00	
30	Hannah Miller	14,699.20	18,900.50	18,090.80	16,231.60	$ 67,922.10	
31	Elizabeth Young	12,980.60	11,080.50	13,875.00	12,768.40	$ 50,704.50	
32	Mary Smith	10,890.60	11,545.00	12,457.40	9,873.80	$ 44,766.80	
33		$ 64,796.65	$ 66,678.00	$ 69,617.50	$ 64,154.00	$ 2,65,246.15	

Figure 6-7 Worksheet split into two horizontal panes

Once you split the worksheet, you could find a thin light gray bar, a split bar, along the row or column where the split occurs (just below row 11 in Figure 6-7). If you position the mouse anywhere on the split bar, the pointer changes from a white-cross to a split pointer shape with black arrowheads pointing in opposite directions from parallel separated lines. You can drag the split bar up, down, left or right to increase or decrease the size of the current pane. You can remove the panes either by double clicking somewhere on the split bar or by clicking the Split command button in the Window group on the View tab again.

Freezing Headings

Panes are really great to view different parts of the worksheet simultaneously that can't be normally seen together. Excel allows you to freeze headings in the top row and first column so that headings stay in view all the time even if you scroll through the worksheet.

Figure 6-8 shows a Sales Analysis worksheet for three years where you are not able to see all the rows and columns at one time. If you scroll down to see the rows below and scroll towards the right to see all the columns, then you will not be able to see the headings (Figure 6-9). Instead, you will be able to see only the data. From Figure 6-9, are you able to clearly figure out the sales made by Aaron Turner in the third quarter of 2014-15? As there are fewer number of columns, you might be able to go by assumptions. But it can never be made sure as the headings are not visible.

	A	B	C	D	E	F	(
1		Sales Represntative	Quarter 1	Quarter 2	Quarter 3	Quarter 4	Full Ye
2							
3		Aaron Turner	10,545.20	9,635.10	14,320.20	17,250.80	$ 51,
4		John Smith	589.25	10,258.50	7,548.30	9,602.30	$ 27,
5	Sales (2012-2013)	Hannah Miller	9,632.40	11,560.80	14,597.60	12,500.00	$ 48,
6		Elizabeth Young	8,569.00	10,253.00	13,540.50	8,596.20	$ 40,
7		Mary Smith	10,251.75	10,236.10	8,974.25	6,580.00	$ 36,
8			$ 39,587.60	$ 51,943.50	$ 58,980.85	$ 54,529.30	$ 2,05,
9							
10							
11		Aaron Turner	18,231.95	8,530.40	15,500.45	16,452.60	$ 58,
12		John Smith	4,387.00	9,873.80	8,365.10	8,000.00	$ 30,
13	Sales (2013-2014)	Hannah Miller	10,800.60	13,655.90	20,120.00	14,230.90	$ 58,
14		Elizabeth Young	7,809.00	10,105.70	12,680.15	11,800.40	$ 42,
15		Mary Smith	13,150.50	9,547.25	9,631.00	8,536.50	$ 40,
16			$ 54,379.05	$ 51,713.05	$ 66,296.70	$ 59,020.40	$ 2,31,
17							
18							
19		Aaron Turner	17,569.25	16,256.00	18,450.50	17,368.00	$ 69,
20		John Smith	8,657.00	8,896.00	6,743.80	7,912.20	$ 32,
21	Sales (2014-2015)	Hannah Miller	14 699 20	18 900 50	18 090 80	16 231 60	$ 67

Figure 6-8 Sales Analysis data where not every rows and columns are visible

	B	C	D	E	F	G
12	John Smith	4,387.00	9,873.80	8,365.10	8,000.00	$ 30,625.90
13	Hannah Miller	10,800.60	13,655.90	20,120.00	14,230.90	$ 58,807.40
14	Elizabeth Young	7,809.00	10,105.70	12,680.15	11,800.40	$ 42,395.25
15	Mary Smith	13,150.50	9,547.25	9,631.00	8,536.50	$ 40,865.25
16		$ 54,379.05	$ 51,713.05	$ 66,296.70	$ 59,020.40	$ 2,31,409.20
17						
18						
19	Aaron Turner	17,569.25	16,256.00	18,450.50	17,368.00	$ 69,643.75
20	John Smith	8,657.00	8,896.00	6,743.80	7,912.20	$ 32,209.00
21	Hannah Miller	14,699.20	18,900.50	18,090.80	16,231.60	$ 67,922.10
22	Elizabeth Young	12,980.60	11,080.50	13,875.00	12,768.40	$ 50,704.50
23	Mary Smith	10,890.60	11,545.00	12,457.40	9,873.80	$ 44,766.80
24		$ 64,796.65	$ 66,678.00	$ 69,617.50	$ 64,154.00	$ 2,65,246.15

Figure 6-9 Headings are not visible when the worksheet is scrolled

You can freeze the row headings by clicking the Freeze Panes command button in the Window group on the View tab and then selecting the option Freeze Top Row from the dropdown. Similarly, you can freeze the column headings by selecting the option Freeze First Column from the dropdown. If you want to freeze columns and rows simultaneously, select the cell on the top and left of which you want to freeze the headings and then select the option Freeze Panes from the dropdown that appears when you click the Freeze Panes command button in the Window group on the View tab.

In case of the worksheet displayed in Figure 6-8, if you click cell C2 and then click the option Freeze Panes from the dropdown, you will get a worksheet where the columns A and B and the first row will be frozen. You can easily move to the right or bottom seeing the headings clearly as in Figure 6-10.

	A	B	D	E	F	G
1		Sales Represntative	Quarter 2	Quarter 3	Quarter 4	Full Year
12		John Smith	9,873.80	8,365.10	8,000.00	$ 30,625.90
13	Sales (2013-2014)	Hannah Miller	13,655.90	20,120.00	14,230.90	$ 58,807.40
14		Elizabeth Young	10,105.70	12,680.15	11,800.40	$ 42,395.25
15		Mary Smith	9,547.25	9,631.00	8,536.50	$ 40,865.25
16			$51,713.05	$66,296.70	$59,020.40	$2,31,409.20
17						
18						
19		Aaron Turner	16,256.00	18,450.50	17,368.00	$ 69,643.75
20		John Smith	8,896.00	6,743.80	7,912.20	$ 32,209.00
21	Sales (2014-2015)	Hannah Miller	18,900.50	18,090.80	16,231.60	$ 67,922.10
22		Elizabeth Young	11,080.50	13,875.00	12,768.40	$ 50,704.50
23		Mary Smith	11,545.00	12,457.40	9,873.80	$ 44,766.80
24			$66,678.00	$69,617.50	$64,154.00	$2,65,246.15

Figure 6-10 Column A and B and row 1 is frozen

When Excel sets up the frozen panes, the borders of frozen panes are represented by a single line. You can unfreeze the panes by clicking the option Unfreeze Panes from the dropdown that appears when you click Freeze Panes command button on the View tab.

Adding Comments to Cells

You can add text comments to any cells in an Excel worksheet. Comments can help you to remind something you need to do on your worksheet or to mark your current place in a large worksheet so that next time you can easily start your work from there. To add a comment,

1. Select the cell that you want to add comment to.

2. Click the New Comment button in the Comments group on the Review tab which opens a textbox as in Figure 6-11.

3. Enter your comment in the textbox.

4. Click somewhere outside the textbox once you are done. Excel adds a tiny triangle in the upper-right corner of the cell to mark the location of the comment.

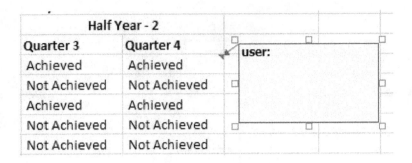

Half Year - 2		user:
Quarter 3	Quarter 4	
Achieved	Achieved	
Not Achieved	Not Achieved	
Achieved	Achieved	
Not Achieved	Not Achieved	
Not Achieved	Not Achieved	

Figure 6-11 Textbox to add comment

You just have to position the thick white cross mouse pointer somewhere in the cell with the location indicator whenever you want to see the comment.

Reviewing All the Comments Together

If your worksheet contains a bunch of comments, it would be practically difficult to position the mouse pointer over each of its cells in order to read each one. In that case, you just need to click the Show All Comments command button in the Comments group on the Review tab. Then you will see all the comments in the current worksheet as in Figure 6-12. You can hide all the comments by clicking the Show All Comments button again.

		Sales (2014-2015)				
13						
14		Half Year - 1		Half Year - 2		
15	Sales Representative	Quarter 1	Quarter 2	Quarter 3	Quarter 4	user: My First Comment
16	Aaron Turner	A [user: Beyond expectation] eved	Achieved	Achieved	
17	John Smith	Not Achieved	Not Achieved	Not Achieved	Not Achieved	
18	Hannah Miller	Achieved	Achieved	Achieved	Achieved	
19	Elizabeth Young	Not Achieved	ieved	Not Achieved	Not Achieved	
20	Mary Smith	N [user: Inconsistent performer] d	Not Achieved	Not Achieved	
21						

Figure 6-12 Showing all the comments simultaneously

You can move back and forth from comment to comment by clicking the Next and Previous command buttons in the Comments group, if your worksheet has Review tab selected in the Ribbon. Once you reach the last comment in the workbook, you receive an alert box asking whether you want to continue reviewing the comments from the beginning.

Editing the Comments

To edit a comment, select the cell that contains the comment and then click the Edit Comment button in the Comments group on the Review tab. You can then change the contents of a comment. You can also right click the cell that contains the comment and click Edit Comment from the shortcut menu to change the contents of a comment.

You can change the placement of a comment in relation to its cell. You just need to select the comment by clicking somewhere on it and then dragging the textbox by positioning the mouse pointer on one of its edges. When you release the mouse button, Excel redraws the arrow connecting the comment's textbox to the new position as in Figure 6-13.

10		**user:**		
11		Beyond expectation		
12				
13			Sales (2014-2015)	
14		Half Year - 1		Half Year - 2
15	**Sales Representative**	**Quarter 1**	**Quarter 2**	**Quarter 3**	**Quarter 4**
16	Aaron Turner	Achieved	Achieved	Achieved	Achieved
17	John Smith	Not Achieved	Not Achieved	Not Achieved	Not Achieved
18	Hannah Miller	Achieved	Achieved	Achieved	Achieved

Figure 6-13 Comment in cell A16 is moved to a new position

You can change the size of a comment's textbox. You need to select the comment, position the mouse pointer on one of its sizing handles and then drag in the required direction. When you release the mouse button, Excel redraws the textbox with the new size wrapping the text to fit in the new size.

You can format the contents of a comment exactly as you format data in a cell. After selecting the content of a comment, you can go to the Home tab and use different formatting options. You can also select the content of a comment, right click the comment's textbox and then click Format Comment from its shortcut menu to open the Format Comment dialog box. You can then use options to change the font, font style, font size, or color of the text displayed in the selected comment.

Deleting the Comments

You can delete either the comment along with the note indicator or delete just the contents of a comment. To delete just the contents of a comment, select the comment and then delete the content of the comment from the comment's textbox so that the note indicator will remain as it is without any comment.

To delete a comment along with the note indicator, select the cell that contains the comment and then click the Delete button in the Comments group on the Review tab. You can also select the cell that contains the comment, right click and then click the option Delete Comment from the shortcut menu. To delete the comments of selected range of cells, click the Clear button in the Editing group on the Home tab and select the Clear Comments option from the dropdown menu.

Printing the Comments

You can print comments along with worksheet data. To print comments, click the Dialog Box launcher in the lower-right corner of the Page Setup group on the Page Layout tab (circled in Figure 6-14). Click Sheet tab from the opened Page Setup dialog box and select either At end of sheet or As displayed on sheet from the Comments dropdown list on the Sheet tab.

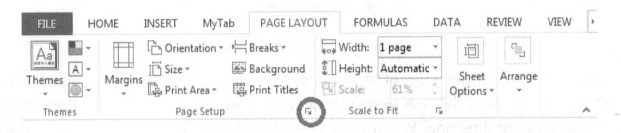

Figure 6-14 Dialog Box launcher in the Page Setup group

Cell/Range Naming Ceremony

It is always easy to remember descriptive names than to remember cell names like B60, IV80 etc or cell ranges like B10:C15, CG23:EK40 etc. Excel allows you to name cells as well as cell ranges. Once you name a cell or cell range, you can use it to designate the cell selection that you want to print or use in other Office 2013 programs. You can also use these unique names to locate cells or ranges using the Go To feature.

There are certain guidelines that you need to follow when naming cells or range of cells.

✓ Names must begin with an alphabet letter, not a number.

✓ Names cannot contain spaces. You can use underscores.

✓ Names cannot correspond to valid cell coordinates in the worksheet.

To name a cell or cell range in a worksheet,

1. Select the cell or cell range that you want to name.

2. Click the cell address that appears in the Name Box on the far left of the Formula bar.

3. Type the name for the selected cell or cell range in the Name Box. Make sure that you follow the naming conventions. (Figure 6-15 shows naming the cell range A4:A8 as Employees)

4. Press the Enter key.

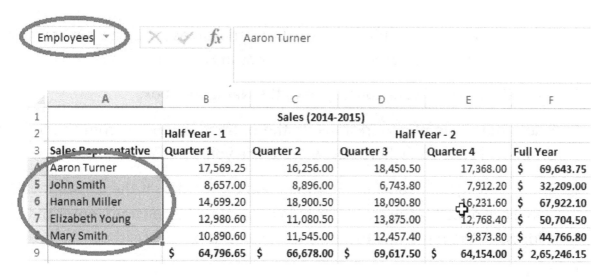

Figure 6-15 Naming the cell range A4:A8 as Employees

To select a named cell or cell range, click the Name box on the Formula bar and select the name from the dropdown that appears to the right of the cell address. You can also click Ctrl+G to open the "Go To" dialog box, select the name and click OK (alternatively double click the name) so that the named cell or cell range will be selected.

Naming Formulas

The formula =Distance/Time would be easier to understand than the one =A3/B3. You can create formulas that use cell or range names instead of cell references exactly as you create normal formulas. Instead of specifying cell references, you have to specify cell names. That is it. Only thing is that you cannot copy formulas that use cell names using fill handle. Because when you copy a formula that uses names, Excel copies the original formula without adjusting the cell references to the new rows and columns.

Naming Constants

There are many formulas that use constant values and if you name constants, chances for making errors are less. Which of the following formulas is prone to less errors, =PI *A1*A1 or =3.141593*A1*A1? Of course, the first formula will be easier to use especially when there are hundreds of formulas that use the constant value.

To create a constant,

1. Click the Define Name button in the Defined Names group on the Formulas tab which opens a New Name dialog box as in Figure 6-16.

2. Enter the name of your constant into the Name: textbox.

3. Select the name of a worksheet or the option Workbook from the Scope: dropdown based on where you want to use your constant.

4. Enter the constant value inside the Refers to: textbox. If the constant value is in a cell or cell range or if a formula calculates the constant, enter the cell address or the formula after the = sign in the Refers to: textbox.

5. Click OK.

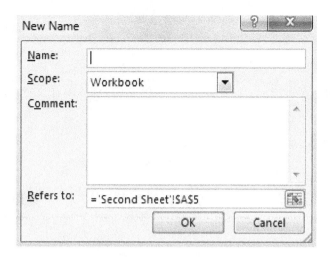

Figure 6-16 New Name dialog box to name constants

Once you assign a constant, you can use it within formulas either by just typing the name where you want to use it in the formula or by clicking the Use in Formula command button in the Defined Names group on the Formulas tab when you want to use it and then clicking the required name.

Seek and Ye Shall Find

It is really easy to locate the information you need in your worksheet using Excel's Find feature. You can open the Find and Replace dialog box by going to Home → Find & Select (in the Editing group) → Find or pressing Ctrl + F or Shift +F5 or Alt +HFDF.

Enter the text you want to locate in the Find what: dropdown. Click the Find Next button or press Enter to start the search. You can have more search options by clicking the Options button as in Figure 6-17.

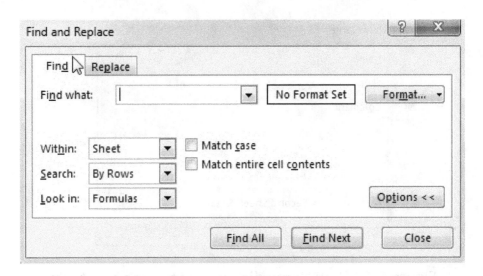

Figure 6-17 Find and Replace dialog box with advanced options

If you select the Match case checkbox, Excel performs a case-sensitive search. For example, if you are searching for aa, the entry Aaron will not be considered a match if you select the Match case checkbox. If you select the Match entire cell contents checkbox, Excel would consider only exact match. For example, if you are searching for Aa, the entry Aaron will not be considered a match if you select the Match entire cell contents check box.

Excel normally searches down the worksheet by rows. To search across the columns first, choose the By Columns option from the Search: dropdown menu. To reverse the search direction and revisit previous occurrences of matching cell entries, press the Shift key while you click the Find Next button in the Find and Replace dialog box.

You can look for data with specific formatting. To have Excel match the formatting assigned to a particular cell,

1. Enter the data you want to look for in the Find what: dropdown.

2. Click the Format button in the Find and Replace dialog box.

3. Select the option Choose Format From Cell... from the dropdown (Figure 6-18) which closes the dialog box and an ink dropper icon appears.

4. Click the ink dropper icon in the cell that contains the formatting that you want to look for (Figure 6-19). The formatting in the selected worksheet appears in the Preview text box in the Find and Replace dialog box.

5. Click the Find Next button or press Enter.

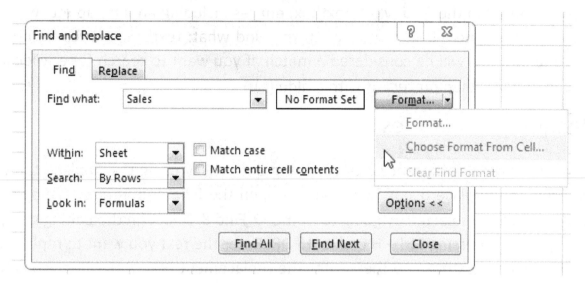

Figure 6-18 Choose Format From Cell option to look for data with specific formatting

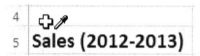

Figure 6-19 Ink dropper icon

Another way to look for data with specific formatting is:

1. Click the Format button in the Find and Replace dialog box.

2. Select the option Format from the dropdown which opens the Find Format dialog box.

3. Select the formatting options to match from various tabs and click OK.

When you use either of these methods to look for data with specific formatting, the No Format Set button located between the Find what: textbox and the Format button changes to a Preview button. The word Preview in this button will have the same format that you are looking for. You can clear the search format by selecting the Clear Find Format option from the dropdown that appears when you click the Format button in the Find and Replace textbox.

If you do not know the exact spelling or the precise value you are looking for, then you can use wildcard search. The question mark (?) stands for a single unknown character and the asterisk (*) for one or more unknown characters. For example, if you enter a? In the Find what: textbox, entries including an, am, ap etc. will be considered a match. If you enter a* in the Find what: textbox, entries including are, and, ant etc. will be considered a match. If you want to search for a wildcard character itself, then precede it with a tilde (~).

Replacing Cell Entries

You can automate the process of replacing data easily using the Replace tab on the Find and Replace dialog box. You can open the Find and Replace dialog box with Replace tab selected by going to Home → Find & Select (in the Editing group) → Replace or pressing Ctrl + H or Alt +HFDR. Enter the text you want to replace in the Find what: textbox and then enter the replacement text in the Replace with: textbox.

Make sure that you select the Match case and the Match entire cell contents checkboxes carefully because otherwise your worksheet could be a total mess with many wanted and unwanted replacements. After specifying what to replace and what to replace it with, you can click the Replace All button to replace all occurrences in a single operation or click the Replace button to replace the occurrences one by one.

Doing Your Research

You can make use of Excel 2013's Research task pane to look for information you want online. You need to click the Research command button in the Proofing group on the Review tab to open the Research task pane (Figure 6-20). When you open the Research pane for the first time, it is a floating pane that you can reposition anywhere in the worksheet by dragging.

Figure 6-20 Research task pane

To search for something in the Research pane, select the cell that contains the phrase you want to research online or enter the word directly into the Search for: text box. Click the type of online reference from the dropdown. To start the online search, click the Start Searching button (the green box with the right arrow). Excel then connects to the designated online resources and displays the search results in the list box below.

When you click any of the links in the list box, the particular site will be opened in your default Web browser. To return to Excel after visiting a particular web page, just close the browser.

Protecting Your Worksheets

You can protect your worksheet and guard it against any unplanned changes once your worksheet is finalized. You can lock or unlock each cell in the worksheet. By default, Excel locks all the cells in a worksheet.

1. Click the Protect Sheet command button in the Changes group on the Review tab to open the Protect Sheet dialog box.

2. Enter a password in the Password to unprotect sheet: text box if you want to assign a password that must be supplied before you can remove the protection from the worksheet.

3. Select the check box options you want to be available when the protection is turned on in the worksheet from the Allow all users of this worksheet to: list box.

4. Click OK or press Enter.

You can go a step further and protect the entire workbook.

1. Click the Protect Workbook command button in the Changes group on the Review tab to open the Protect Structure and Windows dialog box.

2. Enter a password in the Password (optional): textbox if you want to assign a password that must be supplied before you can remove the protection from the workbook.

3. Click OK or press Enter.

Once you protect the worksheet, it is impossible to make further changes to the contents of any of the locked cells in that worksheet or workbook, except for those options that you specifically exempt in the Allow all users of this worksheet to: list box. Once you protect the workbook, it is impossible to make further changes to the layout of the worksheets in that workbook.

Excel displays an alert dialog box with the following message when you try to edit or replace an entry in a locked cell: "The cell or chart you are trying to change is on a protected sheet. To make changes, click Unprotect Sheet in the Review Tab (you might need a password)."

You need to click the Unprotect Sheet or the Unprotect Workbook command button in the Changes group on the Review tab to remove protection from the current worksheet or workbook document and make the worksheet or workbook editable. You would have to enter the password you have already assigned when protecting the worksheet or workbook (if any) in the Password: textbox. You can also protect a worksheet or your workbook from the Backstage by clicking the Protect Workbook button.

7. Maintaining Multiple Worksheets

Introduction

In this chapter, we will learn how to

> ➢ Move from sheet to sheet in a workbook
>
> ➢ Select sheets for group editing
>
> ➢ Add and delete sheets in a workbook
>
> ➢ Name sheet tabs descriptively
>
> ➢ Rearrange sheets in a workbook
>
> ➢ Display parts of different sheets
>
> ➢ Compare two worksheets side by side
>
> ➢ Copy or move sheets from one workbook to another
>
> ➢ Create formulas that span different worksheets

Once you become comfortable in working with a single worksheet, you might have to play with different worksheets in a workbook. By the end of this chapter, you will be comfortable in dealing with multiple worksheets.

Juggling Multiple Worksheets

You could add more worksheets in a workbook when you have to deal with different, still logically related data. For example, if your company has branches in different locations and you want to keep track of the annual sales of these different branches. In such a case, it would be better to create a single workbook with different worksheets for each branch than maintaining separate workbooks for each branch.

By keeping the sales data in different worksheets of the same workbook,

✓ You can enter the stuff that's needed in all the sales worksheets just by typing it once into one of the worksheets.

✓ You can add formulas and macros for any one the worksheets which will be readily available in the other worksheets.

✓ You can quickly compare the data of different branches as they are available in different worksheets in the same workbook.

✓ You can print sales information of all branches as a single report in one printing operation.

✓ You can easily create charts to compare sales of different branches.

✓ You can easily setup a summary worksheet that total the sales of different branches.

Sliding between the Sheets

When you open a new workbook, it contains a single worksheet with the name Sheet1. You just have to click the New Sheet button (the one with plus sign in a circle) on the Status bar to add more worksheets to your workbook (circled in Figure 7-1). Each worksheet added will have a generic Sheet name with the next available number appended to it like Sheet2, Sheet3 and so on. These names appear on tabs at the bottom of the workbook window.

Figure 7-1 The New Sheet button to add more worksheets

You need to click the tab with the name of the sheet you want to see to go from one worksheet to another so that Excel brings that worksheet to the top of the stack and its name is displayed in bold type on the tab.

If there are so many worksheets in your workbook, all the tabs might not be visible at any one time and you would see an ellipsis (three dots in a row) on the

Status bar immediately after the last visible sheet tab. In such a situation, you can move to the next worksheet in a workbook by pressing Ctrl+PgDn and move to the previous sheet by pressing Ctrl+PgUp. You can also use the two tab scrolling buttons, Next (triangle pointing right) and Previous (triangle pointing left), on the Status bar to bring new sheet tabs into view (Figure 7-2).

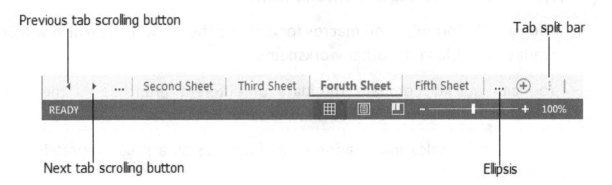

Figure 7-2 Tab scrolling buttons to slide between sheets

When you click the Next tab scrolling button, the next tab of the worksheet on the right is brought into view. If you hold down the Shift key when clicking the Next button, then several tabs are scrolled at a time. If you hold down the Ctrl key when clicking the Next button, then the last group of sheets are brought into view.

When you click the Previous tab scrolling button, the next tab of the worksheet on the left is brought into view. If you hold down the Shift key when clicking the Previous button, then several tabs are scrolled at a time. If you hold down the Ctrl key when clicking the Previous button, then the first groups of sheets are brought into view.

When you right click either of the tab scrolling buttons, the Active dialog box gets opened as in Figure 7-3 showing a list of all the worksheets in the workbook. You can activate a worksheet by selecting it and clicking OK.

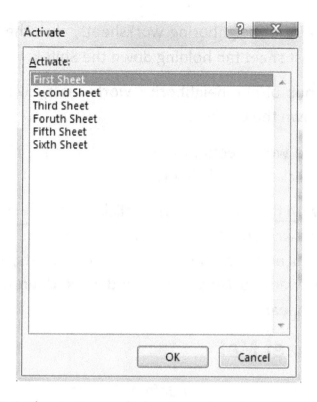

Figure 7-3 The Activate dialog box showing all worksheets

You can drag the tab split bar (Figure 7-2) to the right to select a sheet tab without doing an inordinate amount of tab scrolling.

Editing en Masse

Usually, we make changes to one worksheet at a time. But there could be situations where we have to make changes massively. In other words, we might have to select a bunch of worksheets and make the same change in all of them simultaneously. For example, you might have to enter the names of twelve months in cell A1 through A12 in three worksheets. Excel allows you to complete this operation so easily and quickly.

The changes you make in one worksheet after selecting multiple worksheets will appear in exactly the same way in all selected worksheets. This of course makes the process of doing repeated task lot easier and faster. If you want to delete Sheet2, Sheet4 and Sheet6, you do not have to delete them one by one. You can select all the sheets to be deleted and delete them in just one step.

There are different ways to select a bunch of worksheets in a workbook.

✓ To select a group of neighboring worksheets, click the first sheet tab and then click the last sheet tab holding down the Shift key.

✓ To select a group of non-neighboring worksheets, click the required sheet tabs holding down the Ctrl key.

✓ To select all the worksheets in the workbook, right click any of the sheet tabs and then click Select All Sheets from the shortcut menu that appears.

Once you are done with the massive editing, click a non-selected worksheet tab to deselect the group of worksheets. If you want to make only one of the selected worksheets active and ungroup the remaining worksheets, then right click the worksheet that you want to keep active and click Ungroup Sheets from the shortcut menu that appears.

Don't Short-Sheet Me!

When you open a new workbook, by default it contains a single worksheet. You can of course increase the default number of worksheets if you want so that next time when you open a workbook, you will have more number of sheets opened. To change the default number, go to File → Options which opens the Excel Options dialog box with the General tab selected. Enter a number between 1 and 255 in the Include this many sheets: text box under the When creating new workbooks section (circled in Figure 7-4) before you click OK.

Adding worksheets to and deleting worksheets from a workbook even after opening a workbook is as simple as that in Excel 2013. You can add up to 255 worksheets in a workbook. You just need to click the Insert Worksheet button to insert new worksheets.

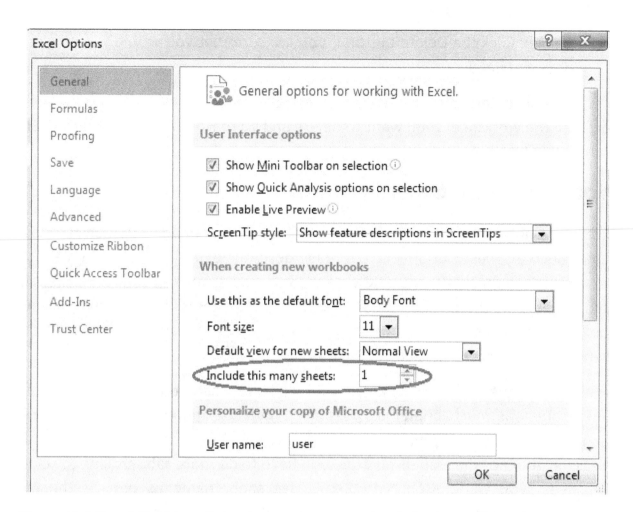

Figure 7-4 Excel Options dialog box to increase the default number of worksheets

You can also add a bunch of worksheets to the workbook at a time. Select a group with the same number of tabs as the number of new worksheets you want to add, starting with the tab where you want to insert the new worksheets. Now go to Home → Insert (in the Cells group) → Insert Sheet to insert new worksheets.

To delete a worksheet from the workbook,

1. Click the tab of the worksheet that you want to delete.

2. Go to Home → Delete (in the Cells group) → Delete Sheet. (You can also press Alt + HDS or right-click the tab and choose Delete from its shortcut menu to delete a sheet.)

3. If the sheet you are trying to delete contains any data, Excel displays an alert message, "You can't undo deleting sheets, and you might be removing some data. If you don't need it, click Delete" with two buttons Delete and

Cancel. Click the Delete button if you are sure that you won't be losing any data you need.

You can also delete more than one worksheet from the workbook at a time. Select all the worksheets you want to delete and go to Home →Delete (in the Cells group) → Delete Sheet.

Worksheets by Other Names

Excel does not name the worksheets so uniquely or creatively. Do you feel that names such as Sheet1 or Sheet2 are really descriptive? Anyhow, Excel gives you the freedom to rename the worksheets the way you want. You can name them in such a way that the names add an identity to the sheets. For example, if your worksheet contains sales data for the first quarter, you always have the freedom to name that particular worksheet Sales – Q1.

Though the worksheet name can contain up to 31 characters, try to keep your sheet names as much briefer as possible. When the name of your worksheet becomes longer, you are making the sheet tab longer. The longer the sheet tab, the fewer the tabs that can display and you have to do more tab scrolling to select the sheets you want. Moreover, Excel uses sheet name as part of the cell reference when you have to reference cells in other worksheets in your formulas. So, if your sheet names are longer, then your formulas look more complex and difficult to handle though they are actually not. In short, the fewer characters in a sheet name, the better.

To rename a worksheet tab,

Double click the sheet tab and replace the current name on the tab by entering the new name.

Or

Right click the sheet tab, click Rename in the shortcut menu and then replace the current name on the tab by entering the new name.

Sheet Tabs by Other Colors

Excel 2013 allows you to assign colors to different worksheet tabs. You can use this feature to color code the worksheets so that you can differentiate your sheets easily. To assign a color to a worksheet tab, right click the tab and highlight the option Tab Color on its shortcut menu. It opens a submenu containing the Tab Color popup palette as in Figure 7-5.

Figure 7-5 Tab Color popup palette

Once you assign a color to the sheet tab, the name of the active sheet tab appears underlined in the color you just selected (Figure 7-6). When you make another sheet tab active, the entire tab takes on the assigned color and the text of the tab name changes to white if the selected color is sufficiently dark enough that black lettering is impossible to read (Figure 7-7).

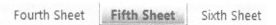

Figure 7-6 The name of the active sheet tab appears underlined in the assigned color, red

Figure 7-7 The entire tab takes on the assigned color when another sheet becomes active

To remove a color from a tab, right-click the sheet tab and highlight the Tab Color option to open the Tab Color pop-up palette. Then, click No Color at the bottom of the Tab Color palette.

Rearranging the Sheets

Sometimes, you might have to change the order in which the sheets appear in the workbook. To rearrange the sheets, you just have to drag the tab of the sheet you want to arrange and then release it to the new position.

When you drag the tab, the mouse pointer changes to a sheet icon with an arrowhead on it as in Figure 7-8. Excel also marks your progress among the sheet tabs. When you release the mouse button, Excel reorders the worksheets in the workbook by inserting the sheet at the place where you dropped the tab off (Figure 7-9).

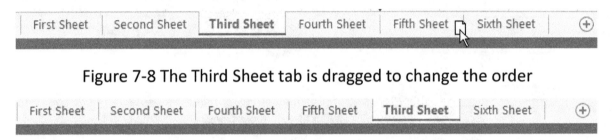

Figure 7-8 The Third Sheet tab is dragged to change the order

Figure 7-9 The Third Sheet tab is dropped between The tabs Fifth Sheet and Sixth Sheet

If you hold down the Ctrl key while dragging the sheet tab, Excel inserts a copy of the worksheet at the place where you release the mouse button. The copied sheet is designated by the addition of (2) after the tab name. For example, if you copy Fourth Sheet to another place in the workbook, the name of the copied tab becomes Fourth Sheet (2).

You can also move or copy worksheets from one part of a workbook to another by right clicking the sheet that you want to move or copy and then choosing Move or Copy from the shortcut menu. The Move or Copy dialog box is opened and you need to select a sheet from the Before sheet: list box based on where (in front of which sheet) you want to insert the moved or copied sheet. Select the check box; Create a copy only if you want to create a copy of the worksheet. Click OK.

Opening Windows on Your Worksheets

In Chapter 6, we have seen how to split a single worksheet into panes so that we can view and compare different parts of that same sheet on the screen. Similarly, you can split a single workbook into worksheet windows and then arrange the windows so that you can view different parts of each worksheet on the screen.

To open the worksheets in different windows,

1. Click the New Window command button in the Window group on the View tab which opens a new window indicated by the :2 that Excel adds to the end of the filename in the title bar.

2. Click the tab of the worksheet that you want to display in this new window.

3. Repeat the steps 1 and 2 if you want to add more windows.

4. Click the Arrange All command button in the Window group on the View tab, select one of the Arrange options in the Arrange Windows dialog box and click OK or press Enter.

You have the following options to select from the Arrange Windows dialog box.

Tiled: Excel changes the size of the windows to arrange them in such a way that they all fit side by side on the screen as in Figure 7-10.

Horizontal: Excel changes the size of the windows equally and place them one above the other as in Figure 7-11.

Vertical: Excel changes the size of the windows equally and place them next to each other as in Figure 7-12.

Cascade: Excel changes the size of the windows to arrange them in such a way that they overlap one another with only their title bars showing as in Figure 7-13.

Windows of active workbook: Excel shows only the windows that you have open in the current workbook.

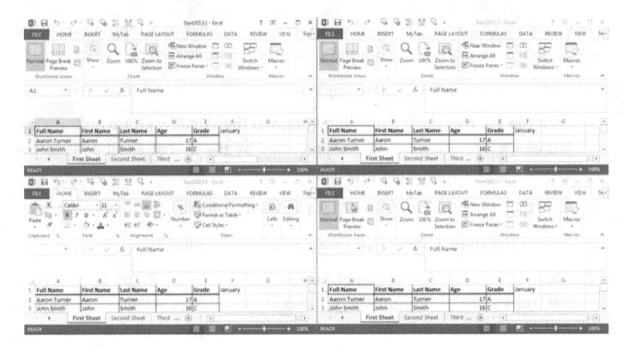

Figure 7-10 Four worksheet windows arranged with the Tiled option

Figure 7-11 Four worksheet windows arranged with the Horizontal option

You can temporarily zoom the window to full size by clicking the Maximize button on the window's title bar. When you finish your work in the full-size worksheet window, you can return to the previous arrangement by clicking the window's Restore button. If you close one of the windows by clicking Close, Excel doesn't automatically resize the other open windows to fill in the gap. To fill in the gap created by closing a window, you need to arrange them again by clicking the Arrange All command button.

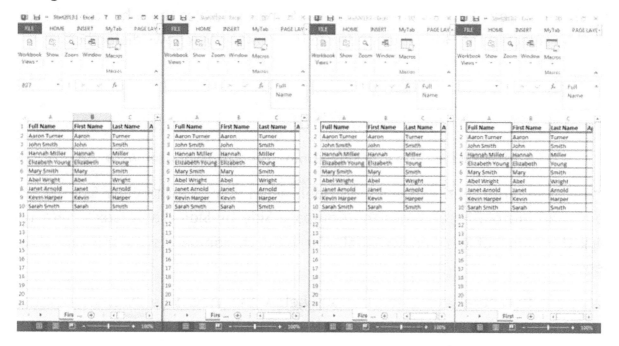

Figure 7-12 Four worksheet windows arranged with the Vertical option

Figure 7-13 Four worksheet windows arranged with the Cascade option

Comparing Worksheets Side by Side

You can compare two worksheet windows side by side easily and quickly using the View Side by Side command button in the Window group on the View tab (Figure 7-14). When you click this button, Excel automatically tiles them horizontally as if you had selected the Horizontal option in the Arrange Windows dialog box.

Figure 7-14 View Side by Side command button on the View tab

If you have more than two windows open when you click the View Side by Side command button, Excel opens the Compare Side by Side dialog box where you click the name of the window that you want to compare with the one that's active.

There are two other command buttons below the View Side by Side command button in the Window group.

Synchronous Scrolling: After selecting this button if you scroll in the active window, the scrolling happens exactly in the same way in the inactive window as well.

Reset Window Position: If you click this button after manually resizing the active window, then the active window and inactive window restore their positions to their previous side by side arrangement.

Shifting Sheets to Other Workbooks

Sometimes, you might have to move or copy a particular worksheet from one workbook to another. To do this,

1. Open both the workbooks, the workbook that contains the worksheet you want to move or copy and the workbook to which you want to move or copy the worksheet.

2. Select the workbook that contains the worksheet that you want to move or copy and select the worksheet that you want to move or copy.

3. Right-click its sheet tab and then click Move or Copy from its shortcut menu which opens a Move or Copy dialog box.

4. Select the name of the workbook to which you want to move or copy the worksheet from the To book: dropdown in the Move or Copy dialog box.

5. Select the name of the sheet, in front of which you want to insert the moved or copied sheet, from the Before sheet: list box in the Move or Copy dialog box. If you want the moved or copied sheet appear at the end of the workbook, choose the (move to end) option.

6. Select the Create a copy checkbox if you want to copy the selected worksheet instead of moving it.

7. Click OK or press Enter.

You can also move or copy worksheets from one workbook to another by just dragging the required worksheet from one window to another. Before trying to drag worksheet from one window to another, make sure that you arrange the windows by clicking the Arrange All command button in the View tab. To move a worksheet, you just need to drag the worksheet to be moved and drop it in the workbook where you want to move it. To copy a worksheet, you should hold down the Ctrl key while dragging the worksheet from one workbook to another.

Summing Stuff on Different Worksheets

It would be great to have a summary worksheet that recaps the values residing in different worksheets in the workbook. When you create a summary worksheet, you might have to add, subtract or compare values in different worksheets and display the result in the summary worksheet. When you reference a cell in a different worksheet, you need to specify the worksheet name along with the cell name. Suppose you want to add the values in cell A1 in the worksheet named Teaching Staff, cell B2 in the worksheet named Non Teaching Staff and the cell C1 in the worksheet named Students and display the result in cell A1 in the worksheet named Summary Sheet. Then the formula in cell A1 in the worksheet named Summary Sheet would be =SUM('Teaching Staff'!A1, 'Non Teaching Staff'! B2, 'Students'!C1).

8. Doing What-If Analysis

Introduction

In this chapter, we will learn how to

> ➤ Perform what-if analysis with one and two variable data tables.

> ➤ Perform what-if analysis with goal seeking.

> ➤ Look at different cases with the Scenario Manager.

Excel is not just a data entry workspace that can be used to keep different types of data or a simple calculator that performs static computations. Excel also excels in performing different kinds of dynamic what-if analysis. As the name indicates (what if?), What-if analysis helps you explore the possibilities in a worksheet by providing different possible inputs into the same equation and analyze different possible outcomes clearly, easily, quickly and effectively.

Excel 2013 allows you to perform what-if analysis in a number of ways. You can use:

> ✓ Data Tables to see how changing one or two variables affect the bottom line.

> ✓ Goal Seeking to find out what it takes to reach a predefined objective.

> ✓ Scenarios to setup and test a wide variety of cases, all the way from the best-case scenario to the worst-case scenario.

Playing What-If with Data Tables

Data tables allow you to provide a series of possible inputs that Excel then plugs into a single formula. You can go for either a one-variable data table or a two-variable data table. As the name indicates, you can only provide possible values for a single input in a formula in case of a one-variable data table and you can provide possible values for two inputs in a formula in case of a two-variable data table.

Once you are ready with the data to be analyzed, go to Data → What-If Analysis (in the Data Tools group) → Data Table (Figure 8-1) to open the Data Table dialog box. The Data Table dialog box contains two text boxes, Row Input Cell and Column Input Cell.

Figure 8-1 What-If Analysis command button in the Data tab

If you plan to create a one-variable data table and enter the possible values in the rows of a single cell, then you need to designate one cell in the worksheet as the Row Input Cell. On the other hand, if you enter the possible values in the cells of a single column, then designate one cell in the worksheet as the Column Input Cell.

When creating a two-variable data table, you need to designate two cells in the worksheet hence using both the Row Input Cell and the Column Input Cell textboxes. One cell serves as the Row Input Cell that substitutes the series of possible values you have entered across cells of a single row and the other cell serves as the Column Input Cell that substitutes the series of possible values you have entered down the cells of a single column.

Creating a One-Variable Data Table

Figure 8-2 shows a loan calculator for which we are going to create a one-variable data table. In this worksheet, cell B2 contains the loan amount, cell B3 contains the loan period in months (300 months means 25 years) and cell B4 contains annual interest rate. The cell B3 is formatted to currency and the cell B4 is formatted to percentage.

The monthly loan amount is calculated using the financial function PMT. The PMT function calculates the payment for a loan based on constant payments and a constant interest rate. The parameters to be passed to the PMT function are interest rate, total number of payments for the loan and the present loan amount. The formula in cell B5 is =-(PMT(B4/12, B3, B2)) and this cell is also formatted to currency. We negated the resulting value because the value calculated by the PMT function will be otherwise negative as it is the loan amount.

Suppose you want to check how much you would have to pay if the interest rate is only 6%. What will you do? You can change the value in cell B4 and see the output value in cell B5. What if you want to check the monthly payment for different interest rates? Instead of changing the value in cell B4 each time, you can create a one-variable data table.

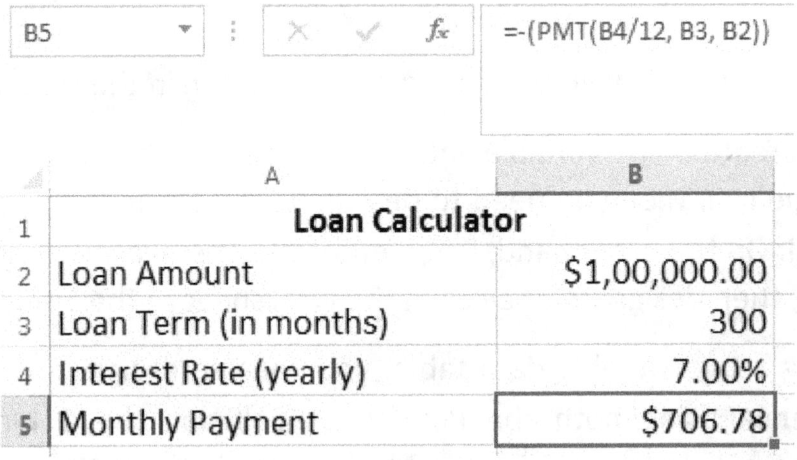

| B5 | ▼ | : | ✕ | ✓ | f_x | =-(PMT(B4/12, B3, B2)) |

	A	B
1	**Loan Calculator**	
2	Loan Amount	$1,00,000.00
3	Loan Term (in months)	300
4	Interest Rate (yearly)	7.00%
5	Monthly Payment	$706.78

Figure 8-2 The loan calculator

Enter a column of interest rates you want to analyze. Here I am entering interest rates ranging from 6% to 8.5% in cells D3 through D13 (also formatted them to percentage) and I get a screen as shown in Figure 8-3.

	A	B	C	D	E
1	**Loan Calculator**				
2	Loan Amount	$1,00,000.00			
3	Loan Term (in months)	300		6.00%	
4	Interest Rate (yearly)	7.00%		6.25%	
5	Monthly Payment	$706.78		6.50%	
6				6.75%	
7				7.00%	
8				7.25%	
9				7.50%	
10				7.75%	
11				8.00%	
12				8.25%	
13				8.50%	

Figure 8-3 The loan calculator with a possible column of interest rates to use as the input for the one-variable data table

Now follow the steps given below to create a one-variable data table that plugs each of these interest rates:

1. Copy the formula entered in cell B5 into cell E2 by typing = and then clicking cell B5.

2. Select the cell range D2:E13.

3. Go to Data → What-If Analysis → Data Table which opens the Data Table dialog box.

4. Click the Column input cell: dialog box (as we have interest rates in a column) and click the cell B4 as it contains the original interest rate.

5. Click OK to close the Data Table dialog box.

6. Click cell B5 and then click the Format Painter command button in the Clipboard group on the Home tab and drag through the cell range E3: E13.

Now your worksheet will look as shown in Figure 8-4.

	A	B	C	D	E
1	**Loan Calculator**				
2	Loan Amount	$1,00,000.00			$706.78
3	Loan Term (in months)	300		6.00%	$644.30
4	Interest Rate (yearly)	7.00%		6.25%	$659.67
5	Monthly Payment	$706.78		6.50%	$675.21
6				6.75%	$690.91
7				7.00%	$706.78
8				7.25%	$722.81
9				7.50%	$738.99
10				7.75%	$755.33
11				8.00%	$771.82
12				8.25%	$788.45
13				8.50%	$805.23

Figure 8-4 The loan calculator worksheet after creating the one-variable data table in the range E3:E13

If you modify any interest rate value in the cell range D3:D13, Excel updates the associated monthly payment value then and there. If you do not want that to happen, then click the Calculation Options command button in the Calculation group on the Formulas tab and select the option Automatic Except for Data Tables. Then Excel updates the data table only if you click the Calculate Now or Calculate Sheet command button in the Calculation group on the Formulas tab.

You cannot delete any single value in the range E3:E13. If you try to delete any one of the values, you will get a message saying "Cannot change part of a data table". You must select the entire range of values, E3:E13 in this case, before you press Delete or click the Clear or Delete button on the Home tab.

Creating a Two-Variable Data Table

The process of creating a two-variable data table is fairly similar to that of creating a one-variable data table. Only thing is that you need to enter two ranges of possible input values for the same formula: one range of values for the Row Input Cell and the second range of values for the Column Input Cell. You then enter your formula in the cell located at the intersection of this row and column of input values.

Considering the same loan calculator example, suppose you want to calculate the monthly loan payment you would have to make for different loan amount and interest rates. It would be really tiresome to try different combinations by changing the values in cell B2 (loan amount) and cell B4 (interest rate). Here a two-variable data table can help you.

To set a two-variable data table, I added a row of possible interest rates in the range E2:J2 and a column of possible loan amounts in the range D3:D9. I also copied the original formula in cell B5 to cell D2 which is the cell at the intersection of the row of interest rates and the column of loan amounts (see Figure 8-5).

| D2 | | ⅹ ✓ fₓ | =B5 | | | | | | |

	A	B	C	D	E	F	G	H	I	J
1	Loan Calculator									
2	Loan Amount	$1,00,000.00		$706.78	6.00%	6.50%	7.00%	7.50%	8.00%	8.50%
3	Loan Term (in months)	300		$70,000.00						
4	Interest Rate (yearly)	7.00%		$80,000.00						
5	Monthly Payment	$706.78		$90,000.00						
6				$1,00,000.00						
7				$1,10,000.00						
8				$1,20,000.00						
9				$1,30,000.00						

Figure 8-5 Loan calculator with a series of possible loan amounts and interest rates to use as the inputs for the two-variable data table

Now follow the steps given below to create a two-variable data table that plugs each of these interest rates:

1. Select the cell range D2:J9.

2. Go to Data → What-If Analysis → Data Table which opens the Data Table dialog box.

3. Click the Row input cell: dialog box and click the cell B4 as we have interest rates in a row.

4. Click the Column input cell: dialog box and click the cell B2 as we have loan amounts in a column.

5. Click OK to close the Data Table dialog box.

6. Click cell B5 and then click the Format Painter command button in the Clipboard group on the Home tab and drag through the cell range E3: J9.

7. Click the cell ranges D2:J9 and then click the Format command button in the Cells group on the on the Home tab. Then click the AutoFit Column Width option on its dropdown menu.

Now your two variable data table will appear as shown in Figure 8-6.

	A	B	C	D	E	F	G	H	I	J
1	**Loan Calculator**									
2	Loan Amount	$1,00,000.00		$706.78	6.00%	6.50%	7.00%	7.50%	8.00%	8.50%
3	Loan Term (in months)	300		$70,000.00	$451.01	$472.65	$494.75	$517.29	$540.27	$563.66
4	Interest Rate (yearly)	7.00%		$80,000.00	$515.44	$540.17	$565.42	$591.19	$617.45	$644.18
5	Monthly Payment	$706.78		$90,000.00	$579.87	$607.69	$636.10	$665.09	$694.63	$724.70
6				$1,00,000.00	$644.30	$675.21	$706.78	$738.99	$771.82	$805.23
7				$1,10,000.00	$708.73	$742.73	$777.46	$812.89	$849.00	$885.75
8				$1,20,000.00	$773.16	$810.25	$848.14	$886.79	$926.18	$966.27
9				$1,30,000.00	$837.59	$877.77	$918.81	$960.69	$1,003.36	$1,046.80

Figure 8-6 Loan calculator worksheet after creating the two-variable data table in the range E3:J9

Playing What-If with Goal Seeking

Goal Seek feature can be considered as the opposite of formulas. We create formulas to calculate some results based on the provided inputs. The Goal Seek feature works in the opposite way. It starts with the required result and calculates the input value that will give that particular result. For example, you might want to know the sales you need to make to achieve a specific target. In such a scenario, Excel 2013's Goal Seek feature can help you.

To use the Goal Seek feature, you have to first select the cell containing the formula that returns the result you are seeking. Then you need to select the Goal Seek option from the dropdown that appears when you click the What-If Analysis command button in the Data Tools group on the Data tab. It opens the Goal Seek dialog box and the cell that contains the formula is referred to as set cell in the Goal Seek dialog box. Next, you need to specify the target value that you want as the result of your formula and also the location of the input value that Excel can change to reach this target.

Figure 8-7 shows a simple BMI (Body Mass Index) Calculator. The BMI is calculated using the following formula:

BMI = (weight in kilograms)/(height in centimeters)^2

The cell B2 contains height in centimeters and cell B3 contains weight in kilograms. Cell B5 contains the formula to calculate BMI.

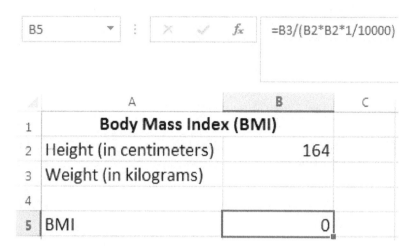

Figure 8-7 The BMI calculator worksheet

Now a person wants to know his ideal weight to have a BMI of 21.5. To find out an ideal weight value for a target BMI of 21.5, follow the steps given below:

1. Click cell B5 that contains the BMI formula.

2. Go to Data → What-If Analysis (in the Data Tools group) → Goal Seek to open the Goal Seek dialog box. The Set cell: textbox now contains the value B5.

3. Click the textbox To value: and enter the target result, 21.5.

4. Click the textbox By changing cell: and click the cell B3 as we need to calculate the weight value.

5. Click OK which will close the Goal Seek dialog box and open a Goal Seek Status dialog box as in Figure 8-8. The OK button will not be enabled until Excel adjusts the BMI value to reach the desired weight.

6. Once it calculates the input value for the specified target, the OK button in the Goal Status dialog box becomes enabled as in Figure 8-9.

7. If you want to keep the values entered in the worksheet as a result of goal seeking, click OK to close the Goal Seek Status dialog box. If you want to return to the original values, click the Cancel button.

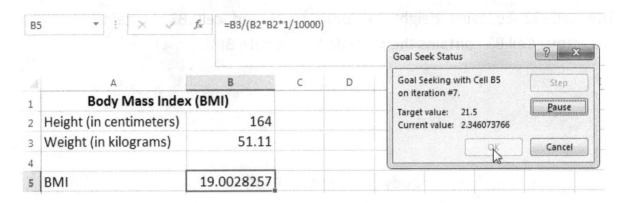

Figure 8-8 The Goal Seek process in proceeding status

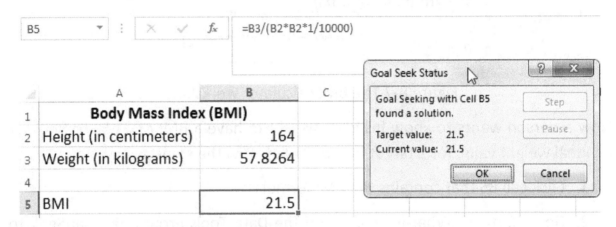

Figure 8-9 The Goal Seek process in completed status

Here it is obvious that to have a BMI of 21.5, your weight should be 57.8264 (provided the height is 164 centimeters).

Making the Case with Scenario Manager

You can create and save sets of different input values that produce different calculated results (referred to as scenarios) using Excel's Scenario Manager feature. These scenarios will be saved as part of your workbook and you can see these saved scenarios to have a detailed what-if analysis whenever you want. Once you setup different scenarios, you can ask Excel to create a summary report as simple as that and see all the input values used in each scenario and the results they produce in the formula.

Setting Up Various Scenarios

The first thing you should do before creating the various scenarios is identifying the input values that are going to vary in a scenario. You then select these cells in the worksheet before opening the Scenario Manager dialog box by going to Data → What-If Analysis (in the Data Tools group) →Scenario Manager.

B12				f_x	=(B3+B4)-(SUM(B6:B10))

	A	B	C
1	Monthly Budget Planner		
2	Income		
3	Salary	$1,000.00	
4	Others	$600.00	
5	Expenses		
6	Rent	$240.00	
7	Car loan	$220.00	
8	Food	$150.00	
9	Credit Card	$350.00	
10	Others	$175.00	
11			
12	Monthly Savings	$465.00	

Figure 8-10 Monthly Budget Planner worksheet

Figure 8-10 shows a simple monthly budget planner worksheet. In this worksheet, it is assumed that the values in cells B4 (Other income), B8 (Food expenses), B9 (Credit card expenses) and B10 (Other expenses) vary from month to month.

Now we are going to add three scenarios: Best, OK and Worst. The Best scenarios is when the person is able to save an amount of $750, the OK scenario is when the person is able to save an amount of $550 and the Worst scenario is when the person is able to save only $250.

To create the Best scenario,

1. Click the cells that contain changing inputs (here B4, B8, B9 and B10).

2. Go to Data → What-If Analysis (in the Data Tools group) →Scenario Manager which opens a Scenario Manager dialog box as in Figure 8-11.

3. Click the Add button to open the Add Scenario dialog box as in Figure 8-12.

4. Click in the Scenario name: textbox and enter the value Best. The currently selected cells, B4, B8, B9 and B10, are already listed in the Changing cells: textbox. You can modify the default comment in the Comment: textbox if you want.

5. Click OK to open the Scenario Values dialog box as in Figure 8-13.

Figure 8-11 The Scenario Manager dialog box

6. Change the values in B4, B8, B9 and B10 to 530, 110, 135 and 75 respectively.

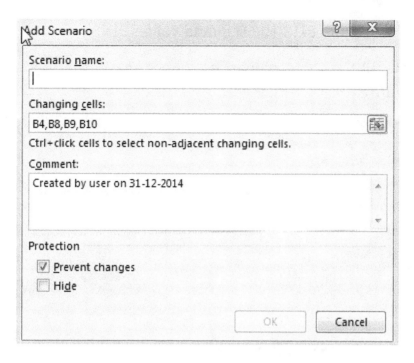

Figure 8-12 The Add Scenario dialog box

7. Click OK to close the Scenario Values dialog box. Now the Scenario Manager dialog box becomes visible with the value Best in the Scenarios: list box. You can click the Add button (instead of OK button) in the Scenario Values dialog box if you want to add more scenarios so that the Add Scenario dialog box will appear instead of the Scenario Manager dialog box.

8. Repeat the process to create OK as well as Worst scenarios. To create OK scenario enter the values 600, 215, 240 and 135 into the cells B4, B8, B9 and B10. To create the Worst scenario, enter the values 420, 215, 305 and 190.

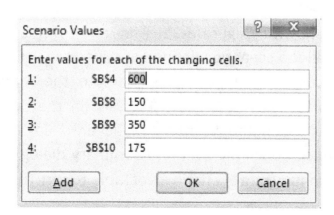

Figure 8-13 The Scenario Values dialog box

Once you create all the three scenarios, your Scenario Manager dialog box will appear as in Figure 8-14.

Figure 8-14 The Scenario Manager dialog box after adding three scenarios

To have Excel plug the changing values assigned to any of these three scenarios into the Monthly Budget Planner table, you need to click the scenario name in this list box followed by the Show button.

Producing a Summary Report

Once you are ready with different scenarios, it is so easy to produce a summary report like the one shown in Figure 8-15. This report displays the changing and resulting values for all the scenarios defined and also the values that are entered into the changing cells at the time you generate the report. To produce a summary report, go to Data → What-If Analysis (in the Data Tools group) → Scenario Manager to open the Scenario Manager dialog box. Now click the Summary button which opens the Scenario Summary dialog box with options to create a Scenario summary or a Scenario PivotTable report.

	A	B	C	D	E	F	G
1							
2		**Scenario Summary**					
3				Current Values:	Best	OK	Worst
5		**Changing Cells:**					
6		B4		$600.00	$530.00	$600.00	$420.00
7		B8		$150.00	$110.00	$215.00	$215.00
8		B9		$350.00	$135.00	$240.00	$305.00
9		B10		$175.00	$75.00	$135.00	$190.00
10		**Result Cells:**					
11		B12		$465.00	$750.00	$550.00	$250.00
12		Notes: Current Values column represents values of changing cells at					
13		time Scenario Summary Report was created. Changing cells for each					
14		scenario are highlighted in gray.					

Figure 8-15 The Scenario Summary report

You can also modify the range of cells in Result cells: textbox if you want. Click the OK button which creates the summary report in a new worksheet named Scenario Summary. If you enter the value B3:B12 in the Result cells: textbox (instead of B12), then you will get a summary report as in Figure 8-16.

			Current Values:	Best	OK	Worst
Scenario Summary						
Changing Cells:						
	B4		$600.00	$530.00	$600.00	$420.00
	B8		$150.00	$110.00	$215.00	$215.00
	B9		$350.00	$135.00	$240.00	$305.00
	B10		$175.00	$75.00	$135.00	$190.00
Result Cells:						
	B3		$1,000.00	$1,000.00	$1,000.00	$1,000.00
	B4		$600.00	$530.00	$600.00	$420.00
	B5					
	B6		$240.00	$240.00	$240.00	$240.00
	B7		$220.00	$220.00	$220.00	$220.00
	B8		$150.00	$110.00	$215.00	$215.00
	B9		$350.00	$135.00	$240.00	$305.00
	B10		$175.00	$75.00	$135.00	$190.00
	B11					
	B12		$465.00	$750.00	$550.00	$250.00

Notes: Current Values column represents values of changing cells at time Scenario Summary Report was created. Changing cells for each scenario are highlighted in gray.

Figure 8-16 The Scenario Summary report with different result cells

9. Playing with Pivot Tables

Introduction

In this chapter, we will learn how to

> ➢ Understand what a pivot table is.

> ➢ Create a new pivot table with the Quick Analysis tool and Recommended PivotTables command.

> ➢ Manually create a new pivot table.

> ➢ Format your pivot table.

> ➢ Sort and filter data in the pivot table.

> ➢ Modify the structure and layout of a pivot table.

> ➢ Create a pivot chart.

Pivot table is nothing but a summary table that is unique to Excel. Pivot tables are really magical in summarizing data. The real magic is that you do not have to even create formulas to analyze the data or to perform any kind of calculation. Pivot tables will do everything for you. You can inspect and analyze the relationships inherent in the data sources easily, quickly and effectively with pivot tables. You can also change the structure of your pivot tables in such a way that data analysis becomes easier and efficient.

Data Analysis with Pivot Tables

Pivot tables are really flexible because by providing a variety of summary functions, they allow you to evaluate and analyze summaries of large amounts of data. Pivot tables also give you the freedom to decide what summary function to use, which fields the summary function is applied to and which fields are to be displayed in the pivot table.

Pivot Tables via the Quick Analysis Tool

Excel 2013's Quick Analysis tool makes creation of a new pivot table a breeze. You can find different pivot table templates, i.e. different types of pivot tables that Excel can create for you on the spot, using your data by following the steps given below.

1. Select the data in your data table, along with the headings, as a cell range.

2. Click the Quick Analysis tool that appears right below the lower right corner of the current cell selection. It opens the Quick Analysis options palette with the Formatting tab opened.

3. Click the Tables tab from the Quick Analysis options palette. Excel displays Table and PivotTable option buttons as in Figure 9-1. The Table button previews how the selected data would appear in a table. The PivotTable buttons preview how the selected data would appear in the chosen pivot table.

4. Highlight the required PivotTable button in the Quick Analysis palette to preview how your data will appear in the specific pivot table.

5. When Excel's Live Preview feature displays a thumbnail of the pivot table you want to create, click its button in the palette to create it. Excel creates the selected pivot table and insert it at the beginning on a new worksheet of the current workbook with a PivotTable Fields task pane on the right of the worksheet.

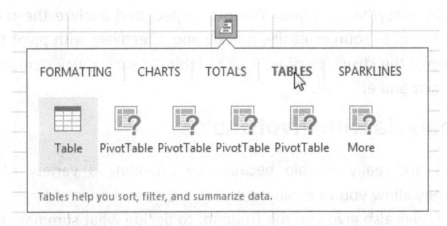

Figure 9-1 The Quick Analysis options palette with Tables tab selected

Figure 9-2 shows a table of sales data and Figure 9-3 shows the pivot table created to analyze that particular data by selecting a PivotTable from the Quick Analysis tool.

	A	B	C
1	Quarter	Employee	Sales
2	Q1	Aaron Turner	$12,000.00
3	Q1	John Smith	$8,750.00
4	Q1	Hannah Miller	$6,900.00
5	Q1	Elizabeth Young	$9,758.00
6	Q1	Mary Smith	$10,300.00
7	Q2	Aaron Turner	$13,500.00
8	Q2	Hannah Miller	$4,300.00
9	Q2	Elizabeth Young	$13,560.00
10	Q2	Mary Smith	$11,255.00
11	Q3	Aaron Turner	$8,230.00
12	Q3	Elizabeth Young	$15,600.00
13	Q3	Mary Smith	$9,300.00
14	Q4	Elizabeth Young	$17,800.00

Figure 9-2 Table of sales data to create a pivot table from

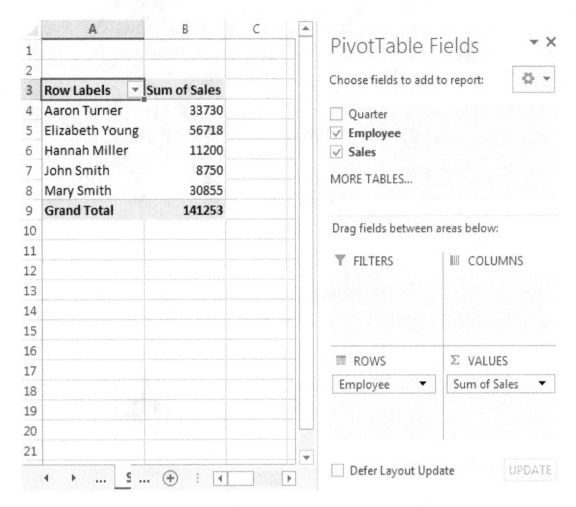

Figure 9-3 Previewed pivot table created on a new worksheet using Quick Analysis tool

Pivot Tables by Recommendation

If you find creating a new pivot table with the Quick Analysis tools difficult, then you can better get the help of Recommended Pivot Tables command button in the Tables group on the Insert tab (circled in Figure 9-4).

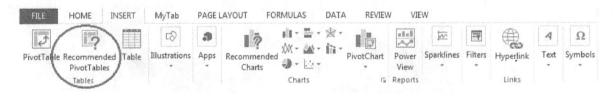

Figure 9-4 The Recommended Pivot Tables command button on the Insert tab

1. Select a cell from the table of data for which you want to create the new pivot table.

2. Select the Recommended Pivot Tables command button in the Tables group on the Insert tab which opens a Recommended PivotTables dialog box as the one shown in Figure 9-5.

3. Select any of the sample pivot table you want from the list box on the left and click OK.

Once you click OK, Excel inserts a new pivot table of the selected type on a new worksheet with a PivotTable Fields task pane on the right of the worksheet. The options on this task pane as well as on the contextual tab can be used to customize your pivot table quickly, easily and effectively.

Manually Producing Pivot Tables

Even if you could not find a pivot table, with structure and appearance that is closest to what you have in mind, from the Tables tab of the Quick Analysis tool palette or the Recommended PivotTables dialog box opened by clicking the Recommended PivotTables command button, you do not have to worry. Excel allows you to create a pivot table from scratch. It is not that difficult or time consuming to create a pivot table that suits your needs and preferences.

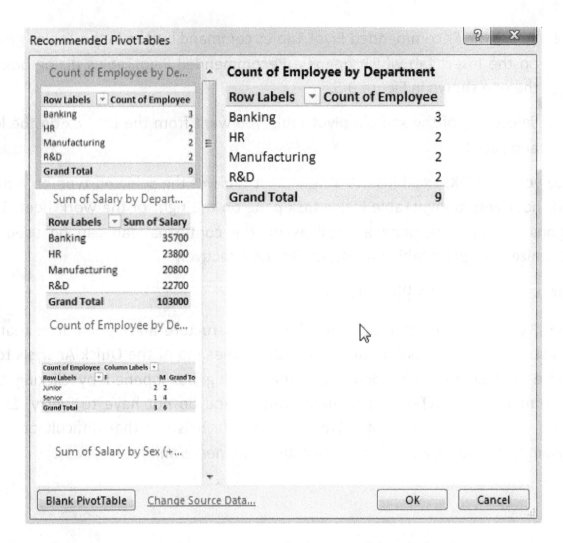

Figure 9-5 The Recommended PivotTables dialog box

To create a new pivot table from the data to be analyzed:

1. Click any cell from the table of data.

2. Go to Insert → PivotTable (in the Tables group) which opens a Create PivotTable dialog box as shown in Figure 9-6.

3. The Table/Range: textbox under the Select a table or range option will be containing the cell range of your table of data. If the range is not correct, you can adjust the cell range and hence modify the value in the textbox. If your data source is external such as Access, then click the Use an external data source option and specify the connection by clicking the Choose Connection button.

4. If you want your pivot table appear on the same worksheet where your table of data resides, then select the option Existing Worksheet under Choose where you want the PivotTable report to be placed. Also click in the Location textbox and select a cell to mark the location of the first cell of the pivot table. By default, Excel adds the pivot table in a new worksheet.

5. Click OK.

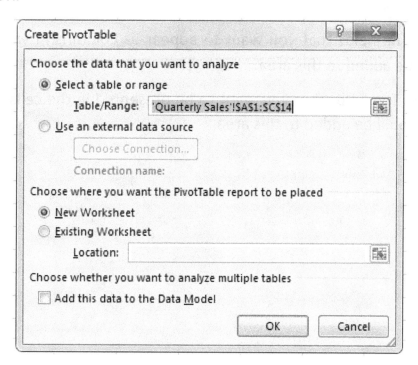

Figure 9-6 The Create PivotTable dialog box

Excel add a blank grid for the new pivot table (Figure 9-7) and opens a PivotTable Fields task pane on the right of the worksheet (current worksheet or new worksheet based on the location specified). It also adds the PivotTable Tools contextual tab to the Ribbon with Analyze and Design tabs.

The PivotTable Field task pane is divided into two areas: the Choose fields to add to report: list box with the names of all the fields in your table of data preceded by empty check boxes and a Drag fields between areas below: section divided into four drop zones: Filters, Columns, Rows and Values.

Now to complete your pivot table, you need to assign the fields in the PivotTable Field List task pane to different drop zones appropriately. You need to drag the required field names from the Choose fields to add to report: list box and drop it one of the four areas under Drag fields between areas below: section.

- ✓ FILTERS: The fields that you want to filter data based on should be added to this area.

- ✓ COLUMNS: The field that you want to appear as columns in your pivot table should be added to this area.

- ✓ ROWS: The fields that you want to appear as columns in your pivot table should be added to this area.

- ✓ VALUES: The fields that you want to be presented in the cells of your pivot table should be added to this area.

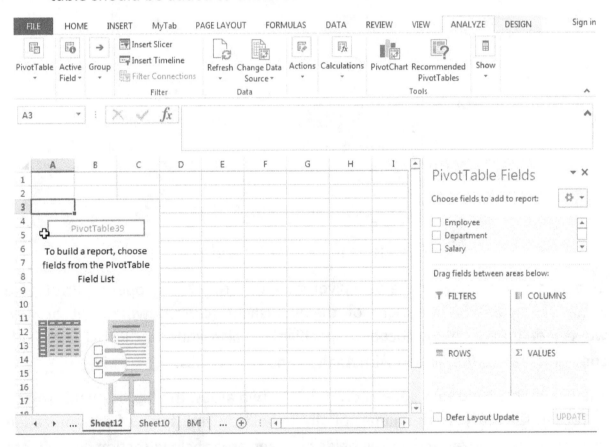

Figure 9-7 Blank grid to add the pivot table (on the left) and the PivotTable Fields task pane on the right

I am going to create a pivot table from scratch for the data in Figure 9-2. I want to analyze the quarter wise sales for each employee. I want to display the employee names as the rows of the pivot table, the quarter names as the columns and the sales information as the data in the table. So drag Employee into the ROWS section, Quarter into the COLUMNS section and Sales into the VALUES section. Now you will have a pivot table as in Figure 9-8.

You can use the command buttons in the Show group on the Analyze tab of the PivotTable Tools contextual tab (Figure 9-9) to hide or show field headers, field list or buttons.

✓ Field List: Click this to hide or show the PivotTable Fields task pane on the right of the worksheet.

✓ +/- Buttons: Click this to hide or show the expand (+) and collapse (-) buttons in front of column fields or row fields that allow you to temporarily remove and redisplay particular summarized values in the pivot table.

✓ Field Headers: Click this to hide or show the headings of your rows and columns.

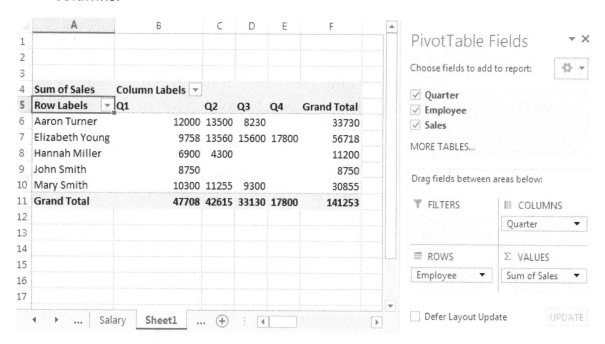

Figure 9-8 Completed pivot table after adding the fields from the list to various drop zones.

Figure 9-9 Command buttons in the Show group on the Analyze tab

Formatting Pivot Tables

Excel 2013 allows you to format your pivot tables quickly and easily just like formatting your tables of data or lists of data. You just need to select a cell within the pivot table so that the PivotTable Tools contextual tab with the Design tab will appear. You could find three groups of command buttons in the Design tab.

- ✓ Layout group contains command buttons that allow you to modify the basic layout of your pivot table and to add subtotals and grand totals.

- ✓ PivotTable Style Options group contains command buttons that allow you to refine the pivot table style using the PivotTable Styles gallery to the immediate right.

- ✓ PivotTable Styles group contains the gallery of styles you can apply to your pivot table by clicking the desired style thumbnail.

Refining the Pivot Table Style

Excel's Live Preview feature will help you check how your pivot table would look in the style that you highlight from the PivotTable Styles dropdown gallery in the PivotTable Styles group on the Design tab. After selecting a style from the gallery, you can still refine the style of your pivot table using check box command buttons in the PivotTable Style Options group. For example, you can add banding to the columns or rows of your table by selecting the Banded Columns or Banded Rows checkboxes.

Formatting Values in the Pivot Table

To format the summed values in the pivot table with an Excel number format,

1. Click the field in the table that contains the words "Sum of" followed by the name of the field whose values are summarized (cell A4 in Figure 9-8 that contains the words "Sum of Sales").

2. Click the Field Settings command button in the Active Field group on the Analyze tab under the PivotTable Tools contextual tab to open the Value Field Settings dialog box as shown in Figure 9-10.

3. Click the Number Format button in the Value Field Settings dialog box to open the Format Cells dialog box with Number tab.

4. Select the number format you want to assign to the numbers in the pivot table from the Category: listbox and modify the format (if required) with the options available for the specific format.

5. Click OK twice to close the Format Cells dialog box as well as the Value Field Settings dialog box.

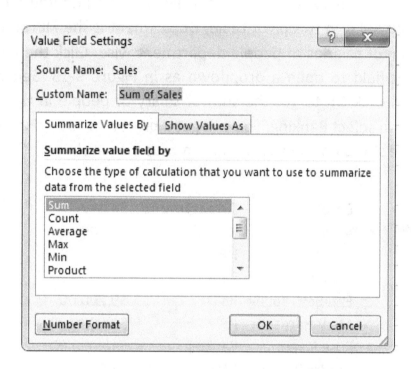

Figure 9-10 Value Field Settings dialog box

Sorting and Filtering Pivot Table Data

Excel automatically adds dropdown buttons to the labels for the row and column fields as well as to the Report Filter field when you create pivot tables. These dropdown buttons known as filter buttons to filter entries in any of these fields and also sort the row and column entries.

If you have more than one column or row fields in your pivot table, you will find collapse buttons (-) to hide subtotal values for a particular secondary field temporarily. Once you click a collapse button, it becomes an expand button (+) to redisplay the subtotals for that secondary field.

Filtering the Report

The most important filter buttons in a pivot table are the ones added to the fields included in the FILTERS. When you select an option from the dropdown attached to the filter buttons, the pivot table includes only the summary data for that option you select.

Suppose you have a salary worksheet as in Figure 9-11 and you created a pivot table as in Figure 9-12. In this pivot table, Department is the FILTER field and you can find the sum of salaries of people department wise. Click the filter button of the Department field to open a dropdown as in Figure 9-13. Select any of the department and click OK to get the sum of salary of people in that department only. Suppose you select Banking, you will get a pivot table as in Figure 9-14. Excel also replaces the standard drop down button with a cone shaped filter icon.

	A	B	C
1	**Employee**	**Department**	**Salary**
2	Aaron Turner	Manufacturing	$12,000.00
3	John Smith	HR	$9,800.00
4	Hannah Miller	Banking	$12,500.00
5	Elizabeth Young	R&D	$9,200.00
6	Mary Harris	HR	$14,000.00
7	Rose Rivera	Banking	$10,000.00
8	Sandra Parker	Manufacturing	$8,800.00
9	Beuna Reed	Banking	$13,200.00
10	Jim Gibson	R&D	$13,500.00

Figure 9-11 Salary worksheet

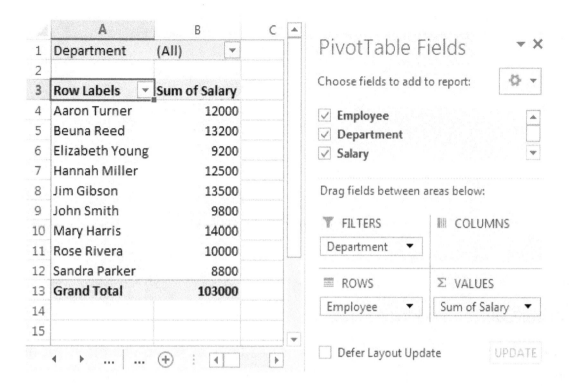

Figure 9-12 Completed pivot table

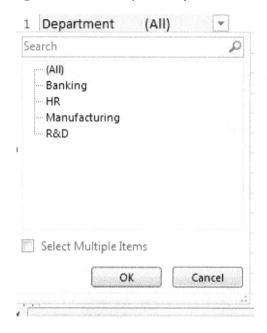

Figure 9-13 Dropdown appeared when Department field's filter button is clicked

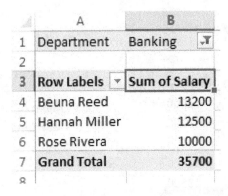

	A	B
1	Department	Banking
2		
3	Row Labels	Sum of Salary
4	Beuna Reed	13200
5	Hannah Miller	12500
6	Rose Rivera	10000
7	Grand Total	35700

Figure 9-14 Data filtered using filter

If you want to redisplay the original pivot table, then select the option (All) (first option from the dropdown as in Figure 9-13) before you click OK.

Filtering Column and Row Fields

The filter buttons on the row and column headings allow you to filter out entries for a particular group. To filter the data in columns or rows, click the particular field's filter button, unselect the (Select All) option, select the entries whose summed values you want in the pivot table and click OK.

Excel replaces the standard drop down button with a cone shaped filter icon as with filtering the filter field. If you want to redisplay the original pivot table, then select the option (Select All) from the dropdown and click OK. Figure 9-15 shows the pivot table with sales information of only Q1 and Q2 for the original pivot table in Figure 9-8.

		Column Labels		
4	Sum of Sales			
5	Row Labels	Q1	Q2	Grand Total
6	Aaron Turner	12000	13500	25500
7	Elizabeth Young	9758	13560	23318
8	Hannah Miller	6900	4300	11200
9	John Smith	8750		8750
10	Mary Smith	10300	11255	21555
11	Grand Total	47708	42615	90323

Figure 9-15 Pivot table after filtering the column label

Filtering with Slicers

Slicers in Excel 2013 make it a snap to filter the contents of your pivot table on more than one field. Slicers also allow you to connect with fields of other pivot tables in the workbook. To add slicers to your pivot table,

1. Click one of the cells in your pivot table.

2. Click the Insert Slicer command button in the Filter group on the Analyze tab under the PivotTable Tools contextual tab to open the Insert Slicers dialog box.

3. Select the fields for which you want to create slicers.

4. Click OK.

Figure 9-16 shows slicers created for the pivot table in Figure 9-8 for Employees and Quarter fields.

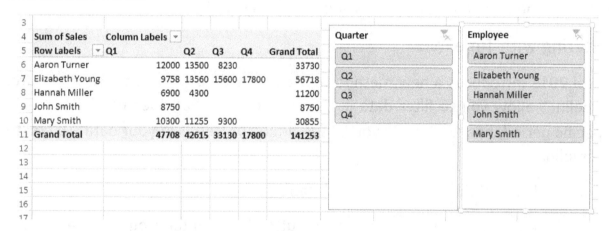

Figure 9-16 Slicers created for Quarter and Employee fields

You just need to click the items in the slicer to select them. Hold down the CTRL key to select non-consecutive items and SHIFT key to select a series of sequential items. When I select Aaron Turner, Elizabeth Young and Mary Smith from the Employee slicer and Q2 and Q3 from the Quarter slicer, I get a pivot table as shown in Figure 9-17.

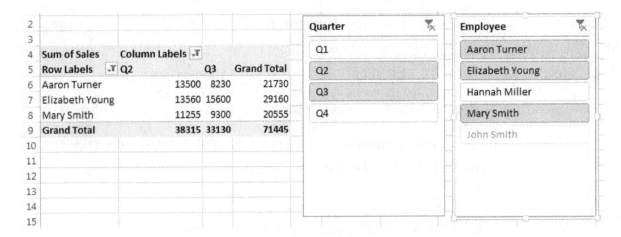

Sum of Sales	Column Labels			
Row Labels	Q2	Q3	Grand Total	
Aaron Turner	13500	8230	21730	
Elizabeth Young	13560	15600	29160	
Mary Smith	11255	9300	20555	
Grand Total	38315	33130	71445	

Figure 9-17 Pivot table filtered using slicers

You can clear the filter by clicking the Clear Filter button on the slicer (delete mark on the top right corner). You can remove a slicer from your pivot table by selecting the slicer and clicking the Delete key on your keyboard.

Filtering with Timelines

Excel 2013 introduces a new method to filter your data with its timeline feature. Timelines allow you to filter data in your pivot table that does not fall within a specific period, hence allowing you to see timing of trends in your data. To create a timeline,

1. Click one of the cells in your pivot table.

2. Click the Insert Timeline command button in the Filter group on the Analyze tab under the PivotTable Tools contextual tab to open the Insert Timelines dialog box.

3. Select the fields for which you want to create timelines.

4. Click OK.

By default, the timeline uses months as its unit. You can change this to years, quarters or days by clicking the MONTHS dropdown button and selecting the required unit (Figure 9-18).

Figure 9-20 shows the timeline created for table of data in Figure 9-19 by selecting the Date Hired field from the Insert Timelines dialog box, selecting

YEARS as the unit and clicking 2004 from the bar on the timeline. You now see the salary details of only employees who joined in 2004.

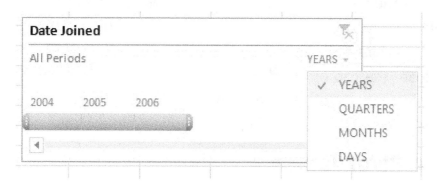

Figure 9-18 Dropdown to change the unit

	A	B	C	D
1	**Employee**	**Date Joined**	**Department**	**Salary**
2	Aaron Turner	03-12-2004	Manufacturing	$12,000.00
3	John Smith	04-10-2006	HR	$9,800.00
4	Hannah Miller	30-06-2005	Banking	$12,500.00
5	Elizabeth Young	26-11-2005	R&D	$9,200.00
6	Mary Harris	11-08-2004	HR	$14,000.00
7	Rose Rivera	09-10-2004	Banking	$10,000.00
8	Sandra Parker	23-06-2004	Manufacturing	$8,800.00
9	Beuna Reed	28-11-2005	Banking	$13,200.00
10	Jim Gibson	16-10-2006	R&D	$13,500.00

Figure 9-19 Table of data to create timeline

Me periods

	A	B	C	D	E	F	G	H
1								
2	Department	(All)						
3				Date Joined				
4	**Row Labels**	**Sum of Salary**		2004			YEARS	
5	Aaron Turner	12000						
6	Mary Harris	14000		2004	2005	2006		
7	Rose Rivera	10000						
8	Sandra Parker	8800						
9	**Grand Total**	**44800**						

Figure 9-20 Pivot table filtered using timeline for the year 2004

Sorting the Pivot Table

You can reorder the data in your pivot table by sorting one or more of the row or columns fields. To re-sort the pivot table, click the filter button for the row or column field you want to use in sorting and click the Sort A to Z option the Sort Z to A option from the top of the dropdown list as in Figure 9-21. The Sort A to Z option sorts the text values alphabetically, values in ascending order and dates from to oldest to newest. The Sort Z to A option sorts in the reverse order.

Modifying Pivot Tables

It is very easy to manipulate and modify Excel pivot tables. You can change its structure by adding or removing fields as simple as that. You can even change the order of the rows or columns by just changing their order in the PivotTable Fields task pane. You can also change the summary function by selecting any of Excel's basic statistical functions.

Modifying the Pivot Table Fields

You can modify the fields in your pivot table from the PivotTable Fields task pane (the window shown on the right of the worksheet). Once the PivotTable Fields task pane appears, you can:

- ✓ Remove a field by dragging the field name out of any of the four drop zones including FILTERS, COLUMNS, ROWS or VALUES and when the mouse pointer changes to an x, releasing the mouse button.

- ✓ Move an existing field to a new place in the table by dragging its field name from its current zone to a new zone.

- ✓ Add a field to the table by dragging the field name from the Choose fields to add to report: list and dropping the field in the desired zone.

Pivoting the Pivot Table's Fields

Will you be actually able to pivot a table, i.e. restructure a pivot table by rotating the row and column fields? Of course, you can pivot a pivot table. You just have to drag the field label in the COLUMNS zone and drop it in the ROWS zone and vice versa to pivot it.

Modifying the Table's Summary Function

By default, Excel uses the SUM function to create subtotals and grand totals for numbers in your pivot table. Sometimes, it might be more logical to use some other summary functions such as AVERAGE or COUNT. To change the summary function used in the pivot table,

1. Click the Sum of field label located at the intersection of first column field and row field in a pivot table (cell A4 in Figure 9-8).

2. Click the Field Settings command button in the Active Field group on the Analyze tab under the PivotTable Tools contextual tab to open the Value Field Settings dialog box as in Figure 9-10.

3. Select the summary function you want from the Summarize value field by list box.

   You can select:

   ✓ Count to show the count of the records for a particular category.

   ✓ Average to display the average of the values.

   ✓ Max to display the largest number.

   ✓ Min to display the smallest number.

   ✓ Product to display the product of the numeric values in that field for the current category and page filter.

   ✓ Count Numbers to display the number of numeric values in that field for the current category and page filter.

   ✓ StdDev to display the standard deviation for the sample.

   ✓ StdDevp to display the standard deviation for the population.

   ✓ Var to display the variance for the sample.

   ✓ Varp to display the variance for the population.

4. After selecting the required summary function, click OK to have Excel apply the new function to the data in the pivot table.

If you apply the AVERAGE function to the pivot table in Figure 9-9, you will get pivot table in Figure 9-21.

	A	B	C	D	E	F
1						
2						
3						
4	Average of Sales	Column Labels ▼				
5	Row Labels ▼	Q1	Q2	Q3	Q4	Grand Total
6	Aaron Turner	12000	13500	8230		11243.33333
7	Elizabeth Young	9758	13560	15600	17800	14179.5
8	Hannah Miller	6900	4300			5600
9	John Smith	8750				8750
10	Mary Smith	10300	11255	9300		10285
11	Grand Total	9541.6	10653.75	11043.33333	17800	10865.61538

Figure 9-21 Pivot table after changing the summary function from SUM to AVERAGE

Creating Pivot Charts

You can have a graphical representation of your pivot table by creating a pivot chart. To create a pivot chart:

1. Click any cell in the pivot table.

2. Click the PivotChart command button in the Tools group on the Analyze tab under the PivotTable tools contextual tab to open the Insert Chart dialog box.

3. Click the thumbnail of the type of chart you want to create in the Insert Chart dialog box.

4. Click OK.

Once you click the OK button, Excel displays the pivot chart in the type you selected which can be moved or resized. Excel also adds a PivotChart Tools contextual tab with three tabs: Analyze, Design and Format.

Figure 9-22 shows a Clustered Colum Chart created for the pivot table in Figure 9-21.

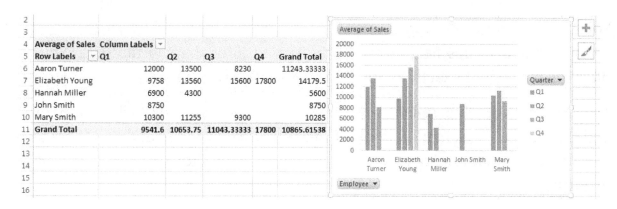

Average of Sales	Column Labels				
Row Labels	Q1	Q2	Q3	Q4	Grand Total
Aaron Turner	12000	13500	8230		11243.33333
Elizabeth Young	9758	13560	15600	17800	14179.5
Hannah Miller	6900	4300			5600
John Smith	8750				8750
Mary Smith	10300	11255	9300		10285
Grand Total	9541.6	10653.75	11043.33333	17800	10865.61538

Figure 9-22 Pivot chart created from pivot table

Moving Pivot Charts to Separate Sheets

By default, Excel creates pivot charts in the same worksheet where the pivot table resides. However, you can move your pivot chart to a separate sheet if you want by following these simple steps:

1. Select the pivot chart.

2. Click the Analyze tab under the PivotChart Tools contextual tab.

3. Click the Move Chart command button in the Actions group to open a Move Chart dialog box.

4. Click the New Sheet button in the dialog box.

5. You can rename the name of the sheet from Chart1 to something descriptive if you want.

6. Click OK to close the dialog box. This will move the pivot chart to the specified sheet.

Filtering Pivot Charts

When you graph the data in a pivot table, the Row labels in the pivot table appear along the x-axis at the bottom of the chart and the Column labels in the pivot table become the data series that are delineated in the chart's legend. The numbers in the Values field are represented on the y axis that goes up the left side of the chart.

You can use the drop-down buttons that appear after the Filter, Legend fields, Axis fields and Values field in the PivotChart to filter the charted data. You can filter the pivot chart exactly as you filter a pivot table.

As with the pivot table, remove the check mark from the (Select All) or (All) option and then add a check mark to each of the fields you want to appear in the filtered pivot chart. Click the following drop-down buttons to filter a different part of the pivot chart:

✓ Axis Fields to filter the categories that are charted along the x-axis.

✓ Legend Fields to filter the data series identified by the chart legend.

✓ Filter to filter the data charted along the y-axis.

✓ Values to filter the data represented in the pivot chart.

Formatting Pivot Charts

You can format and customize your pivot chart using the command buttons on the Design and Format tabs under PivotChart Tools contextual tab. You can use the Design tab buttons to select a new chart style and use the Format tab buttons to add graphics to the chart as well as to refine their look.

10. Charming Charts and Gorgeous Graphs

Introduction

In this chapter, we will learn how to

- ➢ Create great-looking charts with just a few clicks.
- ➢ Customize charts from the Chart Tools contextual tab.
- ➢ Represent data visually with sparklines.
- ➢ Add textbox and arrow to a chart.
- ➢ Insert clip art into your worksheets.
- ➢ Add WordArt and SmartArt to a worksheet.
- ➢ Print a chart only without printing the rest of the worksheet area.

Data visualization is always helpful in understanding data easily, quickly and effectively. Charts and graphs not only make the data representation interesting, but also illustrate trends and anomalies clearer than normal value representation. Excel 2013 offers different types of charts so that you can choose the one that best represents your data.

Making Professional Looking Data

Before explaining different techniques to make beautiful charts, it is assumed that you have the basic knowledge on how to plot different values on a graph. Hey, I am telling about x-axis, that is the horizontal axis usually located along the bottom of the graph and y-axis, which is the vertical axis usually located on the left side of the graph which you might have studied in your high school classes. It is true that

Excel automates the whole process of creating charts. Still, you should have the basic knowledge on graphs and charts so that you can modify your chart if Excel does not do the job the way you want.

In most charts that use x-axis and y-axis, Excel plots the categories along the x-axis (referred to as Category axis) and their values along the y-axis (referred to as Value axis). The chart and the corresponding represented values remain linked so that whenever you make changes to the worksheet values, Excel automatically updates the chart.

Before creating a chart for your data, you need to select any cell within your table of data. If you want to chart only a part of the data, then you should select that specific portion along with headings.

Charts thanks to Recommendation

One of the easiest ways to create charts is with the new Recommended Charts command button in the Charts group on the Insert tab. When you click this command button, Excel opens the Insert Chart dialog box with the Recommended Charts tab opened as in Figure 10-1.

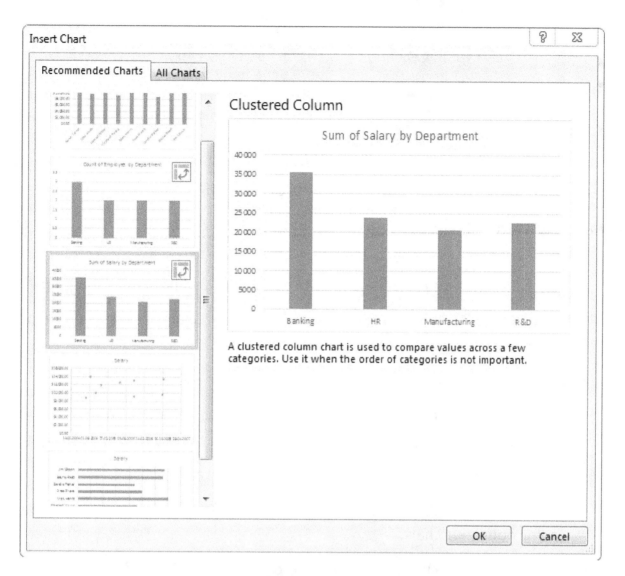

Figure 10-1 The Insert Chart dialog box

If you click any of the thumbnail in the list box on the left, then you will see how your data will appear in that specific chart on the right. Once you find the chart that suits your needs, then click OK button to embed it into a new worksheet.

Charts from the Ribbon

You could find a number of command buttons with dropdowns to the right of the Recommended Charts button in the Charts group on the Insert tab (Figure 10-2).

Figure 10-2 Different Charts command buttons on the Insert tab

You could find the following types and styles of charts there:

- ✓ Insert Column Chart to preview your data as a 2-D or 3-D vertical column chart.

- ✓ Insert Bar Chart to preview your data as a 2-D or 3-D horizontal bar chart.

- ✓ Insert Stock, Surface or Radar Chart to preview your data as a 2-D stock chart, 2-D or 3-D surface chart or 3-D radar chart.

- ✓ Insert Line Chart to preview your data as a 2-D or 3-D line chart.

- ✓ Insert Area Chart to preview your data as a 2-D or 3-D area chart.

- ✓ Insert Combo Chart to preview your data as a 2-D combo clustered column and line chart or clustered column and stacked area chart.

- ✓ Insert Pie or Doughnut Chart to preview your data as a 2-D or 3-D pie chart or 2-D doughnut chart.

- ✓ Insert Scatter (X, Y) or Bubble Chart to preview your data as a 2-D scatter (X, Y) or bubble chart.

After clicking the dropdown attached to any of these command buttons and highlight any of the chart type, you can have a preview of your data with the selected chart type as in Figure 10-3. Once you click any of these chart types from the dropdown, the chart of selected type will be embedded in your current worksheet.

If you are not sure what chart best represents your data, then click the Dialog Box launcher in the lower right corner of the Charts group on the Insert tab. It opens the Insert Chart dialog box with Recommended Charts tab open. Click the All Charts tab to find the complete list of chart types as in Figure 10-4.

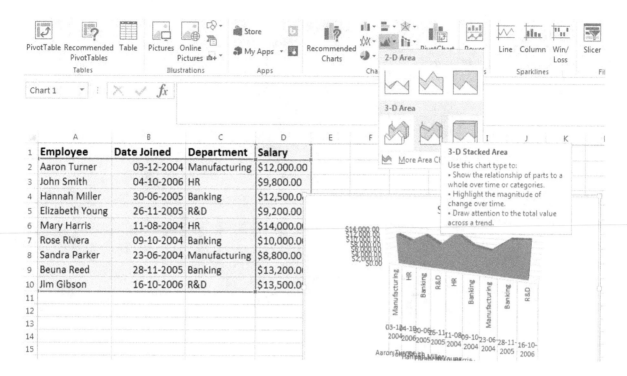

Figure 10-3 Live preview of data with selected chart type

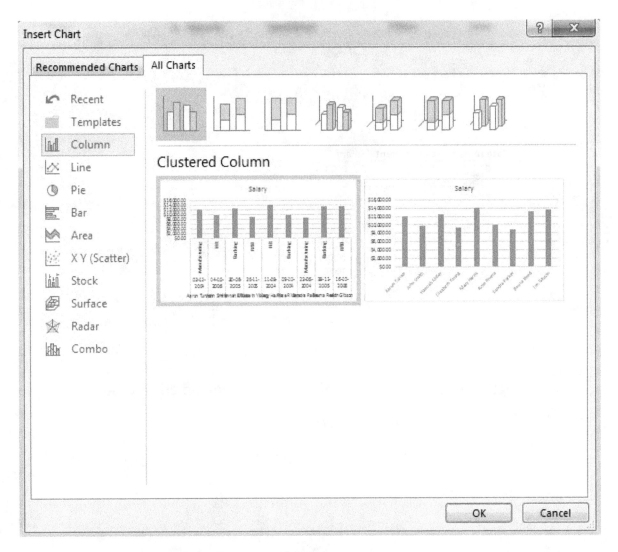

Figure 10-4 The Insert Charts dialog box with all the chart types

Charts via Quick Analysis Tool

Instead of charting the entire table of data (by selecting any cell from your table), you might have to chart only a part of it (by selecting the required part). In such cases, you can use the new Quick Analysis Tool. After selecting the required part,

1. Click the Quick Analysis Tool that appears right below the lower right corner of the current cell selection to open the Quick Analysis options palette.

2. Click the Charts tab from the palette to find a number of chart type buttons and a More Charts button.

3. Hover over any of the chart type button to preview the selected type of chart with the selected data.

4. Once you find the chart of your choice, click its button in the palette to create it.

Figure 10-5 shows the screen after completing Steps 1 and 2. I have selected the required data from the table of data, clicked the Quick Analysis Tool and clicked the Charts tab to get a screen as in Figure 10-5.

Figure 10-5 The Quick Analysis Tool with Charts tab opened

Figure 10-6 shows the screen after completing Step 3. It displays the preview in a thumbnail that appears above the palette when hovering over the second chart type (Clustered Column) in the palette.

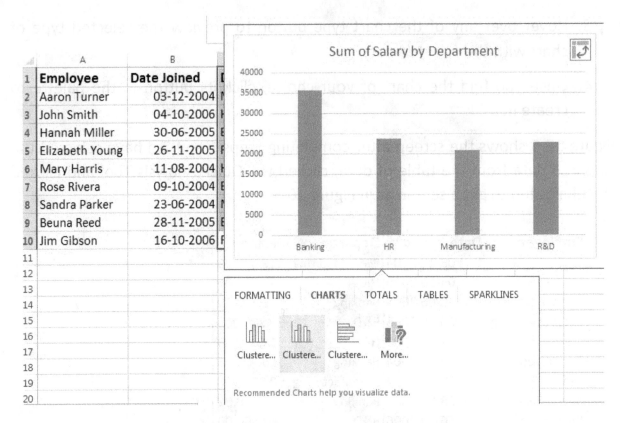

Figure 10-6 Preview of the chart with the selected data

Figure 10-7 shows the embedded chart after completing Step 4. Once the chart is created, you could find that Excel automatically selects the chart area. You could also find PivotChart Tools contextual tab with its Analyze, Design and Format tabs added to the ribbon.

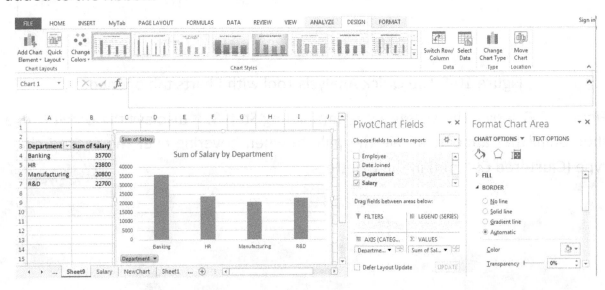

Figure 10-7 Embedded clustered column chart created with the Quick Analysis Tool

Charts on their Own Chart Sheet

Many times, you will require your chart on a separate sheet than embedding it in the same sheet where the table of data resides. To create a chart on a different sheet, after selecting any cell or the cell range from the table of data, just press F11. This will embed the chart in a new sheet that precedes all the other sheets in the workbook. Later you can customize your chart in the new sheet as you want.

Moving and Resizing Embedded Charts

It is so easy to move or resize your charts. Select your chart if it is not selected. When a chart is selected, you could find a thin double-line outline with 8 sizing handles, that are four squares at the four corners and four squares at the center of four sides. You will also find three buttons in the upper right corner of the selected chart:

✓ Chart Elements button (the button with + sign) to modify chart elements such as chart titles, legends, gridlines, error bars and trend lines.

✓ Chart Styles button (the button with the paint brush icon) to modify the chart layout and color scheme.

✓ Chart Filters button (the button with the cone filter icon) to modify the data series represented in the chart or the labels displayed in the legend or along the Category axis.

To move a chart, after selecting the chart, position the mouse pointer in a blank area inside the chart and drag the chart to a new location. To resize the chart, after selecting the chart, position the mouse on one of the sizing handles and drag it when the pointer changes from arrowhead to a double headed arrow to reduce or enlarge the chart.

Moving Embedded Charts to Chart Sheets

Unless you press F11 before creating a chart, the chart appears in the same sheet where the table of data resides. You can easily move an embedded chart to its own chart sheet by following these steps.

1. Select the chart that you want to move.

2. Click the Move Chart command button in the Location group on the Design tab under the Chart Tools contextual tab to open the Move Chart dialog box.

3. Select the New sheet: option.

4. You can give a more descriptive name to the sheet by changing the default sheet name Chart1 in the textbox if you want.

5. Click OK to close the dialog box and open the new chart sheet with your chart.

After moving the chart to its own chart sheet, if you want the chart to appear on the same worksheet where the table of data resides, then click the Move Chart command button again, select the Object in: option and then select the name of the worksheet from the dropdown. Click OK to embed the chart in the selected worksheet.

Customizing Charts from the Design Tab

You can use the command buttons on the Design tab of the Chart Tools contextual tab to make your new chart appear the way you want. The Design tab contains the following groups of buttons:

- ✓ Chart Layouts: The Add Chart Element command button can be used to modify particular elements in the chart such as titles, data labels, grid lines, legend and trend lines and so on. The Quick Layout command button can be used to select a new layout for the selected chart.

- ✓ Chart Styles: The Change Colors button can be used to display a color palette with different color schemes that you can apply to your chart. You can highlight various chart styles in the Chart Styles gallery to preview and click one to select the particular style for your chart.

- ✓ Data: The Switch Row/ Column button can be used to interchange the worksheet data used for the Series with that used for the Categories in the selected chart. Click the Select Data button to open the Select Data Source dialog box where you can add, edit or remove particular entries to Series or Categories category and the Legend entries.

✓ Type: Click the Change Chart Type button to open the Change Chart Type dialog box with All Charts tab selected where you can preview and select a new type of chart to represent your data.

✓ Location: Click the Move Chart button to move the chart to a new chart sheet or another worksheet.

Customizing Chart Elements

The Chart Elements button (the button with + sign) that you find in the upper right corner of the selected chart contains a list of major chart elements as in Figure 10-8 that you can add to your chart. When you hover over each element in this list, you could preview how your chart will appear when you add those particular element to your chart.

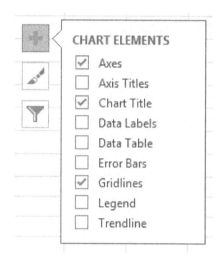

Figure 10-8 The alphabetical list of elements that appear when the Chart Elements button is clicked

To add an element that is currently missing from the chart, select the particular element's checkbox in the list which will put a check mark in it. To remove an item that is currently displayed in the chart, select the element's checkbox to remove the check mark.

If you want to make some changes to the existing elements, you need to click the continuation button (circled in Figure 10-9) and select an option from the continuation menu that appears. The options will be different for different elements.

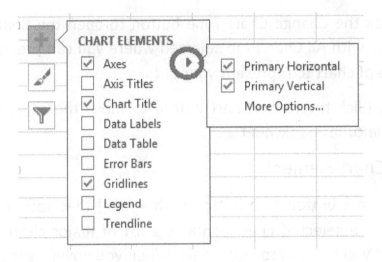

Figure 10-9 The continuation menu of Axes element

Repositioning Chart Title

To change the position of your chart title, click the continuation button attached to the Chart Title on the Chart Elements menu. It will display the following options from which you can select one:

✓ Above Chart: to reposition the chart title so that it appears centered above the plot area.

✓ Centered Overlay Title: to reposition the chart title so that it appears centered at the top of the plot area.

✓ More Options: to open the Format Chart Title task pane on the right side of the Excel window where you can select any of the options from the Fill & Line, Effects and Size & Properties sections under Title Options and Text Fill & Outline, Text Effects and Textbox sections under Text Options to modify different aspects of your chart title.

Adding Data Labels

Data labels display values from the table of data in your chart.

I have added Data Labels to my chart by selecting the Data Labels option from the Chart Elements menu and my chart appears as in Figure 10-10.

Figure 10-10 A chart with Data Labels added

Now if you click the Data Labels continuation menu, you will find the following options:

- ✓ Center: to display the data labels in the middle of each data point.

- ✓ Inside End: to display the data labels inside each data point near the end.

- ✓ Inside Base: to display the data labels at the base of each data point.

- ✓ Outside End: to display the data labels outside of the end of each data point.

- ✓ Data Callout: to add text labels and values that appear within text boxes that point to each data point.

- ✓ More Options: to open the Format Data Labels task pane on the right side of the Excel window where you can select any of the options from the Fill & Line, Effects, Size & Properties and Label Options sections under Label Options and Text Fill & Outline, Text Effects and Textbox sections under Text Options to modify different aspects of your data labels.

Adding Data Tables

Instead of adding data labels in your chart and making your chart more congested, you can add a data table beneath the chart showing the worksheet data it represents. You just have to select the Data Table option from the Chart Elements menu. If you click the continuation button attached to data table, you will find the following options:

- ✓ With Legend Keys: to have Excel draw the table at the bottom of the chart, including the color keys used in the legend to differentiate the data series in the first column.

- ✓ No Legend Keys: to have Excel draw the table at the bottom of the chart without any legend.

- ✓ More Options: to open the Format Data Table task pane on the right side where you can select any of the options from the Fill & Line, Effects and Table Options sections under Table Options and Text Fill & Outline, Text Effects and Textbox sections under Text Options to modify different aspects of your data table.

Editing the Generic Titles in a Chart

When you add axis titles or chart title to a new chart for the first time by clicking the Axis Titles or Chart Title option from the Chart Elements menu, Excel adds generic titles like Axis Title (for both x axis and y axis) or Chart Title. To replace these titles with more descriptive titles, click the title in the chart and then edit the current name after clicking the insertion point in the text at the required point or after selecting the whole title by double clicking it. Press Enter or click somewhere else on the chart area after you change the titles the way you want.

Formatting Chart Titles

Excel displays titles in Calibri font, chart title in 14 point size and axis titles in 10 point size, by default. You can format these titles exactly as you format entries in worksheet cells. You just have to select the titles and then use appropriate command buttons from the Font group on the Home tab.

If you want to make other formatting changes for your chart title or axis titles, you can use the command buttons on the Format tab of the Chart Tools contextual tab.

The Shape Styles group contains the following command buttons to format the entire textbox that contains the title.

✓ Shape Styles thumbnail in its drop-down gallery: to format both the text and textbox for the selected chart title.

✓ Shape Fill button: to select a new color for the textbox containing the selected chart title from its drop-down palette.

✓ Shape Outline button: to select a new color for the outline of the textbox for the selected chart title from its drop-down palette.

✓ Shape Effects button: to apply a new effect like Shadow, Bevel, Reflection, Glow, Soft Edges etc. to the textbox containing the selected chart title.

The WordArt Styles group contains the following command buttons to format the text in chart titles.

✓ WordArt Styles thumbnail in its drop-down gallery: to apply a new WordArt style to the text of the selected chart title.

✓ Text Fill button: to select a new color for the text in the selected chart title from its gallery.

✓ Text Outline button: to select a new outline color for the text in the selected chart title from its drop-down palette.

✓ Text Effects button: to apply a text effect like Shadow, Reflection, Glow etc. to the text of the selected chart title from its drop-down list.

Formatting the x- and y-axis

Excel might not format the values that appear on x- and y-axis always the way you want. If you are not satisfied the way the values appear on either the x- axis or y-axis, you can easily change the formatting as follows:

1. Click the x-axis or y-axis directly in the chart.

2. Click the Format Selection button in the Current Selection group of the Format tab to open the Format Axis task pane (on the right side of the worksheet) with Axis Options under the Axis Options group selected.

3. Change appropriate values under the Axis Options or Text Options to format different aspects of x-axis and y-axis.

4. Click the Close button to close the Format Axis task pane.

Adding Great Looking Graphics

You can add not only charts, but also a number of other graphical elements including sparklines, text boxes, clip art drawings supplied by Microsoft and also images such as digital photos, scanned images and pictures downloaded from the Internet. Excel 2013 also allows you to create fancy graphic text called WordArt as well as process and organizational diagrams known as SmartArt to your worksheet.

Sparking up the Data with Sparklines

Sparklines are special type of information graphic represented in the form of tiny graphs generally about the size of the text that surrounds them. Sparklines can be any of the following chart types:

✓ Line: that represents the relative value of the selected worksheet data.

✓ Column: where the selected worksheet data is represented by tiny columns.

✓ Win/ Loss: where the selected worksheet data appears as a win/ loss chart. The wins are represented by blue squares that appear above the losses that are represented by red squares.

Sparklines via the Quick Analysis Tool

You can use new Quick Analysis Tool to quickly add sparklines.

1. Select your table of data.

2. Click the Quick Analysis Tool.

3. Select Sparklines tab from the option palette to see three buttons for the three types of sparklines as in Figure 10-11.

4. Highlight any of three buttons to preview how your data will look with that type of sparkline.

5. Click the sparkline of your choice to add it to your worksheet.

236

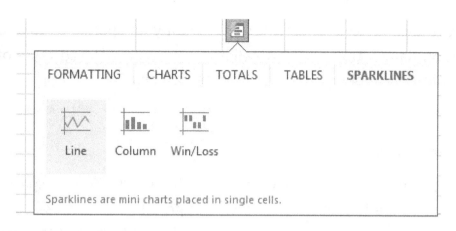

Figure 10-11 Sparklines tab opened from Quick Analysis Tool's option palette

Figure 10-12 represents the sparkline representation of the given data. To get this type of sparkline, I selected cell range B1:F7, clicked the Quick Analysis Tool followed by Sparklines tab and then selected the sparkline type Line. With this visual representation, it is very easy to analyze the performance of each sales representative.

B	C	D	E	F	G
Sales Represntative	Quarter 1	Quarter 2	Quarter 3	Quarter 4	
Aaron Turner	10,545.20	49,635.10	14,320.20	57,250.80	
John Smith	1,589.25	30,258.50	57,548.30	29,602.30	
Hannah Miller	9,632.40	11,560.80	14,597.60	12,500.00	
Elizabeth Young	1,569.00	10,253.00	23,540.50	48,596.20	
Mary Smith	70,251.75	50,236.10	30,974.25	6,580.00	

Figure 10-12 Sparklines added from the Quick Analysis Tool

Sparklines from the Ribbon

You can add sparklines using the Sparklines command buttons on the Insert tab as well. To manually add sparklines to the cells of your worksheet:

1. Select your table of data.

2. Click the chart type you want for your sparklines from the Sparklines group on the Insert tab to open the Create Sparklines dialog box with two textboxes: Data Range: and Location Range.

3. Select the cell or cell range where you want your sparklines to appear in the Location Range: text box. The cell range of your selected table of data will automatically appear in the Data Range: textbox.

4. Click OK.

Formatting Sparklines

Once your add sparklines to your worksheet, Excel 2013 adds a Sparklines Tools contextual tab to the Ribbon with its own Design tab. You can use the command buttons in the Design tab to modify the type, style and format of the sparklines.

The command buttons in the last group called Group can be used to band a range of sparklines into a single group that can share the same charting parameters including axis and/or minimum or maximum values so that they represent the trends equally.

If you want to delete sparklines, right click the cell range that contains the sparklines and go to Sparklines → Clear Selected Sparklines from the context menu. The normal Delete command button or Delete key will not work with sparklines.

Telling All with a Textbox

You can use textboxes to add commentary or explanatory text to the charts just like adding Excel comments to worksheet cells. Unlike Excel comments, you will have to add the arrow separately if you want the textbox to point to something in the chart.

Figure 10-13 shows a textbox with an arrow that points out who performed the best.

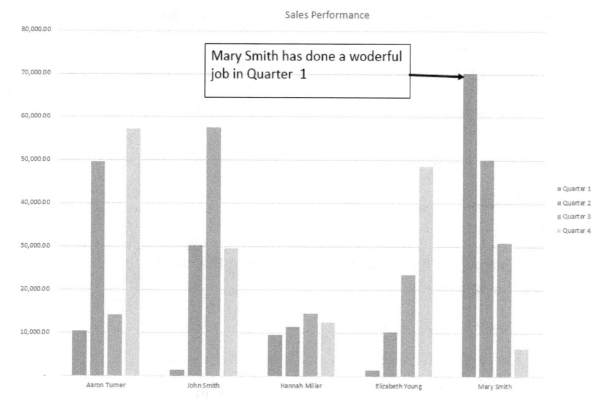

Figure 10-13 Clustered column chart with textbox and arrow added

Adding and Formatting a Textbox

To add a textbox like the one in Figure 10-13,

1. Select your chart.

2. Click the Insert Shapes dropdown in the Insert Shapes group on the Format tab under the Chart Tools contextual tab.

3. Select the Text Box button which is the very first button in the Basic Shapes section.

4. Click the location where you want to draw the textbox and drag the mouse. Release the mouse button to draw the box.

Once a textbox is drawn, Excel positions the insertion point at the top left inside the textbox and you just need to type the text that you want to appear in it. Click anywhere outside the textbox once you are done. You can also

✓ Move the text box to a new location in the chart by dragging it.

✓ Resize the text box by dragging the appropriate sizing handle.

✓ Rotate the text box by dragging its rotation handle in a clockwise or counterclockwise direction.

✓ Change the appearance of the text box using various command buttons in the Shape Styles group on the Format tab under the Drawing Tools contextual tab.

✓ Delete the textbox by selecting it and then pressing the Delete key.

Adding and Formatting a Textbox

If you add an arrow from the textbox to the part of the chart you are referencing, it will make the data presentation clearer.

To add an arrow as in Figure 10-13,

1. Click the textbox to which you want to attach the arrow.

2. Click the Insert Shapes dropdown in the Insert Shapes group on the Format tab.

3. Select the Arrow button which is the second one from the left in the Lines section.

4. Drag the mouse button from the place on the textbox where the end of the arrow is to appear and release the mouse button at the place where the arrow needs to start.

Once an arrow is drawn, you can also:

✓ Move the arrow by dragging its outline into position.

✓ Change the length of the arrow by dragging the sizing handle at the arrowhead.

✓ Change the direction of the arrow by pivoting the crosshair pointer around a stationary sizing handle.

✓ Change the shape of the arrowhead or the thickness of the arrow's shaft by clicking a thumbnail on the Shape Styles drop-down gallery.

✓ Delete the selected arrow by pressing the Delete key.

Downloading Online Images

In Excel 2013, it is so easy to insert images from the Internet. The Insert Pictures dialog box helps you search Office.com for clip art images and also to use the search engine of Microsoft's Bing to search the entire web for the images you want. You also have the freedom to download images that you have in your Windows Live SkyDrive cloud.

To download an online image to your worksheet, click the Online Pictures button in the Illustrations group on the Insert tab which opens the Insert Picture dialog box. You could find the following options in this dialog box:

- ✓ Office.com Clip Art textbox to search for clip art images on Office.com.

- ✓ Bing Image Search textbox to use the Bing search engine to locate images on the web.

- ✓ SkyDrive Browse button to locate images saved on your SkyDrive.

Inserting Clip Art Images

Clip art is nothing but readymade illustrations offered by Microsoft for use in its various Microsoft Office programs including Excel 2013. To locate a clip that suits your needs, type in a keyword describing the image you want in the Office.com Clip Art text box and click the Search button or press Enter. Excel then displays a scrollable list of thumbnails for the images that match the keyword you entered. Click a thumbnail in the list to display a short description and the size of the image in the lower-left corner of the Insert Pictures dialog box as in Figure 10-14.

You can get a better view of a selected image by clicking the View Larger button (the magnifying glass with a plus sign) that appears in the lower right corner of the thumbnail. Excel then displays a slightly larger version of the thumbnail in the center of the dialog box at the same time blurring out all other thumbnails.

To insert a particular clip art image into the current worksheet, click the Insert button if the thumbnail is selected or double-click its thumbnail if it is not already selected.

Figure 10-14 Clipart image collection with details of the selected clipart

Inserting Images from the Web

You can also download pictures from the web using the Bing search engine. To download an image with Bing, open the Insert Pictures dialog box, click in the Search Bing textbox and type your keyword. Once you press Enter or click the Search button, you could find a scrollable list of thumbnails for images matching your keyword. You can then click a thumbnail in the list to display a short description and the size of the image in the lower-left corner of the Insert Pictures dialog box. You can insert an image exactly as you insert a clip art.

Inserting Local Images

You can also insert an image which is saved locally on your computer in one of the local or network drives. Select the Pictures command button in the Illustrations group on the Insert tab to open the Insert Picture dialog box. You can open the folder and select the local graphics file and then import it into the worksheet by clicking the Insert button.

Editing Inserted Images

The image inserted into a worksheet will be automatically selected until you click somewhere outside of the image in the worksheet. When an image is selected, you can:

✓ Move the image to a new location by dragging it.

✓ Resize the image by dragging the appropriate sizing handle.

✓ Rotate the image by dragging its rotation handle in a clockwise or counterclockwise direction.

✓ Delete the image by pressing the Delete key.

Formatting Inserted Images

When an inserted picture is selected in the worksheet, Excel adds the Pictures Tools contextual tab to the Ribbon with a Format tab. The Format tab is divided into four groups: Adjust, Picture Styles, Arrange, and Size.

The Adjust group contains the following command buttons:

✓ Remove Background opens the Background Removal tab and makes a best guess about what parts of the picture to remove. You have the option to mark areas of the picture to keep or further remove. Click Keep Changes when you are finished or Discard All Changes to revert back to the original picture.

✓ Corrections to open a drop-down menu with a palette of options you can choose for sharpening or softening the image and/ or increasing or decreasing its brightness. You can select the Picture Corrections Options item to open the Format Picture dialog box with the Picture Corrections tab selected. You can modify different aspects of image with these different options.

✓ Color to open a drop-down menu with a palette of Color Saturation, Color Tone or Recolor presets you can apply to the image, set a transparent color or select the Picture Color Options item to open the Picture Color tab of the Format Picture dialog box.

✓ Artistic Effects to open a drop-down menu with special effect presets you can apply to the image or select the Artistic Effects Options item to open the Artistic Effects options in the Format Picture task pane where you can apply a special effect by selecting its preset thumbnail from the palette.

✓ Compress Pictures to open the Compress Pictures dialog box to compress all images or just the selected image to make them more compact and thus make the Excel workbook somewhat smaller when you save the images as part of its file.

✓ Change Picture to open the Insert Pictures dialog box where you can find and select a new image to replace the current picture.

✓ Reset Picture button to select the Reset Picture option to remove all formatting changes made and return the picture to the state it was in when you originally inserted it into the worksheet or the Reset Picture & Size to reset all its formatting as well as restore the image to its original size in the worksheet.

You can use the command buttons in the Picture Styles group to select a new orientation and style for the selected picture. You can change the border shape and color by clicking the Picture Border command button, modify shadow or 3D rotation effect by clicking the Picture Effect command button and format a picture with SmartArt styles by clicking the Picture Layout command button.

Adding Preset Graphic Shapes

You can insert preset graphic shapes to your worksheet by clicking the Shapes command button in the Illustrations group on the Insert tab and selecting the required shape thumbnail from the Shapes' dropdown gallery (Figure 10-15).

The shapes in the dropdown gallery are divided into nine groups: Recently Used Shapes, Lines, Rectangles, Basic Shapes, Block Arrows, Equation Shapes, Flowchart, Starts and Banners and Callouts. After clicking the thumbnail of the required shape, you just need to drag and release the mouse button to draw the shape. Once the shape is drawn, Excel activates the Format tab on the Drawing Tools contextual tab.

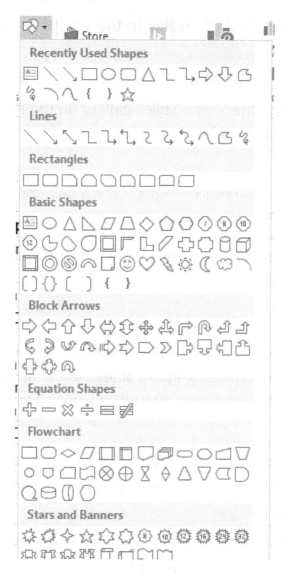

Figure 10-15 Shapes' dropdown gallery

Working with WordArt

Excel allows you to make your worksheet more fascinating by adding some fancy text using the WordArt gallery. To add graphic text to your worksheet,

1. Click the Insert WordArt command button in the Text group on the Insert tab to open the WordArt gallery.

2. Click the A thumbnail in the WordArt style you want to use from the WordArt drop-down gallery which inserts a selected textbox containing "Your Text Here" in the center of the worksheet in the style you selected.

3. Type the text you want to display in the worksheet in the Your Text Here text box.

4. You can format the background of the textbox if you want by applying required style from the Shape Styles gallery on the Format tab. You can also adjust the size, shape or orientation of the text with the selection and rotation handles.

5. After making the required changes, click a cell somewhere outside of the text to complete the WordArt.

Once you click outside of the text, Excel adds the Drawing Tools contextual tab and also deselects the graphic.

Make Mine SmartArt

You can construct fancy graphical lists and diagrams in your worksheet using Excel 2013 Smart Art, a special type of graphic object. Excel provides a wide variety of lists and diagrams to make your own custom graphic shapes. To insert a SmartArt list or diagram,

1. Click the Insert a SmartArt Graphic command button in the Illustrations group on the Insert tab to open the Choose a SmartArt Graphic dialog box as in Figure 10-16.

2. Click a category in the navigation pane on the left followed by the thumbnail of the list or diagram in the center section.

3. Click OK.

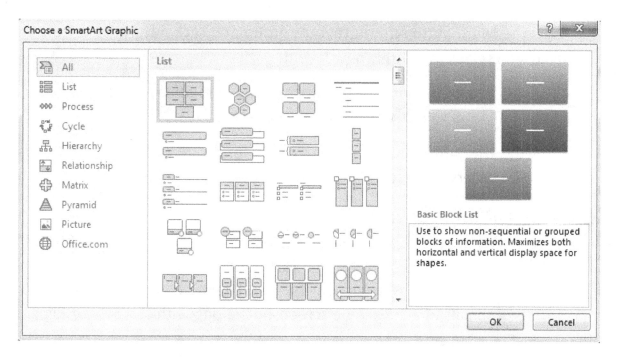

Figure 10-16 The Choose a SmartArt Graphic dialog box

Excel inserts the basic structure of the list or diagram into your worksheet with [Text] inside the shapes where you can enter your text along with a text pane to the immediate left of the diagram. The Design tab of the SmartArt Tools contextual tab includes Layouts and SmartArt Styles galleries for the diagram or list inserted.

Filling in the Text for a New SmartArt Graphic

You just need to type your entry to fill the text in the list or diagram for the first time. To complete the entry, you need to press the down arrow key or click the next list or diagram section. You should never press the Tab key or the Enter key as you normally do in a regular worksheet entry because pressing an Enter key inserts a new section and pressing the Tab key indents the level of the current section.

Formatting a SmartArt Graphic

Even after you close the text pane of your SmartArt list or diagram, you can format its text and graphics. You can format the text as you format worksheet cells, that is, using the appropriate command buttons in the Font group on the Home tab. To format the graphics, you can use the Layouts, Change Colors and SmartArt Styles galleries on the Design tab of the SmartArt Tools contextual tab.

- ✓ Click the More button in the Layouts group and click a thumbnail from the gallery to select an entirely new layout.

- ✓ Click the Change Colors button in the SmartArt Styles group and click a thumbnail from the gallery to change the colors.

- ✓ Click the More button in the SmartArt Styles group and click a thumbnail from the gallery to select a new style for the current layout.

Screenshots Anyone?

Excel 2013 allows you to take screenshots and insert into your worksheets. To take a picture of your screen, click the Take a Screenshot command button's dropdown in the Illustrations group on the Insert tab. Excel opens a dropdown menu with thumbnails of all available screenshots along with the Screen Clipping item. You just need to click a thumbnail to insert it.

To take a screenshot of a portion of your desktop, click the Screen Clipping option. The Excel window will be minimized and the mouse pointer will be changed to a thick black cross. You drag and release the mouse button when you select the required portion. The moment you release the mouse button, Excel automatically reopens displaying the selected screenshot. You can then resize or move this screenshot as you do any other item.

Theme for a Day

You can format all the text and graphics uniformly. Click the Theme command button in the Themes group on the Page Layout tab and click a thumbnail from the gallery after having a Live Preview.

Excel Themes combine three default elements: color scheme applied to the graphics, the font used in the text and graphics and the graphic effects applied. Even after selecting a theme, you can change any or all of these elements by clicking the corresponding command buttons in the Themes group on the Page Layout tab.

- ✓ Colors to change the color scheme by clicking a thumbnail from the palette. You can click the Customize Colors at the bottom to open the Create New Theme Colors dialog box to create a custom color scheme.

✓ Fonts to select a new font by clicking its thumbnail from the list. You can click the Customize Fonts at the bottom to open the Create New Theme Fonts dialog box where you can create a custom font.

✓ Effects to select a new set of graphic effects by clicking its thumbnail from the gallery.

Controlling How Graphic Objects Overlap

By now, you might have noticed that different graphic objects including charts, images, inserted clipart, text boxes and SmartArt graphics float on top of the cells of the worksheet. Most of the objects are opaque and hide information in the cells beneath. Similarly, if you have two graphic objects and move one of them overlapping a part of another, then the one on the top hides the one below. So, there should be some ways to ensure that graphic objects do not overlap one another or do not overlap the worksheet cells that contain information.

Reordering the Layering of Graphic Objects

When two graphic objects overlap, you can decide how they overlay by sending the objects back or forward. You can move a selected graphic object to a new layer in one of two ways:

✓ To move the selected graphic object up toward or to the top layer, select the Bring Forward or Bring to Front option in the Arrange group on the contextual tab. To move the selected object down toward or to the bottom layer, select the Send Backward or Send to Back option in the Arrange group on the contextual tab.

✓ Click the Selection Pane command button in the Arrange group on the Format tab under the contextual tab to display the Selection task pane. Then, click the Bring Forward button (with the triangle pointing up) or Send Backward button (with the triangle pointing down) at the top of the task pane (circled in Figure 10-17).

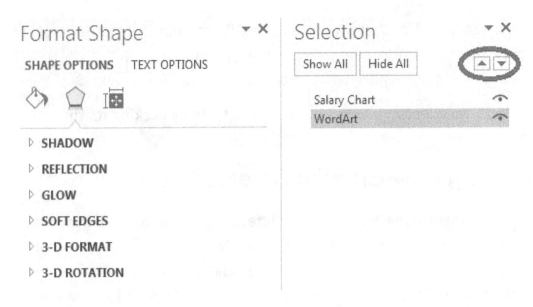

Figure 10-17 Bring Forward and Send Backward buttons in the Selection task pane

Grouping Graphic Objects

Sometimes, you might have to group more than one graphic object so that they act as a single unit and you can move them or resize them in one operation. To group objects, select each object holding the Ctrl key and click the Group command button in the Arrange group on the Format tab under the contextual tab and then select Group from the dropdown menu. After grouping different objects, every object in the group will be selected if you click any one object in the group. You can later ungroup the objects (if you want) by selecting the Ungroup option from the dropdown that appears when you click the Group command button in the Arrange group on the Format tab.

Hiding Graphic Objects

You can hide or show the graphic objects as you want. Select the object you want to hide and click the Selection Pane command button in the Arrange group on the Format tab. You can temporarily hide any graphic object by clicking its eye checkbox. You can click the Hide All button at the top of the task pane if you want to hide all the graphic objects in your worksheet. To redisplay a hidden object, click the empty eye checkbox. You can redisplay all the hidden objects by clicking the Show All button at the top of the task pane.

Printing Just the Charts

To print just a specific chart independent of other graphic objects and worksheet data, select the chart to be printed in the worksheet and go to File → Print. Then you will see the selected chart in the Backstage view. You can click the Page Setup link on the Print Screen in the Backstage view to change the page setup. Once you make the required changes, click OK to close the Page Setup dialog box and click the Print button.

11. Getting on the Data List

Introduction

In this chapter, we will learn how to

- ➢ Set up a data list in Excel.

- ➢ Enter and edit records in the data list.

- ➢ Sort records in the data list.

- ➢ Filter records in the data list.

- ➢ Import external data into the worksheet.

Most of the worksheet tables are created with the intention of performing essential calculations and presenting the information in an understandable form. You can also create worksheet tables just for storing information. This kind of worksheet tables that store lots and lots of information consistently are known as data lists in Excel. You might have heard the term "database table" if you are familiar with software development. Similar to database tables, data lists can also be used to save the names, address and other work related information of all your employees or to store all essential facts about your clients.

Creating Data Lists

You can create a data list in Excel much like you create a worksheet table. The only difference is that data lists have only column headings and no row headings. To create a new data list,

1. Click the blank cell where you want to start the new data list.

2. Enter the column headings (referred to as field names) to identify different kinds of items you need to keep track of.

3. Enter values in the appropriate columns of the row which is the row just below the row containing the column headings.

4. Click the Format as Table button in the Styles group on the Home tab and select a thumbnail from the gallery which opens the Format As Table dialog box (Figure 11-1).

5. Select the My table has headers option if your table has headers. Otherwise unselect it. The cell range of your data list will automatically appear in the Where is the data of your table? Text box.

6. Click the OK button to close the Format as Table dialog box.

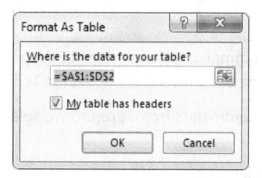

Figure 11-1 The Format as Table dialog box

Now your data list will appear in the selected table format with filters added to each field name in the top row as in Figure 11-2.

Figure 11-2 New data list created in the selected format

Adding Records to Data Lists

One you create your data list with field names (column headings) and first record and also format them as a table, you can start entering the remaining records in subsequent rows of your data list. You just need to press the Tab key when the cell cursor is in the last cell of the first record so that Excel adds an extra row to the data list and you can enter the data for the next record. You can also enter formulas instead of values, so that Excel calculates the entries using the formula and inserts the result into the cell as the field entry.

Using the Form Button

If you find entering records directly in the data list a bit boring, then you can make use of Excel's data form to enter records. But you cannot access the data form so easily because it is not available as a command button in the Ribbon. You have to add its command button to the Quick Access Toolbar or a custom Ribbon tab.

To add data form's command button to the Quick Access toolbar,

1. Click the Customize Quick Access Toolbar button at the end of Quick Access toolbar.

2. Click the More Commands option from its dropdown menu to open the Excel Options dialog box with the Quick Access Toolbar tab selected.

3. From the Choose commands from: dropdown, select Commands Not in the Ribbon option.

4. Click Form from the list box.

5. Click the Add button to get a window as in Figure 11-3.

6. Click OK to close the Excel Options dialog box.

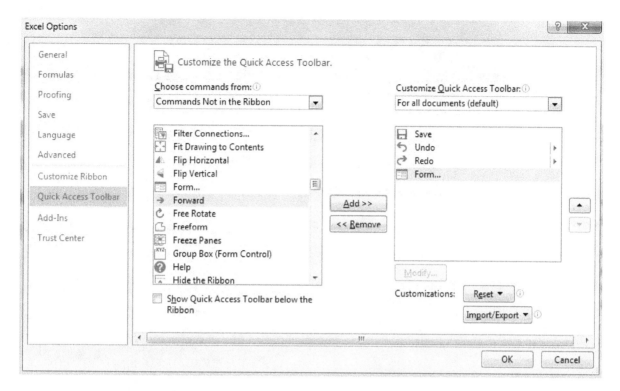

Figure 11-3 Excel Options dialog box after adding Form into Quick Access Toolbar

Now you could see the Form button at the very end of the Quick Access toolbar.

Adding Records via the Data Form

When you click the Form button from the Quick Access Toolbar for the first time, Excel analyzes the row of field names as well as your first record and then creates a data form. The data form displays the field names on the left of the form one below the other with the entries of the first record in the corresponding textboxes as in Figure 11-4.

You could also see a series of buttons on the right of the textboxes including New, Delete, Restore, Find Prev, Find Next and Close. Just above the New button, the number of record you are looking at followed by the total number of records is displayed (here 1/1). When entering new records, you will see a message New Record instead of these numbers.

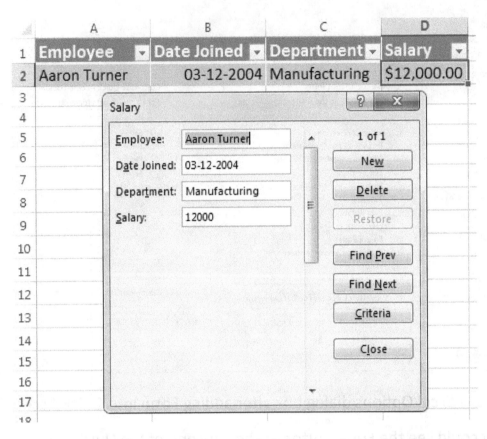

Figure 11-4 The Data Form for the Employee details

Now to add a new record, click the New button so that the entries in the textboxes will become blank and a message New Record appears just above the New button as in Figure 11-5. Enter the data for the first field and press the Tab key to move the cursor to the next field in the same record. Never press the Enter key to advance to the next field in the same record because it will insert the incomplete record and creates a blank data form to enter the next record.

While proceeding, if you realize that you have made an error in a field that you have already completed, then press Shift + Tab to return to that field and just change the entry by entering the new value. If you want to change only certain characters, then place your cursor wherever you want to make changes and enter the value.

Once you complete a particular record, you can press the Enter key or the down arrow key (↓) to insert the current record as the last record into the data list and display a blank data form. Clicking the New button on the form will also do the same. Once you finish adding all the records, you can either press the ESC key or click the Close button at the bottom of the dialog box to close the data form.

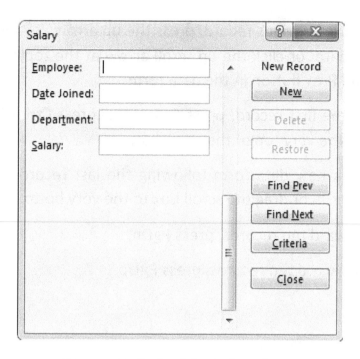

Figure 11-5 The blank data form

Editing Records in the Data Form

You can use the data form not only to enter new records, but also to perform routine maintenance. You can edit or delete the records you want with the help of data form. Locate the record you want to edit using different keys or buttons, move to the required field using Tab or Shift + Tab and then replace the entry if you want or clear the entry by pressing Delete key after selecting it.

To delete an entire record from the data list, click the Delete button in the data form. Excel displays an alert message "Displayed record will be permanently deleted." If you click the OK button, the specific record will be removed from the data list.

Moving through Records in the Data Form

If you want to edit or delete a record in the database through data form, you need to first locate it. You can use the scroll bar to the right of the list of field names or different keystrokes to move through the records.

✓ To move to the next record, press the down arrow key (↓) or Enter key on the keyboard, or click the down scroll arrow at the bottom of the scroll bar (circled in Figure 11-6) or click the Find Next button in the data form.

- ✓ To move to the previous record, press the up arrow key (↑) or Shift + Enter on the keyboard, or click the up scroll arrow at the top of the scroll bar or click the Find Prev button in the data form.

- ✓ To move to the first record, press Ctrl + ↑ or press Ctrl + PgUp or drag the scroll box to the very top of the scroll bar.

- ✓ To move to a new data form following the last record, press Ctrl + ↓ or press Ctrl + PgDn or drag the scroll box to the very bottom of the scroll bar.

- ✓ To move forward ten records, press PgDn.

- ✓ To move backward ten records, press PgUp.

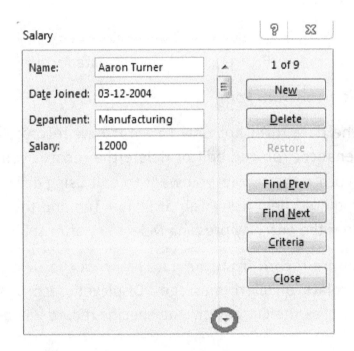

Figure 11-6 Scroll arrow at the bottom of the scroll bar

Finding Records with the Data Form

Finding a particular record by moving from record to record might not be practical in large data lists. In such cases, you can make use of the Criteria button to find the records quickly rather than wasting your valuable time manually looking for it.

When you click the Criteria button, a blank data form appears with the word Criteria in the place of New Record. Now you can enter the criteria to look for in the blank text boxes. Suppose you are looking for the details of an employee named Hannah, but you are not sure how to spell her name correctly. Only thing you know is that her name starts with "Ha". Now enter Ha* in the Name field to narrow your search.

When you enter search criteria, you can use the ? For single and * for multiple wildcard characters. You can also use operators including = (equal to), > (greater than), >= (greater than or equal to), < (less than), <= (less than or equal to) and <> (not equal to) in your search criteria. If you want to find all employees who have salary less than a specific value, say $5000, then you need to enter <5000 in the textbox for the Salary field as the search criteria.

After entering the search criteria, click the Find Next button. Excel displays the first matching record from the database in the data form. If the first record is not that you are looking for, then click the Find Next button again until you locate the record you want. Once you locate the record, you can edit it or delete it as you want. Once you close the data form after making the required changes, the changes will be reflected in the data list.

If there are multiple records that match your criteria, then you may have to click the Find Next or Find Prev button several times to locate the record you want. If no record fits the search criteria you enter, the computer beeps at you when you click these buttons.

Sorting Data Lists

Most of the time, you might want to see the records in your data list in a particular order. For example, you might want to see them in the ascending order of sales made by each employee or in the alphabetical order of the employee names and so on.

When you create your database for the first time, you might enter the records in the order you want. But as you proceed, you might realize that you do not have the option to add the records in the order you want because Excel adds a new record to the bottom of the database regardless of your preferences.

For example, you entered details of all your employees in the alphabetical order of their names. Just after 2 days you complete your database creation, a new employee named Helen Smith joined your company. You need to enter this name between Hannah Turner and Mary Rivera. As there is no other choice, you enter the record and it becomes the last one in the database. After entering the details of many more new employees, what if you want to see their details in the alphabetical order of their names?

This is not the only situation you have to sort out your data list. You enter the records in your preferred order, means the order that you want to use most of the time. But it does not mean that you will never have to use another order. What if you want to see the records in the ascending order of the salary of the employees?

You do not have to worry. Excel makes it so easy to sort the records in the order you want. You only have to specify which field's values decide the order of the records. You also need to specify whether to sort your values in ascending order or descending order. When you sort the entries in ascending order, text entries are placed in alphabetical order from A to Z, values are placed from smallest to largest and dates are placed from oldest to newest.

Sorting on a Single Field

To sort your data list based on only one particular field, you have to just click the AutoFilter button of that field and select the appropriate sort option from its drop down list.

- ✓ Sort A to Z or Sort Z to A in a text field.

- ✓ Sort Smallest to Largest or Sort Largest to Smallest in a number field.

- ✓ Sort Oldest to Newest or Sort Newest to Oldest in a date field.

Excel rearranges all the records in the data list based on the sorting order in the selected field. Excel also adds an up or down arrow to the AutoFilter button of the sorted field (circled in Figure 11-7). An up arrow indicates that the field was sorted in ascending order and a down arrow indicates that the field was sorted in descending order.

	A	B	C	D
1	Name	Date Joined	Department	Salary
2	Aaron Turner	03-12-2004	Manufacturing	$12,000.00
3	Beuna Reed	28-11-2005	Banking	$13,200.00
4	Elizabeth Young	26-11-2005	R&D	$9,200.00
5	Hannah Miller	30-06-2005	Banking	$12,500.00
6	Jim Gibson	16-10-2006	R&D	$13,500.00
7	John Smith	04-10-2006	HR	$9,800.00
8	Mary Harris	11-08-2004	HR	$14,000.00
9	Rose Rivera	09-10-2004	Banking	$10,000.00
10	Sandra Parker	23-06-2004	Manufacturing	$8,800.00

Figure 11-7 An up arrow added to the AutoFilter button indicating that the data is sorted in ascending order

Sorting on Multiple Fields

You might have to use more than one field in sorting when the first field you use contains duplicate values and you want a say in how the records with duplicates are arranged. In the data list shown in Figure 11-8, suppose we want to sort the employee names alphabetically for each department. So, we need to sort records on multiple fields, first by department and then by name.

	A	B	C	D
1	Name	Date Joined	Department	Salary
2	Aaron Turner	03-12-2004	Manufacturing	$12,000.00
3	John Smith	04-10-2006	HR	$9,800.00
4	Hannah Miller	30-06-2005	Banking	$12,500.00
5	Elizabeth Young	26-11-2005	R&D	$9,200.00
6	Mary Harris	11-08-2004	HR	$14,000.00
7	Rose Rivera	09-10-2004	Banking	$10,000.00
8	Sandra Parker	23-06-2004	Manufacturing	$8,800.00
9	Beuna Reed	28-11-2005	Banking	$13,200.00
10	Jim Gibson	16-10-2006	R&D	$13,500.00

Figure 11-8 Employee data list

1. Select any cell from the data list.

2. Click the Sort & Filter command button in the Editing group on the Home tab.

3. Click Custom Sort from the dropdown to open the Sort dialog box.

4. Click the name of the field you first want the records sorted by in the Sort by drop-down list and select the order of sort from the Order dropdown.

5. Click the Add Level button if you want to sort on another field as well.

6. Select a second field to sort on in the Then by dropdown and also select the order. Now your screen will look as in Figure 11-9.

7. If required, repeat Steps 5 and 6 to add as many additional sort levels as required.

8. Click OK or press Enter to close the dialog box.

Figure 11-9 Sorting records on multiple fields

Once you click the OK button, the data list in Figure 11-8 will appear as in Figure 11-10 where the employee names are arranged in alphabetical order for each department. You could find arrows added to the AutoFilter buttons of both Department and Name fields. Sorting records on multiple fields is really useful when you have to deal with a database that has thousands of records.

Excel automatically excludes the first row of the data list from the sort assuming that the first row is a header row containing field names. If you have to include the first row as well in the sort, make sure that you deselect the My Data Has Headers check box before you click OK.

	A	B	C	D
1	Name	Date Joined	Department	Salary
2	Beuna Reed	28-11-2005	Banking	$13,200.00
3	Hannah Miller	30-06-2005	Banking	$12,500.00
4	Rose Rivera	09-10-2004	Banking	$10,000.00
5	John Smith	04-10-2006	HR	$9,800.00
6	Mary Harris	11-08-2004	HR	$14,000.00
7	Aaron Turner	03-12-2004	Manufacturing	$12,000.00
8	Sandra Parker	23-06-2004	Manufacturing	$8,800.00
9	Elizabeth Young	26-11-2005	R&D	$9,200.00
10	Jim Gibson	16-10-2006	R&D	$13,500.00

Figure 11-10 Data list sorted on Department and Name fields

Filtering Data Lists

It is so easy to get only the records you want in a data list with Excel's Filter feature. To get records that contain a particular value, click the AutoFilter button of the appropriate field to display a dropdown list containing all the entries made in that field. Select the one you want to use as a filter and Excel displays only those records that contain the value you selected.

For example, I want to see only employees working in Banking department from the data list in Figure 11-8. To filter the data list, I clicked the Department field's AutoFilter button and then clicked the Select All checkbox to remove all the check marks. Then I clicked Banking check box before clicking OK. Now the data list is filtered as shown in Figure 11-11.

	A	B	C	D
1	Name	Date Joined	Department	Salary
4	Hannah Miller	30-06-2005	Banking	$12,500.00
7	Rose Rivera	09-10-2004	Banking	$10,000.00
9	Beuna Reed	28-11-2005	Banking	$13,200.00

Figure 11-11 Filtered data list

Even after filtering your data list by a single value, if your data list contains more records than you want, then you can still filter your data list by clicking the

AutoFilter button of some other field and then selecting only the records you want.

If you want to display all the records in your database (remove filter), then click the filtered field's AutoFilter button which is now a cone filter and then click the Clear Filter From followed by the name of the filtered field in double quotes option. This will remove the filter and display all the records.

Using Readymade Number Filters

Excel offers a number filter option named Top 10 which can be used on a number field to display only a certain number of records with highest or lowest values. To filter a database using the Top 10 option,

1. Click the AutoFilter button on the number field you want to filter.

2. Highlight Number Filters from the dropdown.

3. Click Top 10 from the submenu to open the Top 10 AutoFilter dialog box.

4. Change the default values in the three inputs if you do not want to see the top 10 items in the selected field.

5. Change Top to Bottom if you want to see the bottom records.

6. Change the value 10 in the middle textbox (currently holds 10) if you want to see more or fewer records.

7. Change Items to Percent in the right most dropdown if you want to see the top or bottom percent.

8. Click OK or press Enter to close the dialog box and filter the database using your selected number filter.

If you filter the data in Figure 11-12 using the settings given in Figure 11-13, you will get a data list as shown in Figure 11-14.

	A	B	C	D
1	Name ▾	Date Joined ▾	Department ▾	Salary ▾
2	Aaron Turner	03-12-2004	Manufacturing	$12,000.00
3	John Smith	04-10-2006	HR	$9,800.00
4	Hannah Miller	30-06-2005	Banking	$12,500.00
5	Elizabeth Young	26-11-2005	R&D	$9,200.00
6	Mary Harris	11-08-2004	HR	$14,000.00
7	Rose Rivera	09-10-2004	Banking	$10,000.00
8	Sandra Parker	23-06-2004	Manufacturing	$8,800.00
9	Beuna Reed	28-11-2005	Banking	$13,200.00
10	Jim Gibson	16-10-2006	R&D	$13,500.00
11	Abel Wright	10-10-2004	Banking	$11,000.00
12	Janet Arnold	04-06-2006	HR	$10,600.00
13	Kevin Harper	11-03-2005	R&D	$7,500.00
14	Sarah Smith	01-02-2006	Manufacturing	$11,300.00

Figure 11-12 Data list which will be filtered using readymade number filters

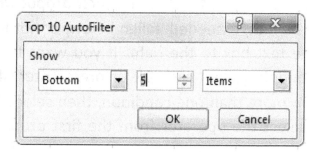

Figure 11-13 Top 10 AutoFilter dialog box

	A	B	C	D
1	Name ▾	Date Joined ▾	Department ▾	Salary ▾
3	John Smith	04-10-2006	HR	$9,800.00
5	Elizabeth Young	26-11-2005	R&D	$9,200.00
7	Rose Rivera	09-10-2004	Banking	$10,000.00
8	Sandra Parker	23-06-2004	Manufacturing	$8,800.00
13	Kevin Harper	11-03-2005	R&D	$7,500.00

Figure 11-14 Bottom 5 records

Using Readymade Date Filters

Similar to readymade number filters, Excel also offers readymade date filters to filter data list by entries in a date field. These readymade date filters include Tomorrow, Today, Yesterday, as well as Next, This, and Last for the Week, Month, Quarter, and Year. Excel also offers Year to Date and All Dates in the Period filters. To filter data list using date filter, click the AutoFilter button of the date field, highlight Date Filters on the dropdown list and then click the suitable date filter option from the continuation menu.

Using Custom Filters

If you could not filter your data list the way you want using any of the previously specified options, then you can create your own filters using custom filters. To create a custom filter for a specific field, click the AutoFilter button of the specific field and then highlight Text Filters, Number Filters or Date Filters on the dropdown list based on the type of your field. Click the Custom Filter option at the bottom of the submenu to open a Custom AutoFilter dialog box.

Select the operator that you want to use in the first dropdown list box and enter the value that should be met, exceeded, fallen below, or not found in the records of the database in the text box to the right. If you want to filter your data list based on only one condition, then click OK or press Enter. If you have to filter your data list based on more than one condition, then select And or Or based on your filter and then select the operator from the first dropdown and enter the value in the textbox.

Suppose you want to filter the details of employees from Figure 11-10 who earn less than $13,000 and greater than $10,000. I clicked the AutoFilter button of the Salary field and highlighted Number Filters and then clicked the Custom Filter option. It opened the Custom AutoFilter dialog box and I changed the values as in Figure 11-15. Then, I get my filtered data list as in Figure 11-16.

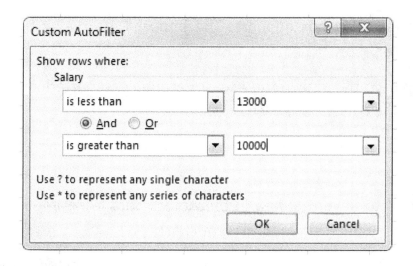

Figure 11-15 The Custom AutoFilter dialog box

Figure 11-16 Data list filtered using custom autofilter

Importing External Data

Excel 2013 makes it so easy to import data from external sources such as Microsoft Access into your worksheet and this process is known as external data querying. You can use web queries to import data directly from various web pages containing financial and other types of statistical data that you need to work with in the Excel worksheet.

Querying Access Database Tables

To query data from an Access database table, click the From Access command button in the Get External Data group on the Data tab. Excel opens the Select Data Source dialog box where you select the name of the Access database and then click Open. The Select Table dialog box appears from which you can select the data table that you want to import into your worksheet. Once you click OK, the Import Data dialog box appears. The Import Data dialog box contains the following options:

- ✓ Table to have the data in the Access data table imported into an Excel table in either the current or new worksheet.

- ✓ PivotTable Report to have the data in the Access data table imported into a new pivot table.

- ✓ PivotChart to have the data in the Access data table imported into a new pivot table with an embedded pivot chart.

- ✓ Only Create Connection to link to the data in the selected Access data table without bringing its data into the worksheet.

- ✓ Existing Worksheet to have the data in the Access data table imported into the current worksheet starting at the current cell address listed in the text box below.

- ✓ New Worksheet to have the data in the Access data table imported into a new sheet that's added to the beginning of the workbook.

You can access data not only from Microsoft Access, but also from a variety of external data sources. To import data from other sources, click the From Other Sources command button in the Get External Data group on the Data tab. Excel opens a dropdown menu with the following options:

- ✓ From SQL Server to import data from an SQL Server table.

- ✓ From Analysis Services to import data from an SQL Server Analysis cube.

- ✓ From Windows Azure Marketplace to import data from any of the various marketplace service providers.

- ✓ From OData Data Feed to import data from any database table following the Open Data Protocol.

- ✓ From XML Data Import to import data from an XML file that you open and map.

- ✓ From Data Connection Wizard to import data from a database table using the Data Connection Wizard and OLEDB.

✓ From Microsoft Query to import data from a database table using Microsoft Query and ODBC.

Performing Web Queries

To make a webpage query, click the From Web command button in the Get External Data group on the Data tab. Excel opens the New Web Query dialog box containing the Home page for your default web browser. To select the web page containing the data you want to import into Excel, you can:

✓ Type the URL web address in the Address: textbox at the top of the Home page in the New Web Query dialog box.

✓ Use the Search feature available on the Home page to find the web page containing the data you wish to import.

Once you get the web page containing the data you want to import displayed in the New Web Query dialog box, Excel indicates which tables of information you can import from the web page into the worksheet with a yellow box and an arrowhead pointing right. To import these tables, you just have to click this box to add a check mark to it.

Once you check all the tables you want to import, click the Import button. Excel closes the New Web Query dialog box and opens a version of the Import Data dialog box with only the Table option available where you can indicate where the table data is to be imported by selecting either Existing Worksheet or New Worksheet. Once you click OK in the Import Data dialog box, Excel closes the dialog box and then imports all the tables of data you selected into a new worksheet starting at cell A1 or in the existing worksheet starting at the specified cell.

12. Linking, Automating and Sharing Spreadsheets

Introduction

In this chapter, we will learn how to

➢ Use Office Apps and Excel add-ins to automate and enhance Excel 2013.

➢ Add hyperlinks to other workbooks, worksheets, Office documents, web pages or email.

➢ Create and use macros to automate common spreadsheet tasks.

➢ Share your worksheets on the web.

➢ Edit your worksheets with Excel Web Applications.

Apps for Office, Excel add-ins, hyperlinks and macros are four main ways to make Excel more powerful and versatile. Add-ins, as the name indicate, add a number of features to Excel. Hyperlinks allow you to link to other worksheets and Office documents. Macros help you automate complex command sequences. Excel Web Applications are simply superb as they allow you to share your worksheets by attaching them to email messages or to publish them to the web which in turn makes communication and collaboration so quicker and effective.

Using Apps for Office

Apps for Office are small programs that run inside various Microsoft Office 2013 programs to extend their functionality. You can do a bunch of things with Apps for Office. You can learn about Excel's features, use a dictionary to get the meaning of different words and also enter dates into your spreadsheet by selecting them on a calendar.

You can get a number of Apps for Office for free. At the same time, some of the really useful Apps are offered for purchase. You can go to the Office Store, find the one that you want and purchase it if required. Before using any of these apps in Excel 2013, you need to install it.

1. Click the My Apps command button in the Apps group on the Insert tab to open the Apps for Office dropdown with a Recently Used Apps section at the top and a See All link at the bottom. The first time you open this menu, the Recently Used Apps section will be blank.

2. Click the See All link on the dropdown menu to open the Apps for Office dialog box containing My Apps and Store links.

3. Click the Store link to display a list of apps available in the store. Each app in the list is identified by icon, name, its developer, its current user rating and its price.

4. Click the name or icon of an app to get more information about it.

5. Click the Add button of an app to install it.

6. You would have to sign in to your Microsoft account in order to install an app. If you're not already signed in, your browser takes you to a sign-in page and if you are already signed in, your browser takes you directly to a confirmation web page.

7. Once the purchase is over, whether free or paid, your browser takes you to the web page explaining how to insert your newly installed app into Excel.

8. Click the Close button on your web browser to close it and return to Excel.

Once you install an app, you can easily insert it into the current worksheet.

1. Click the My Apps command button in the Apps group on the Insert tab to open the Apps for Office dropdown.

2. Click the See All link on the dropdown menu to open the Apps for Office dialog box.

3. Click the My Apps link in the dialog box to see all the currently installed apps.

4. Click the app you want to use in your worksheet.

5. Click the Insert button or press Enter to insert the app into your worksheet.

Once the app is installed, you can start using its features. Some Office apps open in task panes docked on the right side of the worksheet whereas some other apps open as graphic objects that float above the worksheet. Office apps opened in task panes can be closed by clicking the pane's Close button. To close apps that open as floating graphic objects, you need to select the graphic and then press the Delete key. This just closes the app without uninstalling it.

Once you start using different apps in Excel, they will be added to the Recently Used Apps section of the Apps for Office button's dropdown menu. So, you can quickly access any closed app by clicking it from the dropdown menu.

Using Excel Add-Ins

Excel add-in programs are small modules that extend the power of Excel. Add-ins give access to a wide array of features and functions that are not usually offered in the program. There are three types of add-ins:

✓ Built-in add-ins available when you install Excel 2013.

✓ Add-ins that you can download for Excel 2013 from Microsoft's Office Online website at www.microsoft.office.com.

✓ Add-ins developed by third-party vendors that often need to be purchased.

As soon as you install Excel 2013, all the built-in add-ins are fully loaded and ready to use. To load any other add-in program:

1. Go to File → Options to open the Excel Options dialog box.

2. Click the Add-Ins tab.

3. Click the Go button while Excel Add-Ins is selected in the Manage dropdown list to open the Add-Ins dialog box (Figure 12-1) displaying the names of all the built-in add-in programs.

4. Click the name of the add-in to display a brief description of its function at the bottom of this dialog box.

5. Select the check box of the add-in program that you want to load.

6. Click OK to close the Add-Ins dialog box.

Excel automatically places command buttons for the activated add-ins in either in the Analysis group on the Data tab or in the Solutions group on the Formulas tab, depending on the type of add-in.

If you do not want a particular add-in you have loaded anymore, you can unload it by opening the Add-Ins dialog box from the Excel options dialog box's Add-Ins tab, removing the check mark from the corresponding add-in and then clicking OK.

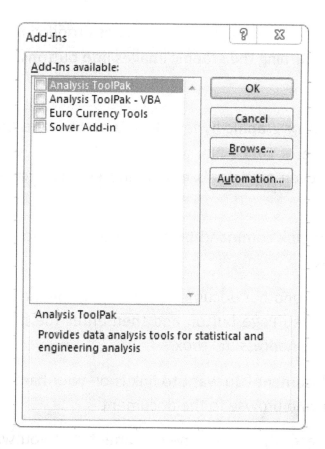

Figure 12-1 The Add-Ins dialog box

Adding Hyperlinks to a Worksheet

You can add hyperlinks to your worksheet and hence make the process of opening other Office documents, Excel workbooks and worksheets a breeze. You can add links not only to documents located on your local hard drive or local network, but also to web pages on the Internet or a company's intranet. Excel also allows you to set up e-mail hyperlinks attaching Excel workbooks or other types of Office files that automatically address messages to co-workers with whom you regularly contact.

You can add the following types of hyperlinks to your worksheets:

- ✓ Text entries in cells known as hypertext, normally formatted as underlined blue text.

- ✓ Clip art and imported graphics from files you have inserted into the worksheet.

- ✓ Graphics you have created from the Shapes dropdown gallery on the Insert tab and hence turning the graphic images into buttons.

When creating a text or graphic hyperlink, you can make a link to another Excel workbook, other type of Office file, a website address, a named location in the same workbook or even a person's e-mail address. To create a text or graphic hyperlink,

1.   Click the Hyperlink command button in the Links group to open the Insert Hyperlink dialog box.

2a.   To add a link to another document, a web page on intranet or Internet, click the Existing File or Web Page button and then enter the file's directory path or web page's URL in the Address: textbox.

2a. i. If the document you want to link is on your hard drive, click the Look in: dropdown and browse to the document.

2a. ii. If you recently opened the document that you want to link to, then click the Recent Files button and select it from the list.

2a. iii. If the document you want to link is located on a website and you know its web address, type it into the Address: textbox.

2a. iv. If you recently browsed the webpage you want to link to, then click the Browsed Pages button and select the address from the list box.

2b.   To add a link to another cell or cell range in the same workbook, click the Place in this Document button. Type the address of the cell or cell range in the Type the cell reference: textbox or select the required sheet name or range name from the Or select a place in this document: list box.

2c.   To open a new email message addressed to a particular recipient, click the E-mail Address button and then enter the email address in the E-mail address: textbox.

2c. i. If the recipient's email address is displayed in the Recently used e-mail addresses: listbox, click the address to enter it into the E-mail address: textbox.

3. Enter the text that you want to appear as the hyperlink text in the Text to display: textbox (optional).

4. To add a screen tip that appears when you hover over the hyperlink text, click the ScreenTip button, enter the text in the ScreenTip text: textbox and click OK.

5. Click OK to close the Insert Hyperlink dialog box.

Once you click a hyperlink, you will be redirected to the destination associated with the hyperlink. To follow a hyperlink, hover over the underlined blue text if you assigned the hyperlink to a text or hover over the graphical image if you assigned the hyperlink to an image. When the pointer changes to a hand with the index finger pointing upward, click the text or image and Excel redirects you to the designated document, web page, cell or email message.

If the hyperlink text is clicked once, the hyperlink text color will change from blue to dark purple though it will have the same blue color when you open the workbook file again. If you want to edit a hyperlink, instead of clicking on it, right click the cell that contains the hyperlink or the image and click the Edit Hyperlink or Remove Hyperlink option from the shortcut menu.

Automating Commands with Macros

You can record complex command sequences using Macros and hence automate Excel worksheet. Macros help you speed up your routine processes considerably and also make sure that they are done without any errors. Excel uses a language called Visual Basic for Applications (VBA) to record your commands and keystrokes.

Recording New Macros

You could find a Record Macro button on the Excel Status bar at the bottom of the Excel 2013 program. The button appears to the immediate right of the Ready status indicator looking like a worksheet with a red dot. Also the View tab contains a Macro command button in the Macros group with a dropdown menu containing a Record Macro option.

Excel also allows you to add an optional Developer tab to the Ribbon that has its own Record Macro command button. To add the Developer tab,

1. Go to File → Options to open the Excel Options dialog box.

2. Click the Customize Ribbon tab.

3. Select the Developer checkbox under Main Tabs in the Customize the Ribbon: list box on the right of the dialog box (circled in Figure 12-2).

4. Click OK which will add the Developer tab to the Ribbon.

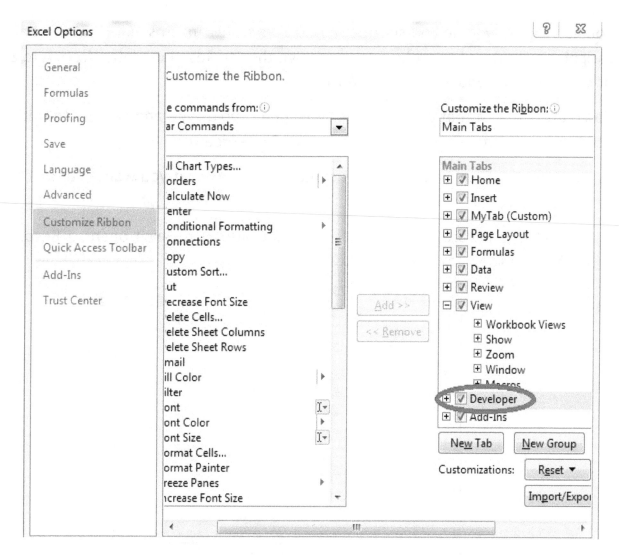

Figure 12-2 The Excel Options dialog box to add optional Developer tab

When you turn on the macro reader by clicking the Record Macro button on the Status bar, clicking the Record Macro option on the Macros button's drop-down menu on the View tab or clicking the Record Macro button in the Code group on the Developer tab, the macro recorder records all your actions in the worksheet.

The macros that you create can be stored as part of the current workbook, in a new workbook or even in a globally available personal macro workbook named PERSONAL.XLSB. When you record a macro as part of this personal workbook, you can run that macro from any workbook. When you run macros as part of the current workbook, you can run those macros only when that particular workbook is open.

You can assign a name and shortcut keystrokes to the macros you create. When assigning a shortcut keystroke, you can assign the Ctrl key plus a letter from A to Z or the Ctrl + Shift and a letter from A to Z.

To create a macro that enters a title in 14-point, bold type and centers the title across rows A through D with the Merge and Center feature:

1. Open the Excel workbook that contains the data that you want your macro to work with.

2. Click the Record Macro button on the Status bar which opens a Record Macro dialog box as in Figure 12-3.

Figure 12-3 Record Macro dialog box

3. Enter the name of your macro in the Macro name: textbox replacing the value Macro1.

4. Click the Shortcut key: textbox and enter the letter if you want to assign Ctrl + a letter or enter Shift plus a letter if you want to assign Ctrl + Shift + a letter to your macro (optional).

5. Select Personal Macro Workbook (if you want to run the macro anytime), New Workbook (if you want to record and save the macro in a new

workbook) or This Workbook (if you want to run the macro only when the current workbook is open) from the Store macro in: dropdown.

6. Click the Description: box and enter the purpose of your macro (optional).

7. Click OK to close the Record Macro dialog box. The Record Macro button on the Status bar and the Developer tab becomes blue square Stop Recording button.

8. Click the Use Relative References option that appears in the Macros command button's dropdown menu in the Macros group on the View tab, if you want to record the macro relative to the position of the current cell.

   In our example, if you want to enter a title not only across cell A1 through D1, but also across A10 though D10 or C5 though F5, then you should of course click the Use Relative References option.

9. Perform the tasks that you want to record using your keyboard, mouse or both.

   In our example, enter the title in cell A1 and click the Enter button on the Formula bar to complete the entry. Select the font size from the Font Size drop down and click the Bold button on the Home tab. Select cells A1 through D1 and click the Merge and Center command button on the Home tab.

10. Click the Stop Recording button on the Status bar.

   The blue square Stop Recording button on the Status bar changes back into circular red Record Macro button.

Running Macros

You can run a recorded macro by clicking the View Macros option on the dropdown of Macros button in the Macros group on the View tab, the Macros button on the Developer tab or by pressing Alt + F8 to open the Macro dialog box (Figure 12-4). You could see all the macros in your current workbook and in your Personal Macro Workbook in the Macro Name list box in the Macro dialog box. Just click the name of the macro you want to run before clicking the Run button or pressing Enter.

If you have assigned a shortcut keystroke to your macro, then you just have to press the shortcut key to run the macro instead of accessing it from the Macro dialog box.

Figure 12-4 The Macro dialog box

Assigning Macros to the Ribbon and the Quick Access toolbar

You can assign your macro to a custom tab on the Ribbon or a custom button on the Quick Access toolbar so that you do not have to open the Micro dialog box to run a macro.

To assign a macro to a custom group on a custom Ribbon tab,

1. Go to File → Options and click the Customize Ribbon tab in the Excel Options dialog box.

2. Click Macros in the Choose commands from: dropdown. All the macros in the current workbook and PERSONAL.XLSB are displayed in the list box.

3. Click the name of the custom group on the custom tab to which you want to add the macro in the Main Tabs list box on the right of the window. If you have not added a custom tab and custom group, then add a tab using

New Tab button and a new group using New Group button and rename them the way you want using the Rename button.

4. Click the name of the macro you want to add to the custom group from the list box on the left.

5. Click the Add button to add the selected macro in the selected group on the custom tab.

6. Click OK to close the Excel Options dialog box.

Now you could see the name of your macro as a button with a programming diagram chart icon on the custom tab. You just have to click this command button to run the associated macro.

To assign a macro to a custom button on the Quick Access toolbar,

1. Click the Customize Quick Access Toolbar button at the end of the Quick Access toolbar.

2. Click More Commands from its dropdown menu.

3. Click Macros in the Choose commands from: dropdown.

4. Click the name of the macro to add to a custom button on the Quick Access toolbar from the Choose commands from: list box.

5. Click the Add button.

6. Click OK to close the Excel Options dialog box.

Now you could see a custom button appears on the Quick Access toolbar with a generic icon. You just need to click this button to run the macro.

Sharing Your Worksheets

If you want to share your spreadsheets with your employees, clients or colleagues, you can use the options on the Share screen in the Backstage view. If you have Microsoft's Lync online meeting software installed on your device, you can present the worksheet to other attendees as part of a Lync meeting. If you save your files in the cloud on your Windows Live SkyDrive, you can easily share the worksheets by inviting others to open them in Excel on their own devices or in their web browser with the Excel Web App if they don't have Excel.

Sharing Workbooks via SkyDrive

To share Excel workbooks you have saved on your SkyDrive,

1. Open the workbook file you want to share and then go to File → Share which opens the Share screen with the Invite People option selected.

2. Click the Type Names or E-mail Addresses text box and then begin typing the e-mail address of the first person with whom you want to share the workbook. As you type, Excel matches the letters with the names and e-mail addresses entered in your Address Book and if it finds possible matches, they are displayed in a drop-down menu. You just need to click it from the list. To find e-mail addresses in your Address list and add them to this text box, click the Search the Address Book for Contacts button and then use the options in the Address Book: Global Address List dialog box. To share the workbook with multiple people, type a semicolon after each e-mail address you add to this text box.

3. Click the Can Edit dropdown button and select Can View option to prevent the people you invite from editing the workbook you share (optional).

4. Select the Require User to Sign-in Before Accessing Document check box if you want the people with whom you share the workbook to have to log in to a Windows Live account before they can open the workbook (optional). If you do not give the login information to the email recipients, then do not select this check box.

5. Click the Share button.

Once you click the Share button, Excel sends the invitation email to all the specified recipients to share the workbook. The program also adds their e-mail addresses and the editing status of each recipient in the Shared With section at the bottom of the Share screen.

All the email recipients will get an email message containing a hyperlink to your workbook on SkyDrive. When they click this link, a copy of the workbook opens on a new page in their default web browser using the Excel Web App. If you have given the user permission to edit the file, the web app contains an Edit Workbook button.

When the user clicks this button, he has a choice between selecting an Edit in Excel and Edit in Excel Web App option on its dropdown menu. When he selects Edit in Excel, the workbook is downloaded and opened in his version of Excel. When he selects Edit in Excel Web App, the browser opens the workbook in a new version of the Excel Web App, containing a Home, Insert, and View tab with a limited set of command options.

Getting a Sharing Link

Instead of sending email invitations to the recipients with links to your workbook, you can create hyperlinks to your workbook and make them available to all those with whom you want to share them. To create a hyperlink to a workbook saved on your SkyDrive, select the Get a Sharing Link option from the Share screen in the Backstage view. To create a link that does not allow online editing, click the Create Link button to the right of the View Link option that appears on the right of the Share screen under the Get a Sharing Link heading. To create a link that enables online editing, click the Create Link button to the right of the Edit Link option in its place.

Excel displays a long hyperlink for sharing your workbook under the View Link or Edit Link heading. The program also displays a list of any of the people with whom you have already shared the workbook using the Invite People option under a Shared With heading and buttons.

Posting Links to Social Networks

You can now post links to your workbooks saved on SkyDrive on any of the social networking sites including Facebook, Twitter, LinkedIn etc. To do this,

1. Open the workbook saved on your SkyDrive that you want to share.

2. Select the Post to Social Networks option on the Share screen.

3. Select the checkbox associated with the social network to which you to post the link under Post to Social Networks on the right of the Share screen.

4. If you want to add any message, enter it in the Include a Personal Message with the Invitation textbox.

5. Click the Post button to post the link.

E-Mailing Workbooks

To email a copy of your workbook, go to File → Share → Email. When you click this, a panel appears with the following five options:

1. Send as Attachment to create a new email message using your default email program with a copy of the workbook file as its attachment.

2. Send a Link to create a new email message using your default email program that contains a hyperlink to the workbook file. This option is available only when the workbook file is saved on your web server.

3. Send as PDF to convert the Excel workbook to Adobe PDF format and attach it in a new email message.

4. Send as XPS to convert the Excel workbook to a Microsoft XPS format and attach it in a new email message.

5. Send as Internet Fax to send the workbook as a fax through an online fax service provider.

Once you select any of these options, Windows opens a new email message in your email program with a link to the workbook file or the file attached to it. To send the link or file, fill in the recipient's e-mail address in the To text box and any comments you want to make about the spreadsheet in the body of the message before you click the Send button.

Sharing Workbooks with IM

If you have access to Skype IM or Microsoft's Lync software on the device running Excel, you can share a workbook saved on your SkyDrive by sending a link to those whom you want to share your workbook via instant messaging. To do this,

1. Open the workbook saved on your SkyDrive.

2. Select the Send by Instant Message option on the Share screen in the Backstage view.

3. Enter the name of the recipient in the To: textbox.

4. Type any message you want to include in the Type Your Message Here textbox (optional).

5. Click the Send IM button.

Presenting Worksheets Online

If you have Microsoft's Lync 2013 software on the device running Excel 2013, you can present your worksheets even in online meetings. To do this,

1. Open the workbook you want to present in online meeting.

2. Select the Present Online option from the Share screen in the Backstage view.

3. Click the Share button under the Present Online heading.

To present your worksheet, highlight the Manage Presentable Content button and then click the name of your workbook from the Presentable Content section near the bottom of its popup palette. When you select the workbook on this palette, the Conversation window closes and the active worksheet of the Excel workbook appears in a presentation window. At the very top of the window containing your worksheet, you see a Currently Presenting mini menu.

You would have control over your worksheet when you present it. The actions you perform on your sheet will be visible to all others who attend the online Lync meeting. If you select the name of an attendee from the Give Control dropdown, that person will get editing control.

If you select the Take Back Control option at the top of the Give Control dropdown, you will get the control of the worksheet back. Once you finish the presentation, click the Stop Presenting button. Then, the Conversation window with your name reappears. You can exit the meeting by clicking the Close button.

Editing Worksheets Online

Microsoft offers several Office Web Apps for Word, Excel, PowerPoint and OneNote as part of its Windows Live Services. You can use these Apps to edit worksheets saved on your SkyDrive within your browser. If you do not have access to the device on which Excel is installed, then you can use this option as long as the device is connected to Internet and runs a web browser that supports the Excel Web App.

To edit a workbook saved on your SkyDrive with the Excel Web App,

1. Launch your web browser that supports Excel Web App.

2. Login to your Windows Live Account from www.live.com.

3. Click the SkyDrive link at the top of the page to open the SkyDrive pages displaying all your folders.

4. Click the link to the folder containing the workbook you want to edit.

5. Select the check box associated to the workbook that you want to edit with Excel Web App.

6. Click the Open button on the SkyDrive toolbar.

7. Edit the worksheet as you want.

8. Once you are done, click the Close button of web browser to save the changes.

Reviewing Workbooks Online

If you work on a device which does not run a web browser that supports Excel Web App, then the browser will open your workbook file with the Excel Mobile Viewer instead of Excel Web App. Though you cannot edit data with Excel Mobile Viewer, it allows you to see the data. If you find some things that require editing, then you can just make a note of them and do it later.

Author's Note

Hello and thank you for reading our book. We would love to get your feedback, learning what you liked and didn't for us to improve. Please feel free to email us at support@i-ducate.com

If you didn't like the book, please email us and let us know how we could improve it. This book can only get better thanks to readers like you.

If you like the book, I would appreciate if you could leave us a review too.

Thank you and all the best to your learning journey in Excel.

www.ingramcontent.com/pod-product-compliance
Lightning Source LLC
Chambersburg PA
CBHW060523060326
40690CB00017B/3367